ETHICS AND NUCLEAR STRATEGY?

Edited by HAROLD P. FORD
and FRANCIS X. WINTERS, S.J.

Published by Orbis Books
in collaboration with
the Woodstock Theological Center, Washington, D.C.,
and
the Institute for the Study of Ethics and International Affairs, School of Foreign Service, Georgetown University

Maryknoll, New York 10545

The Catholic Foreign Mission Society of America (Maryknoll) recruits and trains people for overseas missionary service. Through Orbis Books Maryknoll aims to foster the international dialogue which is essential to mission. The books published, however, reflect the opinions of their authors and are not meant to represent the official position of the Society.

Library of Congress Cataloging in Publication Data

Main entry under title:

Ethics and nuclear strategy?

Updated versions of papers presented at eight seminar sessions held at Georgetown University, Washington, D. C., 1974-75, sponsored by the Woodstock Theological Center and the Institute for the Study of Ethics and International Affairs.

Bibliography: p.

1. United States—Military policy—Addresses, essays, lectures. 2. Atomic warfare—Moral and religious aspects—Addresses, essays, lectures. 3. Atomic weapons and disarmament—Addresses, essays, lectures. 4. Strategy—Addresses, essays, lectures. I. Ford, Harold P., 1921- II. Winters, Francis X. III. Woodstock Theological Center. IV. Institute for the Study of Ethics and International Affairs.

UA23.E83 172'.4 77-5129

ISBN 0-88344-117-9

Printed in the United States of America

To the Memory of
JOHN COURTNEY MURRAY, S.J.
and
REINHOLD NIEBUHR

Contents

Preface

One need not be a professional ethicist to be aware that something is radically askew, politically and morally, when the United States is spending sharply increasing national treasure on weapons at a time of supposed détente and SALT accords. The new U.S. strategic weapons emphases are in large measure responses to the burgeoning military power of the U.S.S.R., yet they have come along incrementally and in the face of earlier expressed assurances to Congress that no such silo-busting weapons systems were being contemplated. In consequence, not only are great new strains put on our national budgets, but the new counterforce emphases doubtless also contribute new pressures on Soviet scientists, technicians, and strategists to develop and deploy still newer offsetting weapons systems. Should such pressures carry the day, we and the Russians will be off once again on another round of weapons development, driven by mutual distrust, competition, bureaucratic momentum, and a certain tyranny of technology.

It is to the sources of such a vicious circle that this book is directed, the distillation of more than a year's inquiry on the part of a distinguished company of strategists and ethicists who met at Georgetown University, Washington, D.C., in eight seminar sessions, 1974–1975, under the joint auspices of the Woodstock Theological Center and the Institute for the Study of Ethics and International Affairs. Titled "Ethics and the U.S. Debate over Nuclear Weapons Strategy," this series purposely brought together participants representing various occupations, religious faiths, and points of view. Neither sponsors nor participants began with any predetermined set of conclusions they wished the seminars to "prove." The intention was simply that the dialogue—informal, continuing, and unique—would bring to the consciousness of participating ethicists a heightened sense of world political reality, while sharpening the foreign-affairs practitioners' sensitivity to dimensions and values beyond those of military hardware and strategic theology. An additional hope was to furnish explicit ethical guidance, whenever possible, to policymakers.

The seminars' results exceeded expectation. Now we wish to share some of these thoughts with a much wider audience.

This book seeks to do just that, though not by reproducing all that was said or written. Rather, the essays here represent some of the most challenging questions which were generated by our inquiry and which have greatest relevance for the concerned public's interests in national policy—and accountability; some of this book's essays are updated versions of papers presented at the seminars, others are subsequent essays stimulated by the seminars' inquiry.

The Georgetown seminars—and this subsequent book—were generated by our concern to clarify and to probe the ethical consequences of the stark new strategic weapons doctrines which Secretary of Defense James Schlesinger suddenly began emphasizing publicly in early 1974. Although somewhat ambiguously and variously voiced by him, these doctrines clearly added up to a new strategy of "counterforce": that is, a strategy and a targeting practice indicating that the U.S. was developing much more accurate nuclear weapons which would give the president many more options (a more "flexible response") in reacting to any future Soviet aggression, by being able to strike only military targets rather than industrial or urban targets. This new doctrine was in one sense merely the latest in a long series which had begun back in the days of U.S. nuclear monopoly, when in the early 1950s Secretary of State John Foster Dulles had coined the policy (or at least the ostensible, "declared" policy), that the U.S. would react massively with nuclear weapons to any serious new "conventional" aggression, say, on the scale of Korea. But this policy, real or declared, had had to give way in the 1960s when the U.S.S.R. itself developed an intercontinental nuclear weapons capability. The new doctrine which then became dominant in U.S. government circles and which more or less still obtained in early 1974, at least among the U.S. general public, was "mutual deterrence," an assumption that nuclear war was very unlikely because of the severe danger that any nuclear war might quickly escalate to a mutual "spasm" nuclear exchange. This "mutual deterrence" concept further assumed that world crises could accordingly be kept from escalating, for fear of "mutual assured destruction," but that if nuclear war should nevertheless come, "countervalue" exchanges could be counted upon: that is, nuclear weapons targeted by both sides at a broad range of civilian and industrial as well as strictly military targets.

Schlesinger's new 1974 emphases were nevertheless of considerably deeper import in several respects: (1) They recognized that the U.S.S.R. had in the meantime been constructing a gigantic new ICBM program, which by 1974 had already given the Soviet Union strategic advantage over the U.S. in certain respects; (2) the new U.S. doctrines also recognized that the U.S.S.R. had never necessarily accepted or shared the previous U.S. assumptions and theoretical distinctions about nuclear strategy, and had all along been giving more attention than had the U.S. to the possibility of perhaps being able to fight a limited nuclear war; (3) the new U.S. doctrines indicated confidence that the rapidly improving technology—*and* accuracy—of U.S. nuclear weapons delivery systems might indeed make it possible for the U.S. to fight a limited nuclear war targeted strictly against military targets, with a chance of keeping that limited war from necessarily quickly escalating into mutual armed destruction; and (4) the new Schlesinger rhetoric reflected, to a few close U.S. strategic weapons-watchers, at least, the *actual* improvement of U.S. strategic weapons delivery systems which parts of the U.S. military had in fact for some time been bringing along secretly, in research and development (R&D), and had been pushing upon the Congress and the Administration—especially since the conclusion of the SALT I accords in the spring of 1972, accords which in the minds of many senior U.S. military figures gave the U.S.S.R. inordinate concessions and strategic weapons potentials.

Aware of this background of the new Schlesinger emphases, general and specialist readers alike will find in this book good arguments for the assets as well as the hazards of counterforce. The readers will also encounter differences of view throughout, on a number of centrally relevant questions, chief among which are: Will the development of counterforce doctrine and weapons make the outbreak of nuclear hostilities more likely? Can nuclear exchanges realistically be kept limited and manageable? Is there such a thing as perceived strategic superiority? Can it be translated into effective political gain in the world? At a more profound level the reader will also find differences of view as to just what are the principal ethical considerations in this or that particular question or situation. More importantly, however, the reader will find a certain broad moral consensus in these essays, on the part of this mixed company of academicians, clergy, civilian and military officers, institute scholars, and so on, that questions of ethics and value *are* relevant, terribly so, to the problem of nuclear weapons, and that the sources of the arms race lie deep within American, as well as Russian, preconceptions and passions.

We appreciate, too, that any such judgments in the extraordinarily complex fields of human motivation and value must be tentative and advanced with considerable humility. We do wish to add to the pioneering, exciting work in ethics and nuclear weapons which the Council on Religion and International Affairs initiated some two decades ago, and so stimulate a broad constituency of readers to the necessity for active and continuing public concern regarding U.S. nuclear weapons doctrines, weapons, expenditures, and priorities. These are not arcane mysteries which must be left just to technical experts. They are matters of life and death.

The glossary (Appendix C) will be of considerable assistance to most readers in clarifying the technical terms which are employed throughout the essays. No glossary of ethical terms has been attempted since the writers presented have used few technical expressions and have defined those they have used themselves. A fairly comprehensive bibliography on the development of ethical thought throughout history, concentrating on the modern era, is included, as is a separate bibliography on the various strategic issues involved.

Acknowledgments for this book are most happily noted. To the Woodstock Theological Center and its first Director, Father Edward L. Glynn, S.J.: for the support which has made this joint undertaking a joyful experience and a success. To Georgetown University's School of Foreign Service and its Dean, Peter F. Krogh: for encouragement and unique stimulus to the seminars' discussions. To Philip Scharper, Editor-in-Chief of Orbis Books, who was able to see promise in a very unfinished manuscript. To our Administrative Officer, Wynn Evenson: for countless procedural triumphs, not least the many times she proved that modern man does not live by bureaucracy alone. To Arlene Sullivan and Ann Bretsch: for invaluable assistance in preparation of the manuscript. And finally to John Suber: for cheerful hospitality.

HAROLD P. FORD
FRANCIS X. WINTERS, S.J.

1

What These Sobering Essays Tell Us

Harold P. Ford

Current U.S. planning for the defense of Western Europe includes a "selective" first strike at the Soviet Union with NATO-based nuclear weapons, Secretary of Defense James R. Schlesinger said Tuesday.... The unmistakable thrust [of his remarks] was to underscore . . . the fact that Pentagon nuclear doctrine now puts more stress on actually fighting a nuclear war than on the abstract theorizing about "deterrence" that used to characterize public official thinking of nuclear war.

Los Angeles Times, July 2, 1975

It seems to me that there is a tendency to call "ethical" those particular moral justifications we tack on to such particular strategic courses as we consider necessary. Should we not, rather, tack on appropriate strategies to those basic ethical courses we consider just and necessary?

Professor Wilfrid Desan
Georgetown University Seminar
May 2, 1975

One purpose of this book's essays and discussion has already been met, as the Preface has indicated, in the germinal seminars at Georgetown University, 1974–1975, which gave practitioners

---

Dr. Ford is a former officer of the Central Intelligence Agency. During 1974–1975 he served as Program Director of the Institute for the Study of Ethics and International Affairs, as Research Fellow of the Woodstock Theological Center, and as Professorial Lecturer at the School of Foreign Service, Georgetown University. Since contributing to this present volume, he has become a staff assistant with the U.S. Senate.

both of ethics and of foreign policy a chance to exchange information, increase the others' knowledge of their respective disciplines, and allow this enhanced knowledge to influence attitudes and policies within the fields concerned. The book now seeks to perform the broader purpose of passing on and updating many of the seminars' insights to all those—ethicists, foreign-policy experts, students, concerned citizens—who share the deeply felt need of our authors to sort out fact and fancy, megatons and morality. (If we had room we would print the entire proceedings of the entire seminar series. I shall, however, make reference in this essay to the thought of various participants which space and other considerations have forced us to omit from the volume.)

The term "concerned citizen" is, perhaps, the key. We offer these essays and their many perspectives in the belief that benefits will accrue in every respect from increased public participation in strategic policymaking, that we citizens should no longer leave such complex matters to the obliging experts, or permit ourselves to be deceived by either wishful thinking or weapons hard-sell, or continue to allow life-and-death decisions on nuclear policies to be made without apparent regard for ethical dimensions and imperatives.

This volume's essays derive strength from the quality and diversity of their authors, perhaps even more so from this book's timing. It appears in the context of our significantly changing times: Not only is there disrupting inflation in arms costs and nuclear proliferation—horizontally to other countries and vertically in qualitative competition between the superpowers; additionally, the present international situation is highly charged and confusing, attendant upon the United States' emergence from its dark Vietnam tunnel into a dazzling, changing world of great Soviet weapons advances, major Soviet-Cuban intervention in Africa, Communist parties' parliamentary advances in Western Europe, strident anti-Americanism in many parts of the world (including much of the United Nations), the tragic self-immolation of Lebanon, and, not least, injured U.S. pride and rekindled U.S. chauvinism.

These last two phenomena reflect the rise and the strengthening of two simultaneous and sharply contradictory sensations within U.S. society: first, that détente is a myth, and that we had better develop great armed strength to protect our interests in an increasingly hostile and refractory world; second, that great arsenals of arms are simply not relevant to most of the more complex questions of our more complex world. The refrains of the first of these sensations were the more dominant during the 1976 U.S. presidential campaign—so much so that, in a real sense, we may be said to now inhabit a post-détente world. The irony is that these simplistic, emotionally kindled sensations make it all the more difficult for the second—and perhaps more accurate—set of sensations to penetrate and guide our thinking. And so we now spend unprecedented sums on arms in a world where most of the problems (and hopes for their mitigation) are primarily psychological, economic, and sociological in character.

Such a context lends added realism to the issues discussed in this volume's essays, insuring them against being an ivory-towered exercise in either strategic theology or the detalia of military hardware. Ethicists and foreign-policy practitioners alike, our authors instruct us about strategic doctrine, bargaining chips, technological momentum, the rhetoric of declaratory policy, bureaucratic realities. More importantly, they tell us about ourselves: our presuppositions, motives, perceptions and misperceptions, and especially about the gap which exists between strategic missiles and moral imperatives—and the absolute necessity of narrowing that gap before we all pass a point of no return. Convinced that heightened ethical sensitivity on the part of the citizenry can make unique contributions to meeting that necessity, I present (and cannot resist commenting on) a few of the principal themes which these essays raise.

In giving increased consideration to fighting a supposedly limited nuclear war, both the United States and the Soviet Union are creating mechanisms which, once set in motion by extreme crisis, ambiguous circumstances, mutual suspicions, and/or incomplete communication, may take charge and carry us all to incredible disaster. Like the momentum set loose by the mobilization machineries in 1914, we Drs. Frankenstein are fashioning the monstrous possibility that, as Francis Winters terms it in "The Nuclear Arms Race: Machine Versus Man," the U.S. and Soviet "machines of war may escape the grasp of their designers and deployers and themselves begin to determine the course of the war." This "eerie possibility," as Fr. Winters calls it, in a sense challenges another of his theses: that the moral questions raised by war are always the same. Moral questions presuppose human rationality and, hence, human control over our destinies; yet this may not obtain, wholly at least, if doomsday, preset mechanisms create a tangled catastrophe beyond moral or physical recall.

From a slightly different perspective, Pierce Corden also finds it necessary to challenge traditional moral criteria, suggesting that modern realities demand the creation of a new framework for value judgments.

The question in "debate" in these essays is not whether the people of the United States should adopt a counterforce strategy; our government has already done so. The questions at hand are what does such a counterforce strategy mean, and what policy and ethical constraints should govern or replace it. Undeniably the U.S. military establishment has been pushing counterforce emphases since at least 1972, and these have now become U.S. government policy. Both the Congress and the public (experts or "mere" concerned citizens) are now, in a sense, onlookers, kibitzing after the *fait accompli* of a basic decision in favor of counterforce. Our great new budgetary and technological marches toward silo-busting weapons are, in turn, deepening the arms race abroad and setting loose potent new bureaucratic-industrial-labor momenta at home. In our setting of neo-Cold War, not even the Congress has been able significantly to blunt this new rush to find meaning and *machismo* in more terrible weapons (except perhaps with respect to the B-1 bomber).

Meanwhile, the supposed purposes of our new counterforce strategy remain many and illusive. Somewhat like past justifications of the U.S. course in Vietnam, counterforce is a many-splendored thing. In its broadest sense it purports to offer a president greater strategic "flexibility," a greater array of nuclear options. But the sales campaigns for counterforce have highlighted various themes at various times, doubtless reflecting countless strands and trade-off considerations, foreign and domestic, which exist among counterforce's assorted champions.

In like manner there are countless strands in this volume's various interpretations of counterforce. Not many of the authors here are persuaded that "flexibility" is, in itself, an adequate justification, given the counterforce capabilities and targeting which the U.S. military has, in fact, long had, but there seems to be a general agreement that the new counterforce emphases do, of course, refine such capabilities and targeting, particularly with respect to silo-busting. Note that there is recognition that the U.S. counterforce declarations have (or have had) strong political-psychological purposes: to dissuade the U.S.S.R. from pushing through to deployment all its strategic programs now in development, and/or to serve as supposed bargaining chips with which to try to manipulate Soviet perceptions in on-going SALT negotiations. Several authors—including Francis Winters, Pierce Corden, and Alain Enthoven—remind us that counterforce is not entirely limited or unique in character, inasmuch as it is a supplement to the United States' existing war plans and contains the option of countervalue attacks (against cities) *in extremis*. Others of our authors feel that counterforce strengthens a sagging U.S. deterrence credibility; still others that it is just an impressive batch of new technological gadgets in search of strategic theoretical justification. There is some concern, expressed especially by Paul Nitze at our Georgetown seminar, that third countries will, rightly or wrongly, come to be impressed by what seems to them to be a decided Soviet strategic superiority (nuclear and conventional), and that such countries may then become psychologically vulnerable to Soviet nuclear blackmail efforts, unless, in the meantime, the United States has taken offsetting (counterforce) steps to maintain at least a perceived equivalence of nuclear-weapons power. Despite these varying interpretations, there does seem to be a certain general agreement among our essayists that the United States' new counterforce emphases do represent: (1) a latter-day effort to redress a strategic disadvantage, real and perceived, caused by the alarming growth of Soviet margins in throw-weight; (2) an effort to emphasize nuclear war-fighting (as well as deterrent) capabilities; (3) an effort to give nuclear weapons a more usable role as political instruments; (4) an attempt to provide weapons and doctrine which would permit various plateaus for negotiation, reassessment, and so forth, once nuclear hostilities had begun, without necessarily escalating at once to spasm war; and (5) a phenomenon which has progressed from RAND-Corporation theory to bargaining-chip childhood, to R&D adolescence, to tomorrow's deployment actuality.

There is, however, no great or general agreement in this volume that these new emphases are mandatory, or that the Soviets are now on the road to gaining an apparent strategic superiority which must be matched, as Paul Nitze implied, by some dramatic new U.S. stroke, such as much more accurate weapons. There does seem to be a general appreciation that the United States still enjoys a strategic weapons advantage, that much of the extreme nervousness over Soviet strategic advances can be atrributed to the zeal with which the Department of Defense and its allies have been selling their new and more accurate weapons to Congress and the public, and that counterforce is nothing new, but simply the latter-day result of theories and technology which have been developing for over a decade. This tendency to discount some of the claims for counterforce obtains even among some of the authors who, on balance, welcome the new strategic emphases. And among even the counterforce champions, the new and more accurate U.S. weapons being developed seem to be considered the more or less normal result of scientific advance—an improved war-fighting capability for situations in which deterrence has failed, and a less immoral instrument of policy than deterrence by the threat of mass destruction.

There is considerable skepticism with respect to a counterforce strategy. For example, go some arguments in this volume, Soviet observers will tend to consider U.S. counterforce weapons to be possible first-strike weapons; or at least these new U.S. developments will strengthen the case of the hawks within Soviet leadership, those who may be advocating doctrines of Soviet first strike and launch-on-warning. There is considerable support for the view of Dr. Herbert Scoville that, with the passage of time, U.S. possession of counterforce weapons will foster more of a general assumption among the public that nuclear-tipped MIRVs and MaRVs are "just more weapons" and, hence, will increase the likelihood that U.S. commanders will cross the nuclear threshold at an early stage in the frustrations and confused pressures of some extreme crisis. To such observers, the possession, cherishing, and temptation to *use* counterforce weapons is a more immoral course than the mere deterrent *threat* to use present nuclear weapons and targeting.

Of most concern to doubters of counterforce is the confidence with which Dr. Schlesinger and his allies have maintained that any future nuclear hostilities can be kept limited, controlled, and well in hand—because "calculations" and "war games" have so indicated. Support for such skepticism certainly derives from the experience of various past wars where ambiguity and accident made quick casualties of pre-existing concepts and confidence—a skepticism supported in more recent history by the less-than-clockwork circumstances of the *Mayaguez* rescue in 1975. Other battlefield arguments can also be used to feed unease about the certainty of some of counterforce's premises: for example, the yet-to-be determined errors and inaccuracies of *actual* weapons strikes and *actual* CEPs; the uncertainties of *real* battlefield command and control; the imperfect *actual* communication between adversaries; the crisis-enhanced pressures to misread an adversary's intentions; and especially the uncertainties of the nuclear fall-out which would be generated by the particular ground-burst necessities of silo-busting targeting. In result, there was considerable sentiment in the seminars that there simply cannot be such a thing as strictly limited nuclear war, and that to preach otherwise so confidently is a gross disservice.

One strong message present in several of this volume's essays is, indeed, that nuclear weapons have a questionable validity as instruments of national political or military policy. Francis Winters makes a particularly strong and convincing case that nuclear weapons have proven to be incompatible with the tradition of civilized warfare, that no conceivable political goals could justify their use, and that one is forced to reexamine nonnuclear options for defense policy. Such a view echoes the judgment voiced by Dr. Hans J. Morgenthau, during the seminars which sparked this book, that the advent of nuclear weapons has brought such revolutionary change to the traditional forces of diplomacy and world balance that to overlook this, in the belief that nuclear weapons, targeting, and strategy can be effectively used to promote political ends, is to be guilty of a conceptual and moral lag of the gravest magnitude and consequence. Pierce Corden, although supporting a countervalue deterrent, speaks of such a declaratory policy as an interim measure to be used for diplomatic purposes while nations work out effective arms-control agreements so that what he terms "the weapons of mass destruction" will never again be used. His point that any survivors of a nuclear holocaust might not even care about the ethics of the particular weapons or strategies used seems especially graphic.

A tragic contradiction presented is the fact that nuclear weapons, despite their questionable usefulness, seem to enjoy a near-universal symbolic value; and that this enchantment with nuclear status constitutes a dangerously destabilizing element in world politics, especially in connection with nuclear proliferation. In truth, a significant part of the hypnosis of competition which has seized the two superpowers and fed their arms races derives from the symbolic value of nuclear weapons. Somehow they have come to represent an index of national power and *machismo*—a sensation of perhaps unique force in the case of the catch-up Soviet competitor. This is clearly evident, too, in the nuclear-weapons motives of France and China. Dr. Alva Myrdal, in particular, stresses the frightening concern that proliferation of nuclear weapons over the next decade may encompass *the* most dangerous threat to world peace. Her very frank and thoughtful essay reminds us in the United States that the superpowers bear significant guilt for proliferation, and that it is they who must show nuclear weapons restraint—that is, demonstrably live up to their obligations under Article VI of the Non-Proliferation Treaty (NPT)—before there can be much realistic hope of worldwide nuclear-weapons restraint. Without in any way exonerating the continuing strategic weapons buildup on the part of the U.S.S.R., we in the United States can only be dismayed that our own particular mix of technological and nationalistic pride certainly contributes significantly to the violation of our NPT obligations.

Another dismaying question (not covered to any extent in these essays) is that of western sales of nuclear materials and enrichment facilities to putative *nth* nuclear weapons countries. And still another source of fear for the future is that of terrorist or other nonstate groups acquiring (and using?) nuclear weapons. Truly, U.S. and Soviet leaders may live to see the day—if they are lucky—when they will sorrowfully recognize what their ingrained suspicions of one another has cost in diverting their attentions from concern for proliferation and according mutual restraint.

A principal question which our essayists leave unresolved is the force of perceptions of power as a key element affecting the arms race, and hence the ability of the United States or the U.S.S.R. to translate visible nuclear weapons power into effective political leverage in the world. Certain authors seem to agree with former Secretary of Defense Schlesinger's insistence that, whether we like it or not, the *apparent* nuclear weapons balance is perhaps as important as the *actual* balance. There are, of course, differences between Soviet and U.S. perceptions and practices, and U.S. inability to convert nuclear strength into explicit and significant political strength does not necessarily mean that Soviet leaders may not give this course a try in the future, once their massive and visible strategic power has been perfected. There is no question, however, that the propensity of certain U.S. champions of more arms to denigrate their country's existing strategic power and to claim that the sky is falling because of its alleged strategic weakness seriously undermines the credibility the United States is seeking to maintain among Soviet and third-nation observers. It is to be regretted that such self-defeating and erroneous rhetoric marked so much of the United States' bicentennial and election year.

An implicit question raised by these essays is whether or not senior government officials have an ethical responsibility not to overstate their cases, especially in speaking of the perfidy of other nations or the alleged highly-controlled precision of their own forces. In the United States, at least, a propensity to overstate performs a great disservice. Whether for declaratory purposes, bargaining chips, promotional enthusiasm, or whatever, there does exist a predilection to overstatement and overcertainty on the part of many officials responsible for strategic decisions. They seem to have compulsions to oversimplification (in order to sell their proposals to the public and the Congress) and to overconfidence (in order to influence adversaries abroad). Such predilections buffet rather than educate the public, confuse and scare the adversary while strengthening the hand of its hawks, and undercut third-country confidence in the United States' judgment and strength.

Clearly, these essays should produce a heightened sensitivity to the pervasive presence of presuppositions in our strategic thinking. "Deterrence" should come in for considerable questioning. Exactly what do all our weapons and weapons expenditures deter: civil war—and foreign intervention—in Angola? The growing power of the Italian Communist Party? Would the Soviets *surely* incinerate the United States if we did not have such a formidable and impregnable (for the moment, at least) sea-based nuclear arsenal? Would not a substantially smaller arsenal still deter the U.S.S.R. from doing something monstrously foolish and self-defeating? Is deterrence in Europe only the product of how many and what kind of U.S. nuclear weapons are targeted at Eastern Europe and the U.S.S.R., or are Soviet calculations not unaffected—militarily, politically, economically, psychologically—by the total deterrent strength and unity of Western Europe, and by uncertainty about the full responsiveness of Eastern Europeans in some extreme crisis? Do the Soviets intend to march into Western Europe at all?

Other presuppositions which deserve close scrutiny include various Defense Department arguments for the new counterforce emphases: for example, that *our* new and more accurate silo-busting weapons should not scare anyone, whereas *their* new weapons show Soviet aggressiveness and possible interest in creating a first-strike capability; that the United States has some kind of mission to support the world; that counterforce weapons help deter "them," and that "they" will move in to any place in the world they can; that investing in the particular DOD arms package of any particular year will permit the United States to shape the future, rather than be shaped by it; that our new weapons will give us bargaining chips, but somehow will not provoke countering developments from the other side. (This last point should evoke a particular caution: Bargaining chip weapons are not, in fact, inexpensive psychological investments, inasmuch as historically they have had a way of slipping down a slope which runs from rhetoric, to R&D, to expensive production and deployment, to countering moves from the other superpower, to a new round of bargaining chips.)

To the degree that there is meaningful discussion of ethics and nuclear weapons today, much of it—even in these essays—seems to concentrate on the ethics of means, to the detriment of more fundamental ethical ends. Often an observer proposes that his or her particular point constitutes "*the* ethical question" at hand. To some, this question is the maintenance of a stable deterrent; to some, the avoidance of nuclear war; to some, the careful control of hostilities once a nuclear threshold has been crossed; to some, the avoidance of an immoral threat to destroy cities. Some couch *the* moral question in terms of this or that particular target; others, the *use* of nuclear weapons; still others, the very *possession* of such arms. Yet to a significant degree such awareness of the ethical dimension in policy questions is often confined only to the *means* of nuclear weapons use (or nonuse). Much more attention must be given to the more profound questions of just what constitutes the ethical good in our nuclear time. For example, do we focus too greatly on freedom, and thus stand ready to commit nuclear genocide in its name? Where does justice come in, and what is justice in a particular situation? To refrain from such focus illustrates, certainly, the abiding, often unconscious force of acculturation and nationalism on foreign-policy discussion. As Professor Wilfrid Desan framed it in the citation that opens this chapter, it is often a question of tacking ethical concerns onto our particular policy preferences, rather than of being grounded in concern for the ethically good and then adjusting our practical policy preferences accordingly. The existence of such preconceptions among groups in the United States—groups which are nearly always congenial, candid, and fairly homogenous—surely demonstrates the enormity of the problems which confront real communication between the proud, suspicious, and wholly dissimilar Soviet and U.S. leaderships.

It is clear, certainly, that the traditional arguments for a just war have lost their efficacy for our age of nuclear weapons. As for limitation, there is considerable doubt that "combatants" could be readily identified and singled out, once nuclear hostilities had begun. As for proportionality, can nuclear war really be kept manageable at every turn, and—again, with the U.S. overkill in the *Mayaguez* incident in mind—can reprisals always be kept proportional to the grievance suffered? As for defensive war, who is the aggressor if hostilities grow out of a long period of mutual fears, developing crisis, and ambiguity, climaxing in a situation where it is not clear just who has committed aggression against whom, and in which every party to hostilities would characterize its own particular resort to arms as being "defensive" and "just"? Such a question has special force because our present situation so resembles that of 1914. Much of our frozen military-political thinking may be conditioned by the events of 1938 to 1950, but our respective weapons build-ups, our alliance systems, our preset mechanisms, our insecurities and suspicions, and our cast of multiple nation-characters might well make war guilt—and hence the aggrieved party's "justified" resort to "defensive" war—an ambiguous commodity indeed, should some new Sarajevo incident ignite an expanding crisis.

Here we face one of the central questions posed by this book of ethical inquiry: Is the serious threat or use of nuclear weapons immoral? Francis Winters answers this question in the affirmative. Although not all our contributors would agree with Fr. Winters, I do and think it appropriate to voice my view that no other conclusion can be drawn in view of the terrible logic, uncontrollability, irrelevance to political purposes, and sheer horror of nuclear destruction.

A further question: Is not our basic strategic problem not merely that of nuclear weapons, but of the very use of force itself as an instrument of state policy in a shrinking, volatile world? If so, what ethical norms should be applied to the use of various nonnuclear weapons? To some, Fr. Winters' resolution—that we must reexamine nonnuclear means of warfare—may provide at least an interim answer. Yet even if all nuclear weapons were effectively banned tomorrow, it is probably a safe estimate that, given our Hobbesian natures, the use of "conventional" weapons would be with us earth dwellers for some years to come. And many of the ethical problems raised in these essays on nuclear weapons still apply. The firebombings of Dresden and Tokyo were no more moral because they were "conventional" and nonnuclear. Indeed, in this volume Pierce Corden classes them, as well as chemical and bacteriological weapons, with nuclear weapons and treats them all in the same category. What about actions such as the deliberate defoliation in Vietnam? Acts of terrorism, such as both Arab and Israeli groups—government sponsored or no—have engaged in? Then, too, there are immense momenta of vested interest set loose in the world of modern nonnuclear weapons: two prime examples are those attending the U.S. Navy's itch to acquire a naval base at remote Diego Garcia—even if it helps fuel a new arms race in the Indian Ocean; and the U.S. Air Force's urge to provide continuing aerial platforms for its many flyboys—even if their desired B-1 bomber is obscenely overpriced and its purposes ambiguous. Surely this volume's interest in sharpening our moral sensitivities with respect to nuclear-weapons decision-making is also relevant to tempering our indulgence in conventional weapons.

Our basic ethical problem may not be that of the mechanical means we are fashioning (which may get out of human control), but of unpredictable people themselves. We know that in everyday life the problem is not our computers, but how we humans program them. If doomsday processes should carry us over the brink some day, it will have been our own frailties which created and programmed those automatons. This volume's essays can perhaps perform their most valuable contribution in questioning the too-great certainties of today's strategic mathematicians, and in giving greater weight to the wild card of the human factor. Deterrence is surely not a science, nor the product of so many budget dollars spent, nor the result of certain new weapons deployed, but of profound subjective questions about our human makeup—our perceptions and misperceptions, our fears and ambiguities, our propensities to bluff, our acquisitiveness and combativeness, our immense technological creativity—alongside the constraints of our finite group and nationalistic identifications and most certainly our finite wisdom. Stated in briefest compass, these essays should heighten one's appreciation of the fact that all the participants in the arms race—Americans, Soviets, whoever—are driven essentially by inordinate self-righteousness, suspicion, competitiveness, and pride.

The dangers of disaster are great and will grow greater; yet however sobering these essays, we need not end on a note of despair. True, humankind has a terribly long way to go in a terribly short time, if we are to avert a disaster no one has planned or expected or desired. But many places offer promising beginnings. Each of us can insist that our own government—and that of the U.S.S.R.—make demonstrable progress in genuine arms limitation and control, valuable in its own right as well as with respect to nuclear proliferation elsewhere. Each of us can demand that our country put tougher restrictions on the export of nuclear materials and facilities to other countries, especially those which are presumably nuclear-capable. Above all, each of us can question—and encourage others to question—our ingrained and sacred preconceptions: deterrence, triad of weapons systems, silo-busting, newer and more horrible is better, "they" are the cause of all evil, and so on.

In short, we must urgently and substantially reorder our practical and ethical priorities to meet the new adversaries of tomorrow. While the United States and the U.S.S.R. have been spending billions to protect themselves against each other, countless new challenges have been welling up in the world—challenges of politics, of expectations, of the environment—which must be constructively and imaginatively confronted by Soviet and U.S. skills and expenditures. For example, there are numerous social and economic weaknesses within U.S. society itself which not only degrade our real strength, but cry out for remedy. As Dr. Marshall Shulman said at one of our seminars, the greatest strategic and ethical tragedy which might befall the United States would be for important segments of our national life and strength to collapse—amidst a plethora of the shiniest new counterforce weapons. Surely this very real danger demands an urgent re-ordering of ethical concerns so as to provide a better basis for moral choice than is provided by nationalistic righteousness, by strategic-technical certainties and strategic-theological incantations, and by the tacking on of a few ethical constraints—after the fact of decision—to the particular favorite strategic cure-all of the moment.

2

Ethics, Diplomacy, and Defense

Francis X. Winters, S.J.

PROLEGOMENON ON POLITICS

There may have existed eras when a discussion of ethics and national security could have turned immediately to the question of ethical norms and specific political-military situations. The present age is not such a time. Before examining the validity of ethical criteria which might be useful in discriminating among alternative national security policies, in our time it is imperative to address the prior question: Why speak of ethics in the context of national security at all? What is the possibility or the worth of discussing the relation between ethics and political-military affairs?

The origins of the current cultural assumption about the incompatibility of ethics and national security are obscure. In the present-day United States, however, three factors contribute significantly to the bias against attempting ethical evaluations of political-military policies: (1) the recognition that the level of violence employed by both sides in World War II was unprecedented, indiscriminate, and unjustifiable by any reasonable moral code whatsoever; (2) the subliminal awareness that the structure of peace between the two superpowers at the present time rests on their capacity and unconscionable willingness to commit genocide (and probably national suicide) if deterrence fails; (3) the vivid

---

Father Winters is Director of the Institute for the Study of Ethics and International Affairs and Assistant Professor of Ethics and International Affairs, School of Foreign Service, Georgetown University.

recollection of the national ordeal of a presidential resignation, in the face of probable impeachment on account of unparalleled usurpation of political power.

In this historical context, the ethically sensitive citizen of the United States tends to adopt one of four stances: withdrawal from politics in despair, turning his or her attention to more interior pursuits; engagement in the theatrical politics of the Catonsville Nine, the Camden Fourteen, and other such groups; living with the tormenting awareness that the ethical sense, which is essential to humanity, cannot be squared with modern military strategies, and hoping that "something will turn up," technologically or politically, to resolve the dilemma of preserving peace by threatening genocide; or commitment to the effort to fashion a national security policy consistent with his or her sense of political values. This essay addresses itself to those who have opted for the fourth alternative—namely, fashioning a defense policy which is not repugnant to the human instinct for ethics. It may be that those who have opted for the other courses—abandoning politics, abandoning political reality, or abandoning ethics—are more numerous. Nevertheless, it seems useful to offer these reflections in service to the minority who insist on attempting the reconciliation between the political and ethical instincts of humankind.

In undertaking the demanding task of elaborating a political ethic adequate for the nuclear age, especially in the face of the widespread despair about the feasibility of this task, it is crucial to reflect on the human context of politics, the place of politics in the scheme of things. Among modern authors, such disparate thinkers as Paul Ramsey, Hannah Arendt, and Albert Camus have contributed to delineating the context within which politics can be adequately understood.[1]

Dr. Ramsey has suggested that the central element in political ethics is an affirmation of the dignity of the political vocation. Pointing to Plato's *Republic* and the book of Genesis as superior treatises on the political vocation of humankind, he suggested that the acme of human achievement is the act of self-governance, whereby the human person, in confrontation with another free person, decides on a course of action and so begets a set of events which otherwise might never have been. Politics is thus a form, and perhaps the ultimate form, of human creativity.[2]

Creativity is also the context in which Hannah Arendt chose to discuss politics. Writing in 1967, when the public image of policymakers was just going into its present decline on account of the seemingly ungovernable momentum of the United States' involvement in Vietnam, she spoke of

> . . . the actual content of political life—of the joy and the gratification that arises out of being in company with our peers, out of acting together and appearing in public, and out of inserting ourselves into the world by word and deed, and thus acquiring and sustaining our personal identity and beginning something entirely new.[3]

Politics, as the apex of human creativity, is not only an opportunity—a realm of activity, such as contemplation or sensuality, that one might engage in or forego—but an imperative, at least for some citizens. The necessity of politics is no less evident to Ramsey and Arendt than is its creative character, for both authors have a profound awareness of the anti-creative potentialities of human beings, of the monumental capacity of humankind to destroy. Arendt has explored this theme of evil thoroughly in a book-length study of the trial of Adolph Eichmann, tracing the human tragedy of Hitlerian politics to the general moral collapse of Europe, not excluding that of the Nazis' victims. In the context of the almost universal acquiescence of German society to Hitler's policies, she clarified the banality of Eichmann's cooperation in the extermination of the Jews. Eichmann was one of those people who couldn't think for himself but merely assimilated the surrounding climate of opinion. He was unable to stand alone. In those desperate circumstances, it was incumbent on others, more thoughtful, more confident, more influential, to stand up and resist. In the absence of such civilized protest, Eichmann was almost certain to acquiesce.[4] Destructiveness, like creativity, is a joint enterprise, the enterprise of politics gone astray.

A picture of such needed resistance against evil, remedial politics, emerges from the life and writings of Albert Camus, who was himself a member of the French Resistance to the Nazis. Interpreting politics under the rubric of rebellion, Camus spoke of such political resistance as one of the essential human dimensions,[5] a necessary component of human experience. Politics for him consisted of actions springing from self-affirmation in the face of threats. In a world of evil, politics is the art of saying "no." As Dr. Rieux, the hero of *The Plague*, said in the closing words of the novel:

Nonetheless, he knew that the tale he had to tell could not be one of final victory. It could be only the record of what had to be done, and assuredly would have to be done again in the never ending fight against terror and its relentless onslaughts, despite their personal afflictions, by all who, while unable to be saints but refusing to bow down to pestilence, strove their utmost to be healers.[6]

Politics, then, for Ramsey, Arendt, and Camus is an act of creativity in the context of encroachment by destructive forces. From this understanding of the political vocation these authors derive their claim for the dignity and exhilaration of political activity as humankind's effort to exercise human creativity in the midst of hostile forces. The dignity of politics stems both from its creativity and from its necessity. If humankind is to prosper, some persons must understand the interaction of individuals and states, make judgments about alternative courses of action, and execute these plans in cooperation with their peers. On the willingness of some to engage in politics rests the security of all.

POLITICAL ETHICS

This affirmation of the dignity of the political realm—of the worth and exhilaration of creative public activity in the midst of impending threats—is the proper starting point for a discussion of political ethics. But it is only the starting point. Even a slight familiarity with the bewildering plurality of political philosophies and structures competing in the international system suggests questions of validity and of the comparative utility of various political perspectives. Are all these modern political systems equally conducive to the creative process of social interaction? Are some political philosophies and structures actually inimical to human creativity? On what grounds is it possible to form a judgment about the forms of political life? Is such a judgment possible at all?

Even if it is possible to evaluate national political structures on the basis of their compatibility with human creativity, is it possible to draw any conclusions about the appropriate conduct of these national societies within the international system? Are domestic politics and international politics commensurable realities? What foreign policies contribute to human creativity in the international system? On what criteria can one rely in making such judgments?

These questions could be amplified and made more specific. The extensive literature on ethics and foreign policy has probed many of these issues without discovering completely satisfactory answers.[7] But rather than further elaborating the questions which cluster around the interrelationship between ethics and politics, I will attempt here to reduce the questions to two principal ones. What moral test should be applied by citizens to their domestic political systems? And what moral tests should be applied to the interaction among diverse political societies in the international system?

The Requirement of Ethical Domestic Politics

The prior question is perhaps the less often asked: Can one be at home in his or her own country? Hannah Arendt, who had been required to choose between political conviction and patriotism, remarked on the sad necessity which forces some people to leave their native lands because political institutions at a certain time are incompatible with the individual's sense of justice:

> Indeed, this is how we all come into the world—lucky if the world and the part of it we arrive in is a good place to live in at the time of our arrival, or at least a place where the wrongs committed are not "of such a nature that it requires you to be the agent of injustice to another."[8]

Speaking for the legions of citizens who have been forced to choose exile over complicity in injustice, Arendt pointed to the primal and radical political decision, the choice among affirmation of one's native political heritage, revolution, emigration, or death. Her own choice of exile makes particularly poignant her study of Eichmann, a former compatriot, who chose to cooperate in the political design of Nazism. Her reflections on the necessity of the radical choice of political allegiance likewise speak eloquently for the many conscientious Germans who embraced the tragic life of émigrés during the 1930s.[9]

The question asked by the German émigrés of the thirties, and more recently by many citizens who fled the United States to avoid service in what they judged an immoral war in Southeast Asia, is not, of course, a new question. It is the perennial radicalism of Socrates, of Antigone, and of religious martyrs over the centuries, men and women such as Thomas More who have finally preferred death to an unacceptable compromise with conscience.[10] Indeed, resistance to the claims of unexamined patriotism is an essential element of the natural-law approach to political ethics, one of the principal systematic approaches to the questions under consideration here. Echoing Camus's insistence that "resistance is one of the essential dimensions of man,"[11] the late Heinrich Rommen, another distinguished German expatriate, traced the natural-law tradition to the intercultural experience of Greece in the fifth century B.C., whereby awareness of conflicting legal systems gave rise to the properly ethical question for citizens: the necessity of choosing among competing legal systems on the basis of a supralegal frame of reference, namely, the sense of justice. This historically crucial distinction between positive (artificial and human-made) law and natural ("divine") law has ever been the basis for validating the claims of conscience against the power of the state.[12] The faithful decisions of Socrates, Antigone, Thomas More, and others are symbolic of the ever-recurring conflict between conscience and the claims of the state. Conscience denies the absolutism of political claims. In this denial, the civil disobedient of all ages has relied on a touchstone beyond the law, on some supralegal norm of conduct which itself invalidates the claims of unjust laws. Beyond law there exists justice.

It is the reality of justice, whose existence has been testified to over the ages by the allegiance of men and women willing to embrace exile or death for its sake, which confirms the possibility, and even the necessity, of relating ethics and politics. To deny the finality of politics, as the exiles and martyrs have done, is to affirm the indispensability of ethics, which includes the study of values transcending politics. The beginning of political wisdom is to understand the limits of politics itself.

The Search for a Positive Political Heritage

Political ethics, however, is not merely a negative inquiry, the delineation of the boundaries of the political realm. Ethics also includes the contemplation of the positive moral resources of various political structures and philosophies. Once we have answered the radical and initially negative question of the ethical legitimacy of our native political culture—once, that is, we have determined that there is nothing in the political society which is inimical to the claims of conscience—then we may begin to explore the positive resources inherent in that tradition for fostering creativity and human well-being. The second moment of reflection in political ethics, then, is the examination and assimilation by each citizen of "the spirit of the laws" of his or her native place. Here political ethics becomes immediately particular and, therefore, pluralistic.

As an example of this second and constructive phase of political ethics, it might be helpful to examine the political heritage of the United States of America in order to discover the characteristic insight and institutions in which we have been educated. From a close study of the spirit of the Constitution and such commentaries as *The Federalist* papers, it is possible to see how a citizen of the United States might go about the task of constructing his or her own political ethics.

Accepting *The Federalist* as an authoritative interpretation of the spirit of the U.S. Constitution, I would draw attention specifically to three of its papers, numbers 10, 51, and 63, which contain particularly crucial observations for the subject under study here. All authored by James Madison, they expressed a balanced belief that self-government is difficult and yet feasible under carefully constructed circumstances. The difficulty of self-government arises from the familiar tendency of power to self-aggrandizement and consequent corruption, while its feasibility stems from the possibility of designing internal checks against these self-aggrandizing tendencies.

After some years of experience with the Articles of Confederation, the colonists felt an urgent need for an increased concentration of power. They came to realize that the people could not prosper without a central government powerful enough to deal with issues of taxation, commerce, foreign relations, and defense. Still fresh in their memories, however, were the excesses to which centralized power had gone in Great Britain. Hence, they insisted on framing a constitution in the light of their awareness that power itself could not prosper without an internal structure of checks and balances. Increasingly appreciative of the indispensability of political power, they nevertheless did not betray their revolutionary heritage, which had arisen out of a sense that power is enhanced by diffusion. To preserve this balance between centralization and diffusion of power, the Constitutional Convention constructed a polity in which there was a division of authority between individuals and government, between local and national government, and within the federal government itself, which was divided into three coequal branches. Thereby the authors of the Constitution strove to establish a creative context in which the inevitable conflicts of interest and perspective could be exercised fruitfully. The essential task of government was to be the prevention of any usurpation of governmental power by any one interest or vision. Unilateralism was the primary evil to be avoided in the republic.

Several citations from the papers themselves testify to this philosophy of power:

It is in vain to say, that enlightened statesmen will be able to adjust these clashing interests, and render them all subservient to the public good. Enlightened statesmen will not always be at the helm: Nor, in many cases, can such an adjustment be made at all, without taking into view indirect and remote considerations, which will rarely prevail over the immediate interest which one party may find in disregarding the rights of another, or the good of the whole.

The inference to which we are brought, is, that the *causes* of faction cannot be removed; and that relief is only to be sought in the means of controlling its *effects*. . . .

The other point of difference is, the greater number of citizens and extent of territory which may be brought within the compass of Republican, than of Democratic Government; and it is this circumstance principally which renders factious combinations less to be dreaded in the former, than in the latter. The smaller the society, the fewer probably will be the distinct parties and interests composing it; the fewer the distinct parties and interests, the more frequently will a majority be found of the same party; and the smaller the number of individuals composing a majority, and the smaller the compass within which they are placed, the more easily will they concert and execute their plans of oppression. Extend the sphere, and you take in a greater variety of parties and interests; you make it less probable that a majority of the whole will have a common motive to invade the rights of other citizens; or if such a common motive exists, it will be more difficult for all who feel it to discover their own strength, and to act in unison with each other. Besides other impediments, it may be remarked, that where there is a consciousness of unjust or dishonorable purposes, communication is always checked by distrust, in proportion to the number whose concurrence is necessary.[13]

But the great security against a gradual concentration of the several powers in the same department, consists in giving to those who administer each department, the necessary constitutional means, and personal motives, to resist encroachments of the others. The provision for defense must in this, as in all other cases, be made commensurate to the danger of attack. Ambition must be made to counteract ambition. The interest of the man must be connected with the constitutional rights of the place. It may be a reflection on human nature, that such devices should be necessary to controul the abuses of government. But what is government itself but the greatest of all reflections on human nature? If men were angels, no government would be necessary. If angels were to govern men, neither external nor internal controuls on government would be necessary. In framing a government which is to be administered by men over men, the great difficulty lies in this: You must first enable the government to controul the governed; and in the next place, oblige it to controul itself. A dependence on the people is no doubt the primary controul on the government; but experience has taught mankind the necessity of auxiliary precautions. . . .

First. In a single republic, all the power surrendered by the people, is submitted to the administration of a single government; and usurpations are guarded against by a division of the government into distinct and separate departments. In the compound republic of America, the power surrendered by the people, is first divided between two distinct governments, and then the portion allotted to each, subdivided among distinct and separate departments. Hence a double security arises to the rights of the people. The different governments will controul each other; at the same time that each will be controuled by itself.

Second. It is of great importance in a republic, not only to guard the society against the oppression of its rulers; but to guard one part of the society against the injustice of the other part. Different interests necessarily exist in different classes of citizens. If a majority be united by a common interest, the rights of the minority will be insecure. There are but two methods of providing against this evil: The one by creating a will in the community independent of the majority, that is, of the society itself; the other by comprehending in the society so many separate descriptions of citizens, as will render an unjust combination of a majority of the whole, very improbable, if not impracticable. The first method prevails in all governments possessing an hereditary or self appointed authority. This at best is but a precarious security; because a power independent of the society may as well espouse the unjust views of the major, as the rightful interests, of the minor party, and may possibly be turned against both parties. The second method will be exemplified in the federal republic of the United States. Whilst all authority in it will be derived from and dependent on the society, the society itself will be broken into so many parts, interests and classes of citizens, that the rights of individuals or of the minority, will be in little danger from interested combinations of the majority. . . . In the extended republic of the United States, and among the great variety of interests, parties and sects which it embraces, a coalition of a majority of the whole society could seldom take place on any other principles than those of justice and the general good; and there being thus less danger to a minor from the will of the major party, there must be less pretext also, to provide for the security of the former, by introducing into the government a will not dependent on the latter; or in other words, a will independent of the society itself. It is no less certain than it is important, notwithstanding the contrary opinions which have been entertained, that the larger the society, provided it lie within a practicable sphere, the more duly capable it will be of self government. And happily for the *republican cause*, the practicable sphere may be carried to a very great extent, by a judicious modification and mixture of the *federal principle*.[14]

Thomas Jefferson himself penned the most succinct summary of the spirit of our laws when he wrote, in his *Autobiography:*

It is not by the consolidation, or concentration of powers, but by their distribution that good government is effected.[15]

The philosophy of power which underlies the Constitution is that power is enhanced by diffusion or shared participation among competing individuals and groups within the political system. Excessive concentration of power in any single part of the system, manifested in unilateral and unchecked influence, is to be avoided because it ultimately undermines political power. Such is the inspiration of the domestic political institutions of the United States.

The Relation Between Domestic and Foreign Political Philosophy

Simply on the basis of the philosophy of the Constitution itself it would be possible to articulate an ethic for domestic politics in the United States, one which would make the maintenance of the structures for the diffusion of power a central ethical concern. My concern in this essay, however, is rather with ethics and *foreign* policy. What are the implications of this philosophy of power for the foreign policy of the republic established on the basis of this Constitution?

A hint of the foreign policy implications of the Constitution can be found in *The Federalist*, in the course of a discussion of the establishment of the Senate. In arguing for the establishment of that body, with its members subject to re-election only every six years, James Madison urged the consideration that such a group, because they would enjoy more security from popular whim and would acquire more extensive experience in government, would thus be better able to formulate a foreign policy sensitive to the perceptions and desires of other nations and, therefore, more attractive and agreeable to the international community.

> An attention to the judgment of other nations is important to every government for two reasons: The one is, that independently of the merits of any particular plan or measure, it is desirable on various accounts, that it should appear to other nations as the offspring of a wise and honorable policy. The second is, that in doubtful cases, particularly where the national councils may be warped by some strong passion, or momentary interest, the presumed or known opinion of the impartial world, may be the best guide that can be followed. What has not America lost by her want of character with foreign nations? And how many errors and follies would she not have avoided, if the justice and propriety of her measures had in every instance been previously tried by the light in which they would probably appear to the unbiased part of mankind?[16]

According to the thought of Madison and the other writers of the Constitution, the Senate, in its oversight of foreign relations, was to exercise voluntarily that self-restraint in the area of foreign policy which the laws of the nation made obligatory for domestic policy: the avoidance of unilateralism and unrestrained self-aggrandizement. It was to be the responsibility of the Senate to insure that the United States conduct itself in foreign affairs in accordance with its native political philosophy: that power, whether domestic or international, is enhanced by diffusion. In the spirit of this philosophy the Senate was to guard against policies based sheerly on partisan interest and was to endeavor to insure all interested parties (nations) a voice in the settlement of international disputes. With the exercise of such restraint by the Senate, the United States could hope to conduct its foreign policy in a spirit consistent with its own political heritage and avoid falling into a schizophrenic stance in which its foreign policy contradicted its own domestic political institutions.

From this paper of Madison's we can conclude that the founding fathers sought to establish a foreign policy which would safeguard, in the contact among nations, that same diffusion of power which they hoped would animate political relations within the United States itself.

POLITICS AMONG NATIONS: THE ART OF DIPLOMACY

The search for a foreign policy consonant with the spirit of the Constitution has been a constant feature of U.S. political thought from the time of *The Federalist* down to the present. In a recent book devoted to the question, *Ethics and World Politics*, several distinguished commentators more or less explicitly pursued this theme and methodology. In this volume, three of the contributors, Arthur Schlesinger, Jr., Sen. Mark Hatfield, and Paul Ramsey, who also delivered the 1971 Christian Herter lectures at the Johns Hopkins University School of Advanced International Studies, approached this question from their distinctive perspectives of history, politics, and political theory.[17]

Schlesinger drew attention to the historical fact that each nation must act internationally in accordance with its own political heritage or run the risk of undergoing a self-destructive schizophrenia. Pointing to the disruptive domestic consequences of French colonial policy in Algeria and of the United States' overinvolvement in Indochina, he concluded:

> The moral question arises particularly in a state's observance or nonobservance of its own best standards. Foreign policy is only the face a nation wears to the world. If a course in foreign affairs implies moral values incompatible with the ideals of the national community, either the nation will refuse after a time to sustain the policy, or else it must abandon its ideals. A people is in bad trouble when it tries to keep two sets of books—when it holds one scale of values for its internal polity and applies another to its conduct of foreign affairs. The consequent moral schizophrenia is bound to convulse the homeland. This is what happened to France during the Algerian War. It is what is happening to the United States because of the Vietnam war.[18]

Consistency between political heritage and present-day actions in the international system is imperative because it is the same people who remember their past and plan their future. If a nation has inherited an understanding of power which regards unilateralism as the primary evil to be controlled by governmental structures, it cannot long pursue unilateral policies internationally without abandoning its own heritage or giving rise to destructive dissent at home. In Schlesinger's words:

> The assumption that other nations have traditions, interests, values, rights and obligations of their own is the beginning of a true morality of states.[19]

Senator Hatfield came, by a different methodology, to a remarkably similar conclusion about the relation between ethics and foreign policy. His starting point was similar to Schlesinger's: the national identity of the United States. Urging that the integrity of the national character is the most essential feature of the national interest, the senator insisted that foreign policies such as those pursued in Southeast Asia are dangerous because they contradict our own political instincts and heritage.

> We must recognize that actions claimed to be in the national interest can be an utter refutation of the ideas and values that give us our identity as a nation. Such a contradiction is unnecessary and it can destroy our national integrity. Preserving our integrity and our identity as a humane, compassionate society must be our foremost aim. Our national interest must never be allowed to subvert our national integrity. . . .
>
> The entire meaning of "national security" must be reexamined if we are to take seriously the perspectives that have been previously presented. Most Americans would maintain that we should use force beyond our borders and intervene in revolutions when our national security is threatened. But the real issue is that we must redefine and clarify what we mean by "national security." Security should mean the survival and the continued existence of the nation and its fundamental social and political institutions. Where are the threats to that security? Are they from an invading foreign army? From revolutions abroad? Or do they come from within, from unresponsive, archaic machinery of government; from estranged, disenfranchised citizens who insist that the "system" does not work; from racial strife and antagonism; and from deteriorating, hopeless cities and their embittered, impoverished citizens? These are far more direct "threats" to our security. Yet, such conditions persist, in part, because of the billions spent to protect against supposed "security threats" in distant lands.[20]

Arguing against the prevalent U.S. assumption that ethics and foreign policy cannot be related, Dr. Ramsey said that political and moral values are part of the national heritage which any statesman has assimilated in the normal process of socialization. Hence it is impossible for him or her to make policy judgments without relying to some extent on his or her inherited sense of values:

> Instead, the truth is that moral considerations are behind the eyeballs of the statesman; they precede the exercise of calculating reason. The values of a people are within a statesman; they are not matter with which he deals or which he handles. The values of a people are the spirit and purposes animating the community, pervading its institutions and voluntary associations, forming consciences, including the consciences of citizen and magistrate alike. The values are in the ethos, the traditions of a people; they are inculcated by the institutions, the laws, the activities of the community; these are in charge of the upbringing of Socrates and any

man who has lived in an Athens worth living in. Mr. C. S. Lewis in *The Abolition of Man* makes the striking statement: "I am very doubtful whether history shows us one example of a man who, having stepped outside traditional morality and attained power, has used that power benevolently." That states the historic role of moral values in relation to politics better than any statement I know. Men get to know justice first of all through the *jus gentium* animating the historical community into which they are born; a man's conscience and moral sensibilities have their origin in identity with the purposes of a particular people. To step outside the morality that was handed down to us and then to attain power sets raw power against a weak and abstract morality and sets truth and goodness against power. Still, families, schools, churches, and the writers of a nation's songs should not mistake the most telling way in which anyone speaks truth and righteousness to decision-makers in power. That is through their upbringing and moral development in a society whose moral purposes, values, and outlook they (perhaps inarticulately) share.[21]

A similar position on the relation between ethics and foreign policy has been taken by two distinguished political theorists who have helped to shape the public discussion of the relationship between political and moral values. K. J. Holsti devoted a chapter of his textbook, *International Politics*, to "Ethics in Explanation of Foreign Policy." Insisting that the long and fruitless debate between realists and idealists on this question has vastly oversimplified the issues, he pointed to the same phenomenon of socialization as it affects policymakers.

But explanations of foreign policy which claim that all statesmen are immoral, concerned only with their own power and prestige, and indifferent to the consequences of their actions are surely not warranted by facts. To condemn policy makers as a group overlooks the fact that in their values and moral predispositions they are probably a fairly representative sample of the educated people in the world. We could not deny that often their calculations are wrong, that they frequently look only to the short run and fail to analyze the long-run impacts of their decisions, or that they often have a propensity to dismiss information that does not fit with their favorite theories or values. Yet are not all people guilty of these shortcomings? This is not to argue that publics should avoid criticism of their leaders. Rather, it is to suggest policy makers are probably no better or worse, from an ethical point of view, than their compatriots.

One way of relating ethical considerations to policy making is to conceive of ethics as a combination of cultural, psychological, and ideological "value structures" which inhibit consideration of all possible policy alternatives in a given situation. They establish limits beyond which certain types of behavior become inconceivable.[22]

Recalling the famous conversation between Churchill and Stalin on the resolution of the threat of renewed militarism in postwar Germany, the author pointed out that Churchill's cultural conditioning made it impossible for him to accept Stalin's suggestion that fifty thousand German officers be executed to preclude such a military renaissance.

A similar approach to the realist-idealist debate was taken by Hans Morgenthau in his magistral *Politics Among Nations:*

> On the other hand, there is the misconception, usually associated with the general depreciation and moral condemnation of power politics, discussed earlier, that international politics is so thoroughly evil that it is no use looking for moral limitations of the aspirations for power on the international scene. Yet, if we ask ourselves what statesmen and diplomats are capable of doing to further the power objectives of their respective nations and what they actually do, we realize that they do less than they probably could and less than they actually did in other periods of history. They refuse to consider certain ends and to use certain means, either altogether or under certain conditions, not because in the light of expediency they appear impractical or unwise but because certain moral rules interpose an absolute barrier. Moral rules do not permit certain policies to be considered at all from the point of view of expediency. Certain things are not being done on moral grounds, even though it would be expedient to do them. Such ethical inhibitions operate in our time on different levels with different effectiveness. Their restraining function is most obvious and most effective in affirming the sacredness of human life in times of peace.[23]

There appears, then, to be a consensus among these five thoughtful commentators on resolving the dilemma of relating ethics and foreign policy. All these thinkers agree that it is essential for statesmen, when acting in the international system, to conduct themselves in accordance with the spirit of their own national heritages. In the absence of an effective international legal system, the self-restraints arising from various cultural traditions can function as civilizing factors in international politics.

Assured by this consensus, it is tempting to close the books on the long-continued debate about ethics and foreign policy and to rely on statesmen conscientiously observing the best standards of their own societies, even when acting beyond national boundaries. Tempting as this approach may be, brief reflection on its implications suffices to uncover its inadequacy. Holsti, for example, cited Churchill as his example of the unconscious and yet adequate influence of moral socialization, referring to the famous discussion with Stalin on the fate of the German officer corps. Morgenthau used the same example. Yet, the very fact that two such leaders could have come to contradictory conclusions about the proper solution to preventing German remilitarization raises significant doubts about the adequacy of the "unconscious-conditioning" approach to the problem. Even more substantive questions are raised by a comparison of Churchill's stance on this question with how he resolved the fate of a city in his own country: In Coventry 150,000 of his fellow citizens were left as targets for a bombing raid in order to protect the secret of Ultra, the Allies' key to Axis codes.[24] A similar contradiction within the value-perceptions of Churchill, along with those of other Allied leaders, may be evident in their acceptance of unconditional surrender as their political and military goal in the war. Does the fact that Churchill spared the 50,000 German officers and virtually condemned the 150,000 citizens of Coventry make these decisions correct or even consistent with one another? Does the Allied leadership's insistence on unconditional surrender validate this momentous decision, which eventually led to the use of atomic weapons?[25] Not necessarily. The vigorous dispute which is carried on in the United States even to this day about the moral legitimacy of having insisted on unconditional surrender in World War II gives evidence that the U.S. political heritage can lead to differing views.[26] Although the moral impact of political socialization is an important element in understanding the proper relationship between ethics and foreign policy, other elements must be considered as well. Finally, it is the *critical assimilation* of one's political heritage which provides the basis of a morally adequate decision in the field of foreign policy.

This task of critical assimilation of the national political heritage brings us once more to reflection on the Constitution and to a renewed study of its distinguished commentators. In recent times, one of the ablest political theorists to undertake the task of discovering the implications for foreign policy of our Constitutional heritage has been the late Secretary of State Dean Acheson. In a series of talks and essays during the last twenty years of his life, Acheson continually addressed himself to this question. Several of these essays have appeared in a posthumous collection, entitled *This Vast External Realm.* In the mid-1950s, on the basis of his own experience of diplomacy during some of the brightest days of U.S. foreign policy, Acheson concluded that a successful foreign policy for this nation must be inspired by the principles which animate the Constitution. In an effort to identify the political philosophy underlying the Constitution, the late secretary singled out the spirit of free inquiry and reasoned consent as the essence of the U.S. political experience. From this interpretation of the national heritage, he drew some clear conclusions about foreign policy, particularly vis-à-vis our allies.

> In my belief, what we need is not less spirit of free inquiry, but more. It has been the central idea of our nation, from the days of 1776 and earlier, that a free society is one in which diversity may flourish, in which the spirit of inquiry and of belief is free to explore and express. The advent of Communism has not changed this. We do not become stronger by imposing a uniformity of thinking upon ourselves; we become weaker. We lose, in fact, what we are fighting for; we take upon ourselves the face of our adversary.[27]

Lecturing at Amherst College a decade later, on the topic of "Ethics in International Relations Today," Acheson returned to the same theme of free inquiry:

> The end sought by our foreign policy, the purpose for which we carry on relations with foreign states, is, as I have said, to preserve and foster an environment in which free societies may exist and flourish. Our policies and actions must be tested by whether they contribute to or detract from achievement of this end.[28]

Acheson's understanding of the spirit of free inquiry was one derived from his interpretation and experience of the functioning of the United States Constitution, specifically in the systematic struggle which characterized relations between the executive and legislative branches of the government. When the secretary sought to cultivate the spirit of free inquiry abroad through diplomatic efforts, he presumably anticipated the same struggle among nations to fashion consent out of sharply divergent starting positions. He expected NATO policies to be arrived at through sharp conflict and to be adhered to because all the participants had genuinely contributed to the final solution. From these observations and experiences, Acheson derived certain rules of diplomacy, or qualities for a diplomat, essential to the successful formulation of U.S. foreign policy:

> The spirit of free inquiry, free thought, is the kernel of what we are defending, and it is also the strongest weapon in our arsenal. What is

more, it is the principal binding force in our coalition. The tradition of 1776 is still the most powerful and attracting force in the world today; it is this that draws to our leadership people all over the world. Without this idea, we are to them just another powerful nation, bent upon interests which are not theirs. If we are narrow, dogmatic, self-centered, afraid, domineering, and crabbed, we shall break apart the alliance on which our future depends. But if we behave, in our dealings among ourselves and with our allies, as a free society should, we shall succeed in that most difficult task of leading a group of diverse peoples, doing unpleasant and burdensome things, over a long period of time, in the quiet defense of their precious liberty. It may be that this is the highest test of our American civilization which destiny has in store for us.[29]

To "behave, in our dealings among ourselves and with our allies, as a free society should" was Acheson's perceptive distillation of the lessons of the Constitution for the conduct of foreign policy. Another distinguished commentator, Alistair Cooke, came to the same conclusion about the spirit of our laws, when he summarized the philosophy of the U.S. Constitution in three principles: "compromise, compromise, compromise."[30]

The spirit of compromise which characterizes the U.S. political system is one well suited to international diplomacy, which has been aptly described as the art of compromise or accomodation. Harold Nicolson, in his definitive study, *Diplomacy*, traced the rise of modern diplomacy to the emergence of a mercantile class, who saw that the common interests of various nations should provide counterbalance to their conflicting interests. "It was through trade and commerce that people first learnt to apply common sense in their dealings with each other."[31] Contrasting this mercantile spirit, which sought conciliation, compromise, and credit, with the "heroic" (or military) approach to foreign relations, Nicolson insisted that the commercial approach was more constructive. In this civilian conception of diplomacy, compromise was understood to be more profitable than the destruction of the opponent; negotiation could be seen as the attempt to reach a common understanding by mutual concession. Writing on the eve of World War II, the author (perhaps naively) felt that commercial interests and influence had made obsolete earlier "heroic" diplomacy with its tendency to compare diplomatic negotiations to a military campaign in which conciliation would mean defeat.[32]

Whether or not Nicolson was historically correct in tracing the emergence of the art of negotiation to the rise of the mercantile class and in predicting the eclipse of the "heroic" diplomacy of victory and defeat, it seems clear that he did correctly understand the art of diplomacy as accommodation; a foreign policy based on victory and defeat is, after all, nothing more than a military policy.

Support for this interpretation of the art of diplomacy can be found in Hans Morgenthau's analysis of international relations. Coming to the conclusion of his subtle and nuanced study of the contemporary international system, Morgenthau traced the acute instability and volatility of the system to the fact of its domination by the untraditional approach of the two superpowers to the issues of international politics. The United States and the Soviet Union, who both dismantled their experienced diplomatic corps, virtually simultaneously, but for divergent reasons, now face each other as inflexible crusaders for antagonistic political religions. In order to restore security to the international system, one or both of these superpowers will have to achieve what Morgenthau called the recovery of diplomacy, or the search for peace through accomodation. In other words, the nations will have to determine more realistically what is essential to their real interests, distinguishing real advantage from its shadow, and set out on a course of traditional diplomacy, with its three moments of persuasion, negotiation, and the exertion of pressure (the threat of force). Reminding the reader that force must remain an instrument of diplomacy and that the military sector of society must be controlled by political leaders, Morgenthau recalled the distinction between the traditional aims of war (to break the will of the enemy) and that of diplomacy (to bend his will). With a renewed understanding of the distinction between the unconditional goals of war and the conditional objectives of foreign policy, the United States (and the Soviet Union) can return to the pursuit of diplomacy, whose main purpose is to avoid the absolutes of victory and defeat and to meet the other side on the middle ground of negotiated compromise.[33]

In a passage reminiscent of the political writings of his friend, Hannah Arendt,[34] Morgenthau outlined his interpretation of international politics with an eloquent passage on the nature of power:

> When we speak of power in the context of this book, we have in mind not man's power over nature, or over an artistic medium, such as language, speech, sound, or color, or over the means of production or consumption, or over himself in the sense of self-control. When we speak of power, we

mean man's control over the minds and actions of other men. By political power we refer to the mutual relations of control among the holders of public authority and between the latter and the people at large.

Political power, however, must be distinguished from force in the sense of the actual exercise of physical violence. The threat of physical violence in the form of police action, imprisonment, capital punishment, or war is an intrinsic element of politics. When violence becomes an actuality, it signifies the abdication of political power in favor of military or pseudo-military power. In international politics in particular, armed strength as a threat or a potentiality is the most important material factor making for the political power of a nation. If it becomes an actuality in war, it signifies the substitution of military for political power. The actual exercise of physical violence substitutes for the psychological relation between two minds, which is of the essence of political power, the physical relation between two bodies, one of which is strong enough to dominate the other's movements. It is for this reason that in the exercise of physical violence the psychological element of the political relationship is lost, and that we must distinguish between military and political power.[35]

Political morality, for Morgenthau, as for the Greek theorists whom he understands so well, arises directly from a proper understanding of the nature of power itself as a relationship among people, and from a use of power in accordance with such an understanding. Power is used morally when it supports the psychological relationship among peoples and immorally when it relies on a use of force which is not duly subordinated to the restoration of such a psychological relationship.

Exactly the same political philosophy inspired the effort of Hannah Arendt to interpret the relation between ethics and politics. Although Arendt did not focus principally on international politics, her understanding of the antithetical relationship between power and violence echoed Morgenthau's analysis and led her to insist, as her fellow expatriate did, on the subordination of violence as an instrument of power. She said, for example, in her essay "On Violence,"

Power is indeed of the essence of all government, but violence is not. Violence is by nature instrumental; like all means, it always stands in need of guidance and justification through the end it pursues. And what needs justification by something else cannot be the essence of anything.

. . . Power is in the same category; it is, as they say, "an end in itself."[36]

DIPLOMACY AND DEFENSE

The Uses and Dangers of Violence

Hannah Arendt, in contrasting the characteristics of power and violence (which she admitted never exist in their pure form), perhaps overstated the case for their separability. Although power and violence are not identical, neither are they exact opposites, since such absolute opposition would preclude the employment of violence by power and thus undermine the very principle of the instrumentality of violence which Arendt has insisted on. Nonetheless, the difference between nonviolent power, such as Gandhi exercised so successfully, and the power of violence needs to be stressed continually. As Arendt pointed out, the tragic history of the use of violence to achieve political goals is that, more often than not, violence becomes an end in itself and devours the political goal which had legitimated the resort to violence in the first place.

George Kennan, the distinguished diplomat and scholar, has drawn attention to the same tendency—the tendency of the momentum of violence to replace political power as the governing force during warfare:

> And this leads me to the last thing I have to say. It is that the mistakes made in dealing with the Russians during World War II flowed not just from exaggerated military anxieties and from liberal illusions about the nature of *Soviet* society. A considerable importance must also be assigned to the seeming inability of a democratic state to cultivate and to hold in mind anything like a realistic image of a wartime adversary. The Nazi movement was in many ways a terrible thing: one of the most fearful manifestations modern history has to show of the delusions to which men are prone and the evil of which they are capable when they cut loose from all inhibitions of method and sell their souls to the pursuit of a total end. But this movement was not purely an act of God. It was not an evil miracle. It was a human tragedy, and one of which a great many German people were sufferers no less than others. No one would plead that the Allies should have blinded themselves to the danger of Hitler's ambitions or even to those deficiencies in the German experience and the German character which had made possible his rule. But had the statesmen of the West been able to look at Germany more thoughtfully and more dispassionately, to liberate themselves from the prejudices of World War I, to distinguish ruler from ruled, to search for the true origins of what had occurred, to recognize the measure of responsibility the Western democracies themselves had for the rise of Nazism in the first place, and to

remember that it was on the strength and hope of the German people, along with the others, that any tolerable postwar future for Europe would have to be built—had they been able to comprehend all this it would have helped them to understand the relationship of Russia to Germany in the war, to achieve a better balance in their dealings with both of these troublesome and problematical forces and thus, perhaps, to avoid or mitigate some of the most grievous of the war's political consequences.[37]

Commenting from another perspective, that of the moral philosopher, John Courtney Murray likewise drew attention to the consistent failure of reason to maintain control of violence during warfare. In a footnote to a statement about the possible utility of a theory of just war, Murray made the following pessimistic comment:

I use the subjunctive because I do not know how many wars in history would stand up under judgment by the traditional norms, or what difference it made at the time whether they did or not.[38]

Recalling the unprecedented violations of the precepts of civilized warfare during World War II, including obliteration-bombing, the use of the atomic bomb, and the Allied policy of unconditional surrender, Murray concluded that the doctrine of the just war

is hardly more than a *Grenzmoral*, an effort to establish on a minimal basis of reason a form of human action, the making of war, that remains always fundamentally irrational.[39]

Violence, then, is neither identical with power, nor antithetical to power, but remains an instrument which may be employed for the sake of maintaining or restoring the social relationship among peoples. Yet violence is an instrument ever liable to slip from the guiding hand of politics. Rather than contributing to the creativity which is the purpose of politics, violence is often destructive of political relationships.

It was this melancholy history of violence that led Gandhi to re-examine the foundations of politics and to seek out a new political framework which would dispense with the reliance on violence. Convinced that creativity arises solely from human relationships, Gandhi sought to sublimate the aggressive instinct of the human being through his strategy of *satyagraha*, the effort to establish and maintain a relationship with one's adversary that will force each party to a controversy to examine the validity of various positions. In this distinctively oriental way, Gandhi sought to revitalize the art of diplomacy. The Mahatma's own remarkable political achievements, attained without resort to violence, suggest the need for a re-examination of the dynamics of politics as the effort to maintain psychological relationships.[40]

Hannah Arendt, along with other sympathetic critics, however, has pointed out the special context in which Gandhi was successful, namely, in a relationship between a constitutional monarchy and one of its own colonies during a period when the empire was becoming unwieldy. What, Arendt has asked, would *satyagraha* have availed against Hitler or Stalin?[41] Would capitulation by Gandhi's followers to such a military response have achieved the political truth which is the goal of *satyagraha?* Is it not true that physical resistance may at times be required to maintain the psychological relationships between individuals and nations which are the essence of power? Is there no moral justification possible for self-defense?

It is perhaps only a coincidence that, at the same time that Gandhi was leading a successful nonviolent campaign of persuasion against the British Empire, the representatives of Great Britain were trying to deal with Hitler using only the instruments of persuasion, unenforced by adequate military strength. Striving to reach some accomodation with Hitler at Munich, Chamberlain failed and thereby revalidated the lesson of traditional diplomacy which insisted that the threat of force accompany or follow efforts to persuade and to negotiate. Traditional diplomacy, in other words, which devotes its skill to the effort to persuade the adversary of the validity of its initial claims and, failing this, to negotiate a compromise position which maintains a part of its initial demand, does not hesitate in certain circumstances to threaten the enforcement of its demands by violence. Diplomacy thus draws a sharp distinction between accommodation and appeasement. There are certain elements of its demands on which a nation will not yield, except to superior force.

What is the moral legitimacy of this traditional willingness to threaten, or actually to use, force when it is necessary to protect the interests of the state? What is the moral validity of self-defense? How can the use of force be said to contribute to the maintenance of psychological (and social) relationships among peoples?

A beginning toward solving this perennial political and ethical puzzle can be made by reflecting on the indispensability of *identity* to any human relationship. Without two unique individuals (or groups) there can be no relationship. Whenever, then, one party to a relationship threatens the identity of the other, the defense of the latter individual's (or group's) identity is *required* in order to maintain the relationship itself. If, then, political power is the relationship among individuals (or among groups), the dynamics of power itself require whatever action is necessary to save the identity of the threatened partner.

The phenomenon of identity is perhaps more readily recognized in interpersonal relationships.[42] Here, once more, it might be helpful to recall the figure of Thomas More, whose resistance to the encroachments of Henry VIII has become a cultural symbol of personal identity and integrity. Robert Bolt betokened the fascination that More exerts on the modern imagination. In the preface to his play based on More's struggle with the Crown, Bolt remarked on the relationship between a sense of identity and moral heroism:

> At any rate, Thomas More, as I wrote about him, became for me a man with an adamantine sense of his own self. He knew where he began and left off, what area of himself he could yield to the encroachments of his enemies, and what to the encroachments of those he loved. It was a substantial area in both cases, for he had a proper sense of fear and was a busy lover. Since he was a clever man and a great lawyer he was able to retire from those areas in wonderfully good order, but at length he was asked to retreat from that final area where he located his self. And there this supple, humorous, unassuming and sophisticated person set like metal, was overtaken by an absolutely primitive rigor, and could no more be budged than a cliff.[43]

Resistance is the appropriate personal reaction to encroachments which threaten the identity of individuals. Thus, from the self-affirmation of their own worth springs the apparently negative power of self-defense. There are certain things that individuals will not willingly suffer. Their principles express abstractly the claim of selfhood which they will protect even at the cost of suffering. Although willing to compromise on nonessential differences with their social partners, individuals define certain nonnegotiable commitments. From such commitments spring personal ethics.

States, too, and statesmen acting in their name, are able to define those interests (elements of self-identity) on which they will not compromise—territorial integrity, preservation of political institutions, freedom from internal political interference, freedom to form alliances, access to necessary imports and markets, and so on. These legitimate interests define the prerequisites of national identity and, therefore, the national interest. In pursuing its foreign policy, a sovereign nation rightly defines those interests as limits to compromise. On more tangential issues, its foreign policy may be flexible, but on these points it is firm. When these core values are threatened, the nation's diplomacy abandons the search for compromise and turns to the threat of force. In so doing it does not abandon the political (and moral) order, but rather reaffirms that its own enduring identity is essential to the preservation of those psychological and social relationships which constitute international political power. Self-defense, in other words, is not an abandonment of politics but, as von Clausewitz contended, its continuation by other means.

Force and the Political Heritage of the United States

In this inquiry into the relationship between ethics and foreign policy, I have employed the hypothesis that the philosophy which shapes the domestic political structure can serve as a guide to a morally acceptable foreign policy. Since consistency demands that a nation conduct its foreign affairs in accord with its political philosophy, the traditional diplomatic art of compromise is deeply consonant with the United States' constitutional principles and procedures for resolving conflicts of domestic interest. Is there, however, in the United States' political heritage, any warrant for, or parallel to, the traditional resort to the threat of force when a nation is threatened in its identity or integrity? Is there a domestic political principle which can justify the limits to compromise I have outlined as the prerequisite for national integrity?

The answer comes fairly readily to mind: The Bill of Rights functions in our political system as a limit to compromise, circumscribing the legitimate range of procedural compromise on political disputes within the nation. Although the constitutionally sanctioned procedures for maintaining consent among different parties are accepted as a cornerstone of political society in the United States, these procedures are allowed to resolve only those disputes in which neither party is contesting the validity of any of the rights outlined in the first ten amendments. On these rights of the individual and society, no compromise is possible. The validity and exercise of these rights is not open to dispute, only to interpretation. In addition to the procedural processes the Constitution provides to protect the people of the United States, there are principles found in the Bill of Rights on which the people will admit no compromise.

The domestic polity, then, like the international, is based on the traditional triad of persuasion, negotiation, and the threat of force which is brought to bear on those violating the rights of others. Hence, force cannot be understood as the antithesis of power, but as one of its constitutive features. The threat, or use, of force is morally legitimate, domestically or internationally, provided only that it remains an instrument of political power, an effective safeguard of political identity.

International power (understood as the capacity of a national group to maintain reciprocal relationships with other nations without a loss of its own national identity) may, then, require the use of force, just as domestic political power relies on the police function. Self-defense may be a requirement imposed by the dynamics of power itself. Violence, even lethal violence, can be morally legitimated by the exigencies of power. Killing can be an act of political virtue.[44]

DEFENSE IN THE NUCLEAR AGE

There is, however, a "logic" to military action taken in self-defense (or in defense of an ally)[45] which imposes limits on the *type* of military action which is legitimate. If these limits are transgressed, the use of violence becomes immoral because it ceases to be an instrument of political power and actually subverts power, the maintenance of psychological and social relations among nations, which alone validates the use of force.

The logic of defense is commonly considered to include six elements, three of which pertain to the political objective or goal of military force, while the remaining three delimit the means or strategies that may be employed to effect these goals.[46] A brief delineation of these six elements as they are represented, for example, in the just-war theory, may be helpful in addressing the central question of this volume: whether the traditional moral criteria retain any validity for the task of evaluating nuclear strategic planning.

The logic of self-defense gives rise to the articulation of three limitations concerning the legitimate political objectives of military force: programs of national defense must be (1) defensive,

(2) exclusively defensive, and (3) exclusive of the intention or effect of annihilating the other nation.[47]

The war, and any single military action within a war, must be *defensive* in the sense that it responds to an unjust action by the aggressor nation, who must previously have taken military, political, or economic measures which significantly interfere with the defending nation's national identity, either internally or in its relationship with other nations. (Invasion is the most obvious example of such interference with national power, but an economic blockade or political subversion might also constitute an act of injustice which would warrant defensive military action.)

Such a military response to aggression, taken after the patient work of diplomacy has yielded no settlement of the grievance, must not be allowed to transform itself into a reciprocal act of aggression or retaliation. Neither may military action, undertaken legitimately, be continued in order to achieve concealed aggressive intentions under a cloak of defense. Herbert Butterfield has expressed the traditional criterion of an *exclusively defensive* intention:

> There was one occasion on the eve of the Abyssinian War when the Pope made reference to this tradition and offered a commentary which is relevant to our present discussion. He put forward the significant general thesis: 'A war of defence is justified; but even a war of defence can be pushed too far.' To any dispassionate person the least that this thesis must mean is that, though your enemy may have attacked you first, and you have a right to defend yourself, his sin does not justify you in . . . carrying on the war for the purpose of destroying that enemy or breaking him up. There was a famous case in the eighteenth century of what was called 'a defensive treaty with an offensive *arrière-pensée*.' It amounted to the agreement: 'We will wait until Prussia attacks, but once she has given us the pretext for war, we will combine not merely for defence but for her radical dismemberment.' Such a policy, besides being ethically dubious in itself, is calculated to be harmful most of all (as we shall see) because it is precisely the method by which to destroy the international order.[48]

Finally, it is in the nature of a just, defensive military action that it desist before the aggressor has been annihilated. The destruction of the aggressor nation as a viable society can never be the goal of military force since annihilation evidently exceeds the minimal action necessary to deter aggression.[49]

The Application of Ethical Principles

What implications does this tripartite understanding of morally legitimate defensive goals have for planning defense priorities in a nuclear age? Nuclear weapons might be found acceptable as an instrument of politics if they can be used *defensively*—that is, as the *minimal force* necessary to prevent, diminish, or repel an act of unjust aggression by an enemy—provided that such weapons do not result even in collateral (unintentional) damage equivalent to the destruction of the aggressor society. It is clear that the use of nuclear weapons merely to retaliate against an attacking nation—that is, without plausible defensive purpose or hope of diminishing or repelling an attack—is morally indefensible since it involves a useless sacrifice of human life and social structures. The moral question, then, is this: Short of actual retaliatory strikes against an aggressing society, are there other, legitimate, defensive purposes for which nuclear weapons might be used?

A variety of responses to this question are offered by various authors in this volume. In this paper I will restrict myself to the factors I believe must be considered in searching for answers,[50] starting with an analysis of the second three conditions contained in the logic of defense—namely, the restrictions placed on strategies or military means employed to attain legitimate political objectives.

Within the political and military perspective of justifiable defense arises the second traditional question—the selection of military strategies that are permissible as instruments to carry out such defensive purposes. The necessity for considering these further strategic criteria arises from the very defensive nature of the political decision to go to war. If defense is the rationale for violence, certain strategies, which could only be explained as aggressive measures, fail to qualify as reasonable ends to the objective being sought.

Traditional strategic limitations include: (1) the principle of *discrimination*, which proscribes the intentional attack on noncombatants, as well as deliberate attacks on nonmilitary sectors of the economy which cannot contribute to the military effort during the present conflict; (2) the principle of *proportionality*, which states that the political goal to be achieved by military action must clearly exceed the damage inevitably done by the use of force; and (3) the principle of *political utility*, which requires a reasonable ground of certitude that the means used can indeed achieve the legitimate goal for which they are employed—in other words, that such defensive strategy have a reasonable chance of (at least political) success. These three restrictive principles deserve individual elucidation prior to examining their potential application to the nuclear strategic debate.

The principle of *discrimination*, or selection among militarily feasible targets, limits targeting to those elements of the aggressing society which are actually cooperating in the act of aggression, or which can reasonably be expected to contribute to the aggression during the current hostilities. By insisting on the process of discrimination among targets, the tradition of civilized warfare rejects the excesses inherent in the relatively recent (eighteenth- and nineteenth-century) concept of total war and insists on the necessity of fighting for limited ends by appropriately circumscribed strategies.[51]

Within the principle of discrimination, there are two preeminent subprinciples: that of civilian immunity from intentional attack, and that of the sanctity (inviolability) of nonmilitary sectors of the economy. Each of these subprinciples is, of course, disputed and requires explanation and defense.

The principle of *civilian inviolability* is probably the operatively central element within the tradition of limited war. It insists that even morally legitimate, defensive wars must be prosecuted without resort to terrorization or murder of civilians, even going so far as to prefer surrender to the deliberate targeting of noncombatants. There may be, in other words, unjust wars of aggression which must be allowed to achieve their immoral objectives if the *only* way to resist them successfully is to attack deliberately the civilian sectors of the hostile populace. Another controversial consequence of adherence to this principle might be the necessity of prolonging a war in order to win it without violating the principle of discrimination.[52]

When the principle is viewed in this light, its problematic nature becomes clear and the issue at stake in the debate over its validity is more apparent. How is such a principle validated? On what grounds do moral critics insist that it is always morally illegitimate to murder civilians even though this proscription may result in military defeat or the prolongation of war? What is the source of the obligation contained in the principle of civilian immunity?

The principle of discrimination is the military application of the more universal and comprehensive prohibition against the shedding of blood. Evolving through whatever shrouded history it may have had, the instinct that prohibits the initiation of a violent and lethal attack on a fellow human being represents the perennial recognition of a symbolic boundary whose observance can shield the human community from wanton bloodshed. Students of conflict resolution, such as Thomas Schelling, have suggested that the observance of such symbolic boundaries may function as a process of tacit bargaining between hostile groups who seek to find an upper limit on the amount of violence they are willing to exercise in order to change their overall relationship.[53] Over the ages, this taboo against aggressive killing has gradually been formulated as the prohibition against intended attacks on those who are not themselves aggressors. The incorporation of this traditional limit on violence into the body of international law was detailed by Hans Morgenthau in *Politics Among Nations*. In it Morgenthau drew attention to the affirmation of this prohibition in the Hague Conventions of 1899 and 1907, and in the Geneva Convention of 1949.[54] Another readily available catalogue of international legal restrictions on the targeting of civilians is a survey prepared by the secretariat of the United Nations entitled, "Respect for Human Rights in Armed Conflicts: Part I."[55] According to these moral and legal principles, the intentional targeting of civilians is forbidden.

A second element contained in the principle of discrimination is the prohibition against *directly targeting nonmilitary sectors of the economy* of the aggressing nation. During World War II, both military and moral doctrines were relaxed to allow aerial destruction of the industrial base of the enemy, on the theory that war materiel was as essential to the war effort as combatants, and that those people and industries directly involved in production of such armaments were legitimate defensive targets. The validity of this shift in moral teaching is an issue currently in need of re-examination in the light of the qualitative and chronological differences between conventional and nuclear war. It is, of course, quite likely that armaments or military supplies still in the stage of production at the outbreak of nuclear hostilities will never see service during the nuclear encounter and are, hence, not legitimate defensive targets.

Proportionality is the second criterion traditionally used to judge the moral acceptability of specific strategies in the prosecution of defensive warfare. Assuming that the principle of discrimination is being observed as a strategic limit, the principle of proportionality further delimits the range of morally acceptable strategies by requiring the strategist to weigh the values to be defended by the war (or the particular campaign or attack) against the destruction foreseeable as a result of the military action under consideration. This principle demands a balancing of loss and gain, measured on a moral and political scale: Does the defensive value of the strategy outweigh the combination of *intended and collateral* damage which can realistically be expected to result from the strategy? Any strategy which would prudently be expected to lead to the destruction of either the aggressor's or defender's society (or, *a fortiori*, of both societies) would clearly exceed any conceivable value to be derived from the use of violence. In such a case, violence would have become an end in itself, divorced from the political purpose, which is the maintenance or restoration of relations between societies; the extinction of either society obviously would preclude such a relationship. The almost routine use by military and political leaders in the United States of the phrase "destruction of the U.S.S.R. as a viable society" indicates how much the political control of military power has eroded in recent decades.

Finally, there is the principle of *political utility*. By this criterion, moralists recall the instrumental nature of violence and insist that its use be related to some achievable political purpose —namely, defense of a society's internal or external relations. Any strategy which could prudently be judged futile would, by that judgment, be eliminated as a morally defensible choice.

CONCLUSION

The application of such political-moral criteria to defense planning in the nuclear era constitutes the most profound challenge ever to confront conscience. Conscientious citizens and professionals differ radically on the validity and/or utility of the criteria themselves, on their implications for modern defense planning, and on the political implications of renouncing the use of nuclear weapons on moral grounds. Contributors to this volume themselves witness to the variety of responses which are made to these problems.

Do any of these proposals resolve the dilemma of defense in the nuclear age? What sort of nuclear strategy is compatible with the continued partnership among nations to which the United States is committed by the exigencies of its own political vision? Can we devise a nuclear strategy that will be morally acceptable?

In service of the national debate required to address these questions, I would suggest three conditions which should be verified in any revision of nuclear strategic planning. It may be that attention to these three conditions will facilitate the adoption of a defense policy more consistent with the ethos of the American people than the policy the United States is following now. The three conditions are that the proposed policy be sound *politically*, *constitutionally*, and *ethically*.

The political test may be the most difficult to meet, for it requires that those who finally determine policy understand the ultimate seriousness of politics. Politics is the process of choosing among genuine alternatives and selecting a policy designed to effect the welfare of the society. While the enunciation of this condition may seem banal, I would suggest that, on the contrary, comparatively few Americans approach politics as a matter of ultimate seriousness. The touchstone of political seriousness is a belief in freedom, the genuine capacity for self-governance. Very few Americans, despite their political heritage, really believe that, on a question such as nuclear strategy, they have any policy options available to them. They feel, at least unconsciously, that no alternative to current strategies is conceivable, or at least that no alternative strategy is politically feasible. Until this implicit fatalism is recognized and overcome, no constructive political solution is possible.

It is remarkable to one who teaches in the area of ethics and foreign policy how often he hears an instantaneous and automatic reaction of disbelief to the suggestion of a moral assessment of foreign policy. "Ethics and foreign policy? Is there any such thing?" The quickness and confidence of this endlessly repeated reaction evidences a cultural assumption that one must choose between ethics and politics. Politics itself, however, is precisely the process of choosing among alternative policies. On what grounds does one choose? Surely, anyone who makes policy decisions has some ethical perceptions, as political theorists have noted.[56] Nor would those rejecting the notion of relating ethics and foreign policy deny this ethical impact on the decision of policymakers. What is most often being reflected in this almost universal resistance to the introduction of ethics into politics, I believe, is a deep-seated conviction on the part of the citizenry that policy is determined by someone else, not by the public—that the policy choices of the United States government are not popular decisions, but merely anonymous bureaucratic determinations for which no one is finally responsible.[57] Even in a participatory political situation, such as the United States, very few believe that they are a part of the process of self-government. On all the significant questions, people feel, decisions are made without accountability to the citizens. Hence, any talk of judging policy by ethical criteria is useless because such ethical evaluations would ultimately be ineffectual.

If this assessment of the popular understanding of the political process is correct, the first condition of a situation that can lead to morally acceptable defense postures is a recovery of politics itself, a renewed realization that, at least in the United States, policymaking is a responsibility from which citizens cannot divorce themselves. The decision to allow someone else to determine policy on the ultimate questions of national security constitutes an irresponsible abandonment of politics and an acceptance of fatalism. The recovery of ethics in foreign policy, then, must follow upon a recovery of politics itself, upon a reassertion by the citizenry of their prerogative to influence foreign policy. Without this reawakening to the seriousness of popular political responsibility in a republic, there can indeed be no such thing as a juncture of ethics and foreign policy.

How can this recovery of politics come about? With this question, we come to the second condition of a morally acceptable defense posture—namely the constitutional condition. By this I mean that United States citizens must return to the spirit of the Constitution, by which federal power is diffused among the three branches of the government. Although former Secretaries James Schlesinger and Henry Kissinger have called for "a great national debate" on strategic defense policies to accompany the continuing bilateral SALT proceedings, only a handful of those outside the government have availed themselves of the opportunity to participate in this process of reshaping United States policies. The churches, for example, as institutional representatives of the claims of conscience, have been conspicuously silent on the crucial question of strategic planning. Unless more citizens commit themselves to the demanding intellectual task of entering into this debate, the legislative branch of government will likely continue to accede to the executive on these questions. Without a more broadly based discussion of strategic questions, the legislative counterbalance to administrative pressures will be ineffectual and the constitutionally sanctioned conflict between the interest of the people and those of the military-political bureaucracies will fail to arise. The second crucial condition for framing a morally acceptable defense posture, then, is the renewal of popular participation, through the elected representatives in the legislature, in the shaping of policy.

Finally, this governmental re-examination of defense policy will be morally acceptable only if citizens become conscious of the urgent importance of preserving the traditional taboos against the intentional killing of civilians. If this apparently waning awareness of the necessity to set limits to the use of violence can be revived, the constitutional process of government itself may be able to refashion U.S. defense postures in a way that will be more in accord with our own political heritage.

In summary, I could perhaps do nothing better than to echo the challenge of General T. Dacey, former commander of the Strategic Air Command (SAC), when he was asked about the ethical validity of using the strategic forces at his command. During his years as commander he had often been asked this question and had settled on a response which is politically and morally sound: "If you want us to stand down, tell us."[58]

To careful reflection on this challenge and to the formulation of a responsible reply, this volume is devoted in a spirit of urgency and hope.

NOTES

1. See, for example, Paul Ramsey, "Force and Political Responsibility," in *Ethics and World Politics*, ed. E. Lefever (Baltimore: Johns Hopkins University Press, 1972), pp. 43–73; Hannah Arendt, "Reflections: Truth and Politics," *The New Yorker*, February 25, 1967, pp. 49–88; Albert Camus, *The Rebel*, trans. A. Bower (New York: Random House, Vintage Books, 1956), pp. 13–22, 277–306.

2. Ramsey, "Force and Political Responsibility," pp. 43–50. John Yoder, representing another tradition of theologically grounded political theory, has derived practical conclusions about the validity of pacifism from a profoundly different view of politics. Denying that "making history move down the right tracks" is "a high good," Yoder consistently disallows the use of violence to achieve political goals (*The Politics of Jesus* [Grand Rapids: Eerdmans, 1972], pp. 241–246). Underneath the clash in policy recommendations between Yoder and natural-law thinkers such as Ramsey, there lies the deeper issue of the significance of politics. For a fuller treatment of the issues raised here, see my article "The Violence of Truth," *Worldview*, January 1974, pp. 21–26.

3. "Reflections" p. 88. In her recent commentary, *The Political Thought of Hannah Arendt* (New York and London: Harcourt, Brace, Jovanovich, 1974), Margaret Canovan has drawn attention to a significant lacuna in the system, namely, the failure to integrate the realms of truth and politics. This lapse appears most conspicuously in Arendt's treatment of the *apolitical* nature of con-

science in her essay "On Civil Disobedience," *Crises of the Republic* (New York: Harcourt, Brace, Jovanovich, Harvest Books, 1969), especially pp. 58–68.

4. Hannah Arendt, *Eichmann in Jerusalem, A Report on the Banality of Evil* (New York: Viking Press, Compass Books, 1964).

5. Camus, *The Rebel*, p. 21.

6. Albert Camus, *The Plague*, trans. S. Gilbert (New York: Modern Library, 1948), p. 278.

7. Particularly helpful studies, which include further references to the literature, are Herbert Butterfield, *Christianity, Diplomacy and War* (London: The Epworth Press, 1953); John Courtney Murray, S. J., *We Hold These Truths* (New York: Sheed and Ward, 1960), chaps. 4, 8, 11, 12; Kenneth W. Thompson, *Christian Ethics and the Dilemmas of Foreign Policy* (Durham: Duke University Press, 1959).

8. Arendt, *Crises of the Republic*, p. 60.

9. A catalogue of the German intellectuals who fled to the United States after 1933 would represent a very sizable portion of the creative scholars active in American intellectual life since that time.

10. Writing of More, his gifted biographer R. W. Chambers summarized the universal significance of his decision: "But, if there be indeed some power dwelling in the heart of man, which may give him commands at variance with those of the State to which he is subject; if there be, besides the written laws, what Antigone calls the unwritten and unfailing laws of the gods; if man must render, not only to Caesar the things that be Caesar's, but to God the things that be God's; how is poor man to decide which things belong to which? More placed the right of the State to silence the individual very much higher, and the right of the individual to claim liberty of conscience from the State very much lower than we in England should place them today. Yet he died for the right of the individual conscience, as against the State. Hence he has been attacked on both sides; in his own day, and occasionally since, because he claimed any right whatever against the all-competent, supreme State; by the English historians in the great Whig and Liberal tradition of the Eighteenth and Nineteenth Centuries, because he conceded to the State so much. The problem of what is due to the individual conscience, what to the State, is indeed an eternal one, and not a few people have been surprised and distressed to find it emerging in Europe today [1938], as much alive as ever it was. 'Wherefore our battle is immortal, and the gods and angels fight on our side, and we are their possession. . . . And the things that save us are justice, self-command, and true thought, which things dwell in the living power of the gods' (*Laws*, Book X). So wrote Plato, naming three of the four Cardinal Virtues on which Utopia is founded—fortitude is the fourth. Plato's fine words do not solve the problem for us; every man at need must do it for himself, for the ability to weigh two duties, and balance them against each other, is the measure of human worth and dignity. It rings through the *Antigone* of Sophocles as it does through the *Apology* of Socrates, and nowhere will it be found more clearly than in More's writings in prison. It was as one of a mighty company that, on Tuesday 6 July 1535, he spoke on the scaffold his last words: 'that they should pray for him in this world, and he would pray for them elsewhere, protesting that he died the King's good servant, but God's first' " (R. W. Chambers, *Thomas More* [Ann Arbor: University of Michigan Press, Ann Arbor Paperbacks, 1965], pp. 399–400).

11. Camus, *The Rebel*, p. 21.

12. Heinrich Rommen, *The Natural Law*, trans. T. Hanley (St. Louis: Herder, 1947), part I.

13. *The Federalist*, ed. Jacob E. Cooke (Middletown: Wesleyan University Press, 1961), no. 10, pp. 60, 63–64.

14. Ibid., no. 51, pp. 349–53.

15. Cited by Richard Hofstadter in *The American Political Tradition* (New York: Random House, Vintage Books, 1955), p. 29.

16. *The Federalist*, no. 63, p. 423.
17. *Ethics and World Politics: Four Perspectives*, ed. E. Lefever (Baltimore: Johns Hopkins University Press, 1972).
18. Ibid., p. 35.
19. Ibid., p. 42.
20. Ibid., pp. 79–80, 91–92.
21. Ibid., pp. 51–52.
22. K. J. Holsti, *International Politics* (Englewood Cliffs: Prentice-Hall, 1972), pp. 427–28.
23. Hans Morgenthau, *Politics Among Nations* (New York: A. Knopf, 1967), pp. 224–25.
24. For the recent revelations about the possession of these codes throughout the war, see F. W. Winterbotham, *Ne Plus Ultra* (New York: Harper & Row, 1974).
25. See Giovannitti and Freed, *The Decision to Drop the Bomb* (New York: Coward-McCann, 1965).
26. A moral critique of this decision has been made by Murray in *We Hold These Truths*, p. 265.
27. Dean Acheson, *This Vast External Realm* (New York: Norton, 1973), p. 27.
28. Ibid., p. 137.
29. Ibid., pp. 27–28.
30. In the televised film series, *American Civilization*, in the section entitled "Inventing a Nation."
31. Harold Nicolson, *Diplomacy* (New York: Harcourt, Brace and Company, 1939), p. 50.
32. Ibid., pp. 52–55.
33. Morgenthau, *Politics Among Nations*, pp. 546–47.
34. See Arendt, *Crises of the Republic*, pp. 134–55.
35. Morgenthau, *Politics Among Nations*, pp. 26–27.
36. Arendt, *Crises of the Republic*, p. 150. A similar analysis of power can be found in Murray, *We Hold These Truths*, p. 288.
37. George F. Kennan, *Russia and the West under Lenin and Stalin* (Boston and Toronto: Little, Brown and Co., 1961), pp. 368–69.
38. John Courtney Murray, S. J., *Morality and Modern War* (New York: Council on Religion and International Affairs, 1959), p. 23, no. 8. The same essay appears under the title "The Uses of a Doctrine on the Uses of Force," in *We Hold These Truths*.
39. Ibid., p. 14.
40. For a thoughtful study of the roots and impact of Gandhi's understanding of politics as the art of partnership, see Erik Erikson, *Gandhi's Truth : On the Origins of Militant Non-Violence* (New York: W. W. Norton, 1969).
41. *Crises of the Republic*, p. 152.
42. Erik Erikson has been perhaps the leading theorist of the relation between human development and identity. See his works, *Childhood and Society* (New York: W. W. Norton, 1950), and *Insight and Responsibility* (New York: W. W. Norton, 1964).
43. Robert Bolt, *A Man for All Seasons* (New York: Vintage Books, 1960), xi.
44. On this stark reality moral theorists are sometimes unable to find verbal agreement. Just-war theorists, such as Murray and Ramsey, for example, are more liable to come to such a formulation than writers who have been more fashioned by Protestant approaches to political ethics, such as Kenneth Thompson. For evidence of this difference of accent, which often grows acrimonious, see the exchanges between Murray and Reinhold Niebuhr, as reported only by Murray in *We Hold These Truths*, p. 278 ff., and between Murray and Thompson, both of whom allude to the controversy, in Murray, *Morality and Modern War*, p. 21, no. 1, and Thompson, *Christian Ethics and the Dilemmas of Foreign Policy* (Durham: Duke University Press, 1959), pp. 136–44.

45. It is evident, but sometimes not noted by beginning students of the question, that the resort to violence in defense of an ally can be justified by exactly the same criteria as the resort to self-defense.

46. The literature on the moral doctrine of defense is immense. A good beginning can be made by consulting the literature noted in n. 7 above.

47. Actually, these three qualifications of the political objective of using violence merely constitute a comprehensive interpretation of the legitimate meaning of defense. Yet the separation of the notion of defense into three criteria is helpful in clarifying the implications of the criterion.

48. Butterfield, *Christianity, Diplomacy and War*, pp. 19–20. Another expression of this same *caveat* against the excesses to which any military momentum may drive a nation is the criterion of *right intention.* The meaning of this criterion is that national leaders must actually be intending to rectify the illegitimate interference with their national identity. In other words, they may not use the fact of prior aggression to pursue their own aggressive designs.

49. A classic illustration of the violation of this principle was the Allied policy of unconditional surrender in World War II. Against this policy, which led to more resolute resistance by the Axis powers and ultimately to the use by the Allies of atomic weapons to bring Japan to surrender without terms, moral critics argue that the policy of unconditional surrender violated the nature of international politics, which is the interaction of sovereign states, and ignored the postwar necessity to rebuild the very societies which had been so utterly destroyed.

50. My personal answers may be found in another essay in this volume, "The Nuclear Arms Race: Machine versus Man."

51. See Murray, *We Hold These Truths*, chaps. 11 and 12, and Butterfield, *Christianity, Diplomacy and War*, chap. 2.

52. The question of the surrender of Japan in World War II is the most prominent recent case in question. Discussion of this situation must always be related to the prior issue of the relation between Japanese resistance and the Allied doctrine of unconditional surrender.

53. Thomas Schelling, *The Strategy of Conflict* (London and New York: Oxford University Press, 1960), pp. 70–73.

54. Morgenthau, *Politics Among Nations*, p. 229. A crucial moral distinction is indicated by the traditional qualification implied in the adjective *intentional* (targeting of civilians). By this qualification, just-war theorists insist that it makes a difference where the targeting party aims. Realizing that the act of targeting a legitimate objective may cause damage to other individuals or structures nearby, moralists have claimed that, for sufficient reason, it is allowable deliberately to target the legitimate objective even in the knowledge that some unintended (collateral) damage may be done to innocent or noncombatant personnel. According to this view, the evil of the foreseen but unintended civilian deaths is justified by the comparatively greater value of self-defense, which would be impossible without this regrettable evil. It is, of course, no secret that many critics find this distinction a simple rationalization for utilitarian decisions. Nevertheless, the moral significance of the distinction remains persuasive to a broad spectrum of analysts.

55. United Nations, General Assembly, "Respect for Human Rights in Armed Conflicts: Part I," 28th sess., agenda item no. 96 (A/9915, vol. 1), November 7, 1973, pp. 17–20.

56. See, for example, Holsti, *International Politics*, pp. 427–28, and Morgenthau, *Politics Among Nations*, pp. 224–25.

57. Hannah Arendt referred to this situation as "rule by nobody" (*Crises of the Republic*, p. 137). More succinctly it might be termed "outocracy" (from the Greek for "no one" and "rule").

58. "The American Military in the Seventies," NBC-TV broadcast (January 30, 1970).

3

Politics, Ethics, and the Arms Race

Harold P. Ford

THE SETTING

Both sides have to convince their military establishments of the benefits of restraint, and that does not come easily to either side. . . . What in the name of God is strategic superiority? What do you do with it?

Henry Kissinger (July 3, 1974, upon returning from the Moscow summit conference), *New York Times*, July 4, 1974

The sad fact is that Soviet-American arms-control agreements, to date, have done little more than establish the ground rules for a formally sanctioned, qualitative arms race, permitting both military establishments to perfect most of the new weapons systems they desire. With luck, future arms-control agreements may produce mutual quantitative cutbacks, at least on certain items, but there is danger that the new fears and momentums which SALT-II has set loose will simply bring us all more and better arms—and less security.

The situation is truly Grecian tragedy. U.S. strategic policymakers are uncertain about the U.S.S.R.'s motives and feel that the United States must overinsure against the possibility that Soviet leaders may be seeking strategic superiority and/or a nuclear blackmail capability; Soviet leaders, on their part, justify their weapons buildup by the need to overtake the United States' marked qualitative advantage in nuclear arms and so end the

---

This chapter, now rewritten and updated, derives from an essay the author first prepared for the Georgetown University Seminars. A second, shorter chapter, differing from this present one in various respects but also deriving from that same initial seminar source, is appearing in Kenneth W. Thompson and Robert J. Myers, eds., *Truth and Tragedy: A Tribute to Hans Morgenthau* (New York: New Republic Publishing Co., 1977).

U.S.S.R.'s position of inferiority. Yet the gap—and the Soviet impetus—does not narrow. Thus our anomalous situation of sharply rising arms expenditures amid SALT negotiations and supposed détente. That phenomenon of selective "détente," whether or not explicitly acknowledged by President Ford, of course remains in fact essentially a form of cold peace, a many-faceted continuing struggle for world influence and advantage, fed on both sides by the hypnosis of competition. In the meantime, the accompanying arms race, in many respects, is not only irrelevant to the broader problems of world economic and social turmoil but adds its own new instabilities to the volatile world scene.

And so we have the phenomenon, too, of rising military expenditures, which are distorting other national priorities in both the Soviet Union and the United States. This similarity is but one of countless ways in which the two nations are growing to resemble one another—not with respect to political convergence, but to pride, uncertainty, distrust, outmoded institutions, militarized economies, domestic military influence, technology worship, imperial status, bureaucratic politics, momentum toward ever more weapons, policymaking secrecy, self-righteousness, and international amorality.

The problem is that beyond the SALT talks and the new generation of weapons systems lies the many-dimensioned U.S.-Soviet struggle for supremacy in the world, an evasive goal which will not necessarily translate into demonstrable reward even if strategic "supremacy" can somehow be achieved. Nuclear weapons have, in one sense, not changed the face of world politics at all. The present frailties and insecurities of human beings, their societies, and their military strategies are not appreciably different from those of the ancient past—except that it is now the Politburo vs. the National Security Council, or "assured destruction" vs. "counterforce," rather than Cain vs. Abel, or Alcibiades vs. Nicias.

And yet nuclear weapons have changed everything. One cannot but agree with Andrei Sakharov that a "thermonuclear war cannot be considered a continuation of politics by other means."[1] The problem before the world in 1977, however, is whether *limited* nuclear hostilities qualify under the well-known Clausewitz formula that war is simply a continuation of politics by other means, in view of the fact that both competitors, Soviet and American, are now definitely flirting with the proposition that resort to nuclear arms can be managed and restrained. We observers—and potential victims—simply ask, what would U.S.-Soviet fighting be all about? And how do we know that a war would not degenerate haphazardly into the war *à outrance* that has been so prevalent in major twentieth-century conflicts?

To these questions the antagonists bring considerable similarities and differences. The latter, perhaps the more familiar, involve countless asymmetries of all kinds. Possibly most important is the fact that the Soviet Union is still very much a young, assertive great power, sworn not to accept the status quo; by contrast, the United States is not inaccurately captured in Russell Baker's characterization as no longer the nation of George Washington but of George III.[2] We also differ from the U.S.S.R. in our absence of experience with total war and occupation, a difference which helps explain Soviet insecurities, as well as the dispassionate manner in which many U.S. strategists discuss—and accept—the prospect of nuclear hostilities. Such confidence may result, as well, from the possible two-front war which faces the U.S.S.R. but not the United States at present; Soviet leaders must grind Chinese unknowns into their simultaneous strategic equations, even though they clearly perceive China as secondary to the Western-U.S. threat. We differ also in what we bring from the recent past to the present: The U.S. psyche has been deeply scarred by the events in Indochina, the Watergate scandal, the Nixon resignation, economic trauma, and—not to be overlooked—a widespread sensation among policymakers that some kind of remedial strategic steps are called for, now that the U.S.S.R. is MIRVing its great strategic weapons.

Yet it is U.S.-Soviet similarities that have the greatest relevance for our political-ethical inquiry. At bedrock, each superpower is consumed with distrust of the other, in Harold Nicolson's apt term, that "easiest of all moods to inculcate."[3] Each leadership lacks confidence in its own estimates of the other's likely initiatives and reactions. Each superpower relies on deterrence but is caught in that system's perpetuation of tensions. The tradition-bound bureaucracies of each find it difficult to adjust to rapid technological and political change. Each superpower unilaterally pushes its own interests in the world, even though significant mutual interests increasingly exist. Each uses SALT and other arms-control forums for its own ends: to push and enshrine its own particular weapons advantages; to agree to adjust secondary questions or weapons systems that are not wanted anyway; and (somewhat as the case in the cruiser-building races of the 1920s and 1930s) to appease hard-nosed militarist constituencies by rapidly building up key military items not expressly forbidden by the just-concluded international agreements. Meanwhile, each superpower operates covertly against the other in the world; the CIA and the new KGB headquarters buildings even look alike.

Each power is, in a sense, preparing for yesterday's war, especially in staking so many resources and psychological chips on fixed, land-based intercontinental ballistic missiles (ICBMs), a weapons system which may be about to follow the dreadnought into discard as a symbol of supposed national power and manliness. Yet each has exercised restraint in not crossing the threshold to nuclear conflict, in not permitting escalation of local conflicts or the passions of its clients to involve it in nuclear hostilities not of its own choosing. Each superpower's alliance system is a mixed blessing in many respects. Within each superpower the influence of the military has grown in recent years, adding "take-counsel-of-fears" weight to national-security formulation. Each has shaped its distinctive nuclear arsenal by the same technical judgment that in the late twentieth century the military advantage clearly lies with the offensive. Within each society, countless specialists are caught up in technical *apparatchik* roles, in settings where the actuality of war fades more and more into faceless computer banks and pushbuttons. In a real sense, the scientists and military planners of each superpower have looked into the future and been aghast at what terrible beauties tomorrow's weaponry promises. A few, such as Andrei Sakharov and some of his U.S. counterparts, have been strengthened in their certainty that an end simply must be called to such sophisticated absurdity; but the prevailing reaction, U.S. and Soviet, seems to be that if a weapon can theoretically be produced, the adversary will do so, and thus "we" had better do it first. So, stimulated by the vertical proliferation of ever more complex and expensive weapons, the arms race progresses and the closed circle continues.

THE SOVIET COMPETITOR

Relaxation of tensions must be irreversible and we will fight for that.
Leonid Brezhnev (1974)[4]

Our country has accumulated considerable experience in devising and creating modern weapons. . . . The necessary scientific and technical and economic and military prerequisites are being created for a new, qualitative leap ahead in the development of arms and combat equipment. The widespread generalization of this experience and the understanding of what has been done and what remains to be done is a task of paramount importance.

Former Defense Minister A. A. Grechko (1974)[5]

The division of mankind threatens it with destruction. . . . In the face of these perils, any action increasing the division of man, any preaching of the incompatibility of world ideologies and nations is madness and a crime.

Andrei Sakharov (1968)[6]

The U.S.S.R.'s leaders continue to be committed to détente, a serious endeavor stimulated by numerous Soviet needs, foreign and domestic. This course also apparently springs from confidence that the growing Soviet strategic power can be translated into political gain in the world. Thus, although the existence of domestic U.S. political crises in the past few years may have encouraged those voices within Soviet leadership which champion a more assertive foreign policy, Soviet leaders have not really changed their definition of détente. A principal intention all along has been to try to use it to nudge the historical process of overtaking the United States in the trappings of world power.

Chairman Brezhnev's conduct of détente—and of domestic politics—reflects the presence of increased military influence upon policymaking. It appears that the top military leadership, in return for clearly acknowledging the Party's supremacy and acquiescing in Brezhnev's desired foreign policy style, has been admitted into Politburo decision-making and given a green light on bending the constraints of the SALT accords to the utmost so that they may continue to develop and deploy formidable new generations of strategic weapons.

One of the Soviet leaders' primary problems in recent years has been how to wrestle with the frustration caused by the increasing difficulty of trying to catch up with and surpass a United States whose technology and productivity continue to outclass those of the U.S.S.R. in many respects. This frustration is, of course, but part of the more fundamental Soviet dilemma of how to close the widening gap between rushing modernity and outmoded bureaucracy within Soviet society (in sharper terms, how to continue justifying the Party's authority at a time of rising managerial and technical leaderships).

The seemingly unspectacular Party Chairman Brezhnev appears to have dealt fairly well with this dilemma—through domestic tightening-up, détente, and nailing down of his *primus inter pares* leadership position. At a time when heightened specialized western imports and inputs of détente are somewhat easing the U.S.S.R.'s economic and technological bind, various tough measures on the home front have apparently been addressed to the Soviet leadership's perennial fear of unwanted infection from the West.

Even though détente is not new (it has been proclaimed briefly at various times since 1955), this time it is firmly based in Soviet needs and commitment, which may explain why there has been a certain willingness to conduct détente in less ideological terms. This time détente helps the Soviet leadership neutralize the China threat. And détente is also a useful offensive weapon, in that it enhances Soviet abilities to play upon Western desires for peace in a manner that a Professor Henry Kissinger once called manipulating our preconceptions against us.[7] Indeed, it can be argued that détente helped Soviet leaders to achieve the good deal they got in SALT-I: It supported U.S. hopes and faith in Soviet restraint, yet simultaneously pressed all that the traffic of SALT-I's ambiguities would bear to bring their new advanced weapons programs from bargaining chips to deployed reality. Such an interpretation seems reflected in how the U.S. government has reacted since that time, through its own doctrinal and weapons programs, to the prospect of a sizeable Soviet strategic arms advantage, not only in megatonnage but in significant new silo-busting capabilities, through MIRVing.

These Soviet strategic developments have come atop established doctrinal emphases on fighting and surviving a nuclear war (rather than on deterrence). Having stressed civilian defense (including exercises in evacuating cities) and having much harsher control measures at hand, the Soviet leadership could doubtless conduct nuclear defense much more effectively than could any U.S. administrations, at least in the near future. Soviet doctrine has generally tended to avoid the subject of limited nuclear war, sticking instead to classical defense concepts and to offensive emphases which seem to combine massive retaliation, counterindustrial, and countercombatant elements. Not least, from time to time there have been clear suggestions that the Soviet military was seriously contemplating the preemptive first-strike option in time of crisis.[8] The new Soviet weapons developments, however, do suggest that Soviet military doctrine is in definite process of change, so as to provide for counterforce capabilities and limited nuclear war.

For his part, Brezhnev appears to have narrowed the gap between the Party bureaucracy and the new technical Soviet world (at least the military-industrial part of it). Clearly suggested is a mutually advantageous, post-SALT-I understanding between Brezhnev and the U.S.S.R.'s most influential military figures, in particular the late defense minister, A. A. Grechko. Not only was Grechko made a full member of the ruling Party Politburo, but various of his public statements indicated some Party-military *quid pro quo*'s. He did repeated obeisance to the Party's sole and supreme political authority within the Soviet state; in apparent return for this defense against the extreme conservatives within Party and military, the line has been held against any U.S. proposals at SALT which might freeze Soviet MIRV inferiority, and the Soviet military seems to have received approval for developing great quantities of sophisticated new weapons—at the expense, if need be, of limiting Soviet domestic living standards.

Differences of strategic preference, of course, exist within the Soviet leadership, but given their historical sensitivity on questions of national defense and international status, the new U.S. weapons programs almost certainly served to increase support for what has become the official Politburo weapons line. This suggests that Soviet leaders still buy détente and Brezhnev's apparent long-range expectations for it: that, over time, an expanded Soviet presence in the world, backed up by conventional and strategic power demonstrably superior in appearance to that of the United States, will assist the U.S.S.R. in exploiting numerous western political vulnerabilities all around the globe. Certainly the United States has not been overly successful in translating strategic power into effective political profit. If, however, Brezhnev and his colleagues now truly entertain greater expectations, this may mean that they will be much less hesitant in their conduct of nuclear diplomacy than U.S. leaders have been—or that they are due for countless more political disappointments here and there in the world.

THE AMERICAN COMPETITOR

What we need is a series of measured responses to aggression which bear some relation to the provocation, have prospects of terminating hostilities before general nuclear war breaks out, and leave some possibility for restoring deterrence. It has been this problem of not having sufficient options between massive retaliation and doing nothing, as the Soviets built up their strategic forces, that has prompted the President's concerns and those of our allies.

Former Defense Secretary
James Schlesinger (1974)[9]

The continuation of the nuclear armaments race follows indeed logically from the commitment to a counter-force strategy. . . . Under the assumptions of that strategy, a dynamic relationship exists between the number of targets presented by one side and the number and quality of weapons directed at those targets by the other. . . . Both sides have, then, an incentive to increase targets and counter-force weapons indefinitely.

Hans J. Morgenthau (1964)[10]

We in the United States have harmed our own strategic efforts in various ways:

1. By continuing, widely, to manifest the type of thinking that led to and governed the conduct of the war in Vietnam: making the questionable assumption that strategic problems and war lend themselves to cool and confident prior calculation, apart from broader, random variables of personality, history, ambiguity, change, and chance.

2. By accepting, after the war in Vietnam, a clearly new increase of military considerations in national decision-making—at the expense of diplomacy, economics, and domestic requirements.

3. By permitting various U.S. military and technical figures to push this and that weapons innovation, not because there is a requirement for such weapons, but simply because they can be produced. Sometimes this has even been done under the table or in the face of known Congressional opposition.

4. By permitting a related hard-nosed, short-sighted propensity to play down the consideration that ever-more formidable and diverse weapons developments on our part will—as in the past—spur Soviet leaders, uniquely sensitive to real or imagined threats to Mother Russia, to seek offsetting weapons.

5. By buying, more or less, the presupposition of some of the more conservative U.S. strategists—military and civilian—that the U.S.S.R. actually intends to blow us up some day.

The strategic "debate" in the United States has, in large measure, been after the fact; the country has, in reality, been set upon the new counterforce course for some time, without really having first carefully determined why, what, how much, or whither—and without the courtesy of a by-your-leave to the Congress or the public.

The new U.S. counterforce emphases have some very serious implications. Among them are (1) a growing acceptability of the idea of nuclear war; (2) a confident assumption that nuclear exchanges can be kept managed and limited; (3) a disturbing aura of righteous prudence about possible U.S. recourse to pre-emptive attack; (4) a significant new fueling of Soviet feelings of inferiority and paranoia.

The Nixon and Ford administrations' emphases on counterforce doctrines and the development of counterforce weapons obscure the fact that restraint was a keynote of U.S. strategic conduct for some time. During the 1960s the United States deliberately kept the upper limit of its strategic missile launchers stable; various possible new weapons systems were not pursued to deployment; strategic budgets declined. Many economic and strategic considerations championed this course chosen by then Secretary of Defense Robert McNamara, but one of the most important judgments supporting such conduct was the fairly widely-held thesis that continued U.S. strength plus demonstrable restraint would tend to lay to rest extreme Soviet suspicions about U.S. motives and so promote a slowing of the arms race. This did not occur, in large measure because the U.S. did not simultaneously exercise qualitative restraint, but pressed on with the development and deployment of the MIRV—a technical and economic boon, perhaps, but destabilizing, given the situation of a Soviet competitor qualitatively far behind.

Meanwhile the U.S. public became somewhat inured to strategic competition. No nuclear weapons were detonated in anger. We all got used to the idea of paying annual billion dollar premiums on our deterrent insurance policies. Besides, our attentions were distracted.

Distracted they certainly were. Those were the days of limited war and counterinsurgency, of U.S. "idealized gendarmism," as Elizabeth Young has termed it, when the huge sums and attentions being given to Southeast Asia "tended to mask the fact that American strategic forces were no longer expanding and that the Russian forces were expanding very fast."[11] Indeed, understanding the United States' present strategic predicament must take account of the countless ways in which the war in Vietnam adversely affected our power position: It squandered U.S. lives and national purpose, as well as international respect for U.S. acuity; it siphoned off enormous resources from strategic and other programs and maldeployed U.S. forces; it divided the country, destroyed one president, and contributed importantly to the disgrace of another; it bequeathed great inflationary forces to the 1970s; it gave the U.S.S.R. breathing time and diplomatic leverage; and it generated Congressional and public pressures to arrange future U.S. commitments on a much more discriminating basis.

The war in Vietnam also illustrated certain facets of the United States' operating style which still hinder our best intentions with respect to strategic conduct. This style is reflected especially in certain military and Defense Department arguments, but evident here and there in the postures of various U.S. strategists: conceptual visions tend to be narrow, confidence overly certain, salesmanship slick, underestimation of the adversary's inventiveness and sensibilities self-defeating, and decision-making incremental. No wonder we are stuck. Only this time it is not in rice paddies but in a racing situation where, to use Philip Noel-Baker's description, "there is no technological plateau on which the contestants can pause for breath."[12] Of course it takes two to tangle, and the U.S.S.R. more than contributes its share. But our first concern must be to mitigate our own shortcomings. Thus as citizens we should question the scientific certainty with which weaponry (assured destruction or counterforce—take your choice) is being offered to the U.S. public as an answer to the countless uncertainties and interactions of international life —and at the expense, for example, of such luxuries as greater concern for the aged.

These weaponry cure-alls mirror the growth of military thinking (Schlesinger—Nixon—Kissinger—Ford —Rumsfeld—Reagan —Zumwalt) that has taken place in U.S. society now that Vietnam has become a memory, Soviet strategic capabilities have burgeoned, and former Secretary of Defense James Schlesinger brought new intellectual respectability to his department's strategic views. There is nothing surprising in all of this, but the growth of military influence does heighten tendencies to foresee the worst case and to overinsure against it. The military operates, of course, within a distorting "threat environment." In the past, at least, there have been hundreds of separate, uncoordinated threat assessments on file in the many nooks and crannies of the various armed services and commands—the Joint Chiefs of Staff structure, the Defense Intelligence Agency, the Department of Defense's many levels, defense think-tanks and contractors, and so on. Additionally, when military chieftains request new weapons or budgets they have in the past set aside the judgments of the government's most authoritative assessments, the National Intelligence Estimates (in which the military have participated and often agreed), in favor of "other" assessments which picture the U.S.S.R. in more frightening tones.[13] Also, ever-present among military chieftains and defense secretaries is a tendency to be certain that war can be carefully foreseen, planned, managed; that communications will not break down; that everyone will get the word; that all officers at all levels of command will act rationally and predictably; that all sides will agree at all times on just what level of force is equal to the grievance suffered; that, in sum, war is some preprogrammed game plan and not the confusion and ambiguity described by Tolstoy, Crane, and Solzhenitsyn.

Shaky strategic thinking is by no means restricted only to hard-nosed military types. U.S. administrations and the public want defense on the cheap. We have grown accustomed to the pace of a global role, but we do not wish to support a commensurate conventional establishment. We imagine that we can somehow defend Europe without placing U.S. cities in nuclear hostage. Among some arms-control enthusiasts the view has prospered that technology can back the Soviet Union into political settlement. Many also believe: that the U.S.S.R. and the U.S. have greater common interests than in fact obtain; that certain reasonable academic and official Soviet colleagues carry more weight in their country's policy counsels than they do; that the action-reaction process is far and away the ferment of arms races, underestimating the domestic vintage of bureaucratic and technological momentum; and that peace is maintained because the United States *could* inflict 50 percent fatalities in a retaliatory second strike,[14] whereas the real question is whether it *would* do so if its cities had not yet become prime targets.

Assured destruction has, in any event, clearly run its course. Rapid technological advance and the Soviet march to parity have brought widely recognized new instabilities to the nuclear balance. The credibility of the United States' assured-destruction deterrent has declined. Not least, a vigorous new champion

—counterforce—has appeared on the scene, where it has been given a continuing push by the Department of Defense and the executive since 1972.

Counterforce had actually been incubating a long time; it did not spring suddenly from the brow of Mr. Schlesinger during his early-1974 pronouncements of a new program. Counterforce was current soon after World War II; by the late 1950s it had taken recognizable shape at the RAND Corporation; soon after, it was being touted within U.S. Air Force circles. By 1962 it was developed enough to be given a litmus test by then Secretary of Defense McNamara in his well-known Ann Arbor speech. That trial proved premature, and the idea was discredited as too alarming to the Soviets and possibly a contribution to Khrushchev's equalizing attempt at stationing strategic weapons in Cuba, but it continued to gestate at RAND and elsewhere throughout the 1960s. Labor pangs commenced with President Nixon's February 1972 message to the Congress and were doubtless strengthened by the April 1972 discovery that the U.S.S.R. was preparing to test a huge new ICBM, larger than their SS-9.[15] Certainly the coming birth was heralded in August of that year in an extraordinarily candid and detailed *New York Times* story headlined "Major War Plans Are Being Revised by White House" and describing new counterforce weapons which the U.S. government "has decided to develop."[16] The "new" course was ratified in mid-1973 by the quiet advent of Henry Kissinger's National Security Council Decision Memorandum 242 at the National Security Council,[17] and James Schlesinger's less quiet arrival at the Department of Defense as its new secretary. Finally, it became evident that despite presidential and Defense Department assurances to the Congress that no such weapons development was in view, large sums had in fact begun to go into research and development of counterforce weapons since at least 1972.

There are a number of legitimate arguments for counterforce.[18] It refines the limited-nuclear-war thinking long husbanded by Schlesinger and others at RAND. It recognizes and plays to perceptions of national power. It involves hedges and bargaining chips. It puts the Soviets on notice that the United States can out-spend and out-technique them if they want an all-out arms race. It puts development programs into motion to arrest the U.S.S.R.'s closing of the strategic balance. It may contain better ways of defending Europe. It may stiffen the credibility of the U.S. deterrent since its tones place more emphasis on possibly fighting a war than have previous U.S. doctrines. It promises a system for controlling escalation at various stages or steps of hostilities. It involves more refined targeting than in the past. As the new weapons come along, it will refine U.S. capabilities against force targets. Meanwhile it tells the people of the United States that they are going to have to get used to paying dearly for strategic defense in the late twentieth century. And at least it is new, and not a shopworn soporific.

But counterforce is vulnerable on various counts. Some of its problems relate to the manner in which it is being sold. There is more than a faint sensation of fast shuffle: new contracts and momentum underway, program costs obfuscated, and Congress run through; counterforce is not "counterforce," but simply "flexible response." This problem may be more declaratory than real and Schlesinger may or may not have been guilty of "rewriting scripture to make nuclear war plausible,"[19] but many of his counterforce sales pitches have made it sound as if "flexible response" had never been thought of before and the only options before us now, in a time of national crisis, are dawdling or city-busting. This is of course nonsense. Countertarget weapons and planning have been in the U.S. repertoire for years. All kinds of documentation attest to this; the following two citations should suffice, in terms of time and authenticity:

> It is to the West's interest, if atomic war becomes unavoidable, that atomic weapons of the smallest sizes be used in the smallest area, and against the most restricted target systems possible [Paul H. Nitze, 1956].[20]

> Right at the start it should be clear that the U.S. at no time has had an exclusively "city-busting" strategy. It is absurd to believe that U.S. missile and bomber forces with many thousands of warheads (nearly 8000 force loadings by July '74) have all been targeted on a few hundred built-up areas; it is also fair to surmise that most warheads already are targeted on important military centers, presumably including ICBM silo launchers [Ambassador Gerard Smith, 1974].[21]

The counterforce emphases also raise some serious questions of substance. We are back at the mentality of the war in Vietnam: Everything is scientifically measured, confident, and manageable; we are good, "they" are sneaky; strategic bombing will do the trick; "our" new silo-busting weapons threaten no one, "theirs" mean first-strike; and so on. Did Schlesinger actually believe, as reported at least, that the Soviets might strike a knock-out blow against the United States?[22] Was he really serious in his assurance to a 1974 Senate Foreign Relations Committee hearing that "the best way to help" those within the Soviet leadership who want to halt the arms race was to show the U.S.S.R. that the United States was unmistakably prepared to match the Soviets' strategic weapons programs?[23] What do these counterforce emphases do to previous inhibitions about not crossing the nuclear threshold? Are not these new initiatives creating new bureaucratic constituencies and industrial vested interests that will prove as difficult to control as past ones have?

Most seriously, does emphasis on "flexible response" and "first use" of nuclear weapons reflect U.S. government interest not only in counterforce, but in preemptive strikes? There has been a long and tangled history of U.S. Air Force interest in silo-busting, with much gaming with Congress.[24] Accurate strike-capabilities against silos make little sense if those silos are going to be empty. The United States long eschewed anything which might look like a first-strike capability; but now it goes ahead on just such programs, arousing first-strike fears not only on the part of the Soviets but of western observers.[25] Counterforce proponents answer that it is no longer destabilizing for us to do so, since the Soviets have already skewed the situation by beginning to MIRV their huge weapons. Perhaps so, but it still leaves in doubt just what role young MaRV is supposed to play in strategic life. On technical grounds it is difficult to argue with John C. Baker's judgment that

> the attractiveness of counterforce targets in a second-strike attack could never equal those of a first-strike attack. Consequently, an incentive will exist for the side which seizes the initiative to strike first.[26]

We must, of course, give the Department of Defense the benefit of the doubt and agree for the moment with Ambassador Smith's view that the new counterforce proposals may basically be an attempt to heighten the interest of the U.S.S.R. in SALT-II by stressing the vulnerabilities of its ICBMs, "foreshadowing a day when the entire Soviet ICBM system will be destructible by a part of the U.S. strategic force."[27] We will have to await the playing out of SALT negotiations before seeing whether Smith's view is justified. But meanwhile we can ask of counterforce enthusiasts what a limited war with nuclear weapons would all be about, if at its close we had, as in Schlesinger's previously quoted arguments, simply *restored a situation of deterrence?*[28] That certainly wouldn't be much of a prize for the treasure that would have been spent.

Doubtless there is no single, true motive for counterforce. MaRV and its companions are truly multipurpose weapons, and chances are neither the Soviet nor the U.S military high commands know how their respective counterforce efforts are going to turn out. U.S. administrations, nonetheless, do have the sober responsibility to be forthcoming with the Congress and the public and to take every precaution that, once technical capability has been created, military-technical enthusiasm and momentum do not once again come to fill that capability with some requirement or policy goal, rather than—properly—the other way around.

WE HAVE BEEN HERE BEFORE

Throughout recent history racism of one kind or another has been the ally and support of dehumanization. . . . They who are less than human may differ from us in inherited physical type (race) or in religion or language or national identity or ideology, or in any combination of these. The result is the same; we deny them a true humanity. What I fear, and what I regard as highly probable, is that the robotizing of our weapons will greatly accentuate this process; one form of dehumanization will feed the other. The farther we, individual human beings, are from our target, the less we will be concerned about how others suffer under attack. . . . What does seem well established is that personal insecurity and concern with status are associated with ethnocentricism and chauvinism, and it is reasonable to conclude that, other things being equal, whatever makes people more insecure at the same time creates a propitious climate for the more extreme forms of nationalism. The circle is now complete; nationalistic attitudes lead to the development and acquisition of weapons, new and old, which create uncertainty and add to the feeling of personal insecurity, which in turn contributes to the encouragement of still stronger nationalistic attitudes.

Otto Klineberg (1968)[29]

As a result of the Soviet weapons build-up and the United States' qualitative weapons response, we have arrived at a point where both countries have been before: another round of technological "advances." In the past it was the H-Bomb, then the MIRV and other incrementally determined "decisions"; now, it is MaRV and its generation of ever more accurate, efficient, and expensive weapons.

This situation places significant premiums on the responsibility with which U.S. and Soviet leaders deal with the abounding ambiguity in international life. Dangers exist within each leadership: in the incidence of closed minds, and in tendencies to impose far greater conceptual confidence and pattern upon uncertain situations than they warrant. Given the eternal ambiguity of evidence, leaders' certainty must be based on hard, unambiguous evidence, if we are all to survive in a time of technological temptation to a preemptive strike.

The arms race, stabilized or not by SALT-II, interacts with a broader, destabilizing world scene whose character is still unclear and undergoing transformations. There indeed is political multipolarity: for example, the U.S.-China détente did help hurry the Soviets to SALT-I. But there is not nearly so much multipolarity as Richard Nixon and certain other Americans have conceptually imposed on divided Europe and reluctant Japan. One can go along only in part, for example, with Stanley Hoffmann's 1972 statement that "the Yalta system is coming to an end. For many years the world has ceased to resemble the confrontation of Athens and Sparta."[30] Yalta is still in process of being defined. (Witness the long-dragged-out negotiations of the Conference for Security and Cooperation [CSCE] before Eastern Europe's postwar boundaries could be legitimized at Helsinki.) Moreover, the overwhelming foreign concerns of the U.S. and Soviet governments continue to be about the other: Despite nuclear proliferation there are still only two superpowers, only one series of bilateral SALT negotiations, only one race into space. Remember, too, the Athens-Sparta competition was not a continuous eyeball-to-eyeball confrontation, but a dynamic of wars, détentes, shifting alliance systems, occasional side adventures, and internal differences over foreign policy—in short, not unlike our own times.

But one thing is certain about the world scene: Its character is becoming daily more unpredictable as superpower rivalry interacts with nuclear proliferation, more state actors, more nonstate actors, and new economic and resource constraints. Having seen abuses of analysis (systems and otherwise) in the Vietnamese situation and other cases, we citizens can justifiably insist that U.S. policymakers recognize that tremendous international uncertainties remain—and always will. The world will continue to be a semianarchy of expectations, ambitions, misperceptions, unknowns; there will always be countless interactions—direct and incidental, intentional and fortuitous. At any given time a central conceptual task of the Soviet Party chairman, the U.S. president, and their respective lieutenants will always be how best and most responsibly to reduce those uncertainties.

One of their chief tools will be improved intelligence systems, a technical path to lessened ambiguity which has already helped make the SALT route an acceptable risk to each of the two adversaries; yet intelligence—"national means of verification"—is horribly expensive, it is itself a source of continuing Soviet-U.S. tension, and it often sheds far more light on the other's capabilities than on his intentions.[31] A parallel means of reducing uncertainty will be an increase of communication between Soviets and Americans (and the more communication the better); yet this mix of diplomacy, back channels, Pugwash, exchange visits, signals, news leaks, embassy lobbyings, and type of weapons testing will offer only imperfect results and will continue to lend itself to misunderstanding. In practice, uncertainties will actually continue to be reduced by the patterns which leaders impose on international ambiguities and then sell to rulers and the ruled; yet ruling minds can be locked-in, distorted, prideful and pride-filled, and overly concerned with justifying previous paths, while technical lieutenants often impose a more meaningful pattern—and state it with a far greater degree of confidence—than the situation warrants. The latter tendency has certainly obtained for some years in U.S. military and Department of Defense salesmanship, in the views of various other U.S. strategists, and—we must assume—in certain Soviet counsels as well. Now, as proliferation geometrically expands ambiguity and the opportunities for irresponsibility and error, there simply is no longer room for simplistic certainty and salesmanship. In particular, in any situation in which the use of nuclear weapons might be seriously considered, the eternal ambiguity of evidence must be kept in mind and an enormously increased premium must be placed on *certainty*—not a conceptual or vested-interest certainty imposed on a confusing, fast-moving crisis situation, but an absolute certainty based on hard, unambiguous evidence. At present this caveat applies especially to those very confident officials who peddle new weapons uniquely capable of preemptive roles. First strikes are probably immoral in any circumstance, but what about the morality not to mention the politics of resorting to such strikes in a case of ambiguous evidence and possible cataclysmic error?

WE HAVE NOT BEEN HERE BEFORE

It is worthwhile reminding ourselves that there have been many forms of life on earth that survived far longer than man has, and flourished mightily sometimes for millions of years, and then disappeared and many have followed that course. Wherever that has happened, it would appear that the cause was the same, that particular form of life was not able to make an adequate adjustment to changed circumstances, and so it disappeared. Our circumstances now, as a form of life, have changed just as drastically and radically as the conditions of survival of the dinosaur changed shortly before it disappeared.

Dr. Brock Chisholm (1966)[32]

Given our situation and the now questionable validity of traditional concepts of a just war, a new, broader, and more humane body of strategic and moral thought is an absolute necessity. Such widened vision is especially called for because the superpower competition is, in the largest sense, an anachronism. The United States and the Soviet Union are two dinosaurs threshing about in ancient jungles, half-blind to the fact that their real adversaries are the problems of resources and environment that will determine whether our species is to survive on this planet.

Certainly the most deadly race that the two nations are engaged in is not arms competition, but whether or not their respective peoples and institutions can adjust to the rushing world changes ahead—in technology, awareness, expectations, resource shortages, weather control, laser weapons, terrorist activity, new economic leverages, a plethora of new international actors, and so on. Indeed, the United States and the Soviet Union, before too long, may both face what Arnold Toynbee has called a "permanent state of siege," as they and other modern industrial societies confront massive deteriorating situations in less privileged parts of the world. There is no overstatement in Robert Heilbroner's concern that nuclear proliferation may come to include states or groups that are desperately hungry or disadvantaged; wars of redistribution cannot be excluded when and if such actors, who have nothing to lose, resort to resource raids or even nuclear blackmail threats.[33] Whether or not such a future actually faces us, the enormity of tomorrow's environment and population pressures simply demands mutual Soviet and U.S. restraint *now*—in weapons development, in general one-up-manship, and in all facets of a strategic competition which has become a tragicomic *non sequitur* in relation to the true survival hazards which face us all.

Given this troubled future, U.S. strategic thinking and behavior clearly need new vitality and definition, beyond the present confines of "shall we have counterforce or not," and "if so, what kind of weapon accuracy, yield, targeting, and the like?" The new strategic thought must concern total U.S. relationships: the sources and purposes of political-economic agreements and disagreements in the world, not just their technical weapons, and theoretical models or computer reflections.

A similar need exists for serious rethinking with respect to U.S. ethical concerns and action. Traditional concepts of just war and morality have come to have questionable relevance in a world where practically every nuclear-armed entity would justify use of such weapons as "defensive"; where brutality and lack of conscience are not the monopolies of Communist "aggressors"; where nuclear weapons have made the principle of proportionality an even more difficult aim to achieve once hostilities have broken out; where countless noncombatants would die from fallout, even in the unlikely event that nuclear targets were kept limited; and where the purposes and justification of U.S.-Soviet war have become obscured in mechanistic competition for competition's sake.

Meanwhile, there is much that each of us can contribute to the creation of a deeper and more humane body of strategic and moral thought. Not bemused that existing détente and SALT accords are anything more than a first step toward a less dangerous world, we can recognize that we all feed the arms race in countless small ways. We support officials who are sure that nuclear weapons can be safely and profitably incorporated into U.S. diplomacy. We permit significant arms "decisions" to occur by increment, with no overall debate really being held. We do not hold fast-talking officials to a more searching accountability. We coolly contemplate, calculate, and accept the prospect of megadeaths, whether we be strategists or ethicists. We mentally divide humankind into those people who matter and those who don't; those who bleed, and those who don't. We permit military concerns and contracts to inflate our economy, distort our priorities, and lock parts of our economy into a production momentum that gives us weapons we don't need, to save us from threats that don't exist. We do not realize that U.S. arms and actions look menacing to others, that we are not in our present strategic predicament just because the U.S.S.R. has built up its fearsome ICBMs, but because they have done so in a situation of still-great U.S. weapons advantage and, since 1972 or so, of some increase of U.S. first-strike capabilities. We believe that bayonets or ballistics can take the place of patient, imaginative, compassionate, multidimensioned dealing with the problems—essentially economic, sociological, and psychological—which face the United States and the world. We forget that *all* people seek to bend natural and human situations to their will, and that conflict comes when such drives collide. We underestimate the potential for violence that exists in people. Finally, and perhaps most tragically, we console ourselves that killing is not killing when it is done by remote control or to the accompaniment of bugles and banners.

NOTES

1. Andrei Sakharov, *Sakharov Speaks* (New York: Vintage Books, 1974), p. 65.
2. Russell Baker, *New York Times*, October 1, 1974.
3. Harold Nicolson, "Men and Circumstances," *Foreign Affairs* 23 (April 1945): 477.
4. Leonid Brezhnev in a speech to Soviet leadership. Reported in *New York Times*, June 15, 1974.
5. A. A. Grechko, "The Leading Role of the CPSU in Building the Army of a Developed Socialist Society," *Voprosy Istorii KPSS*, no. 5 (May 1974). In Foreign Broadcast Information Service, *U.S.S.R. Broadcasts*, May 30, 1974, p. A-12.
6. Sakharov, *Sakharov Speaks*, p. 58.
7. Henry Kissinger, *Nuclear Weapons and Foreign Policy* (New York: Harper and Bros., 1957), p. 320.
8. Benjamin S. Lambeth, "The Sources of Soviet Military Doctrine," in Horton, Rogerson, and Warner, eds., *Comparative Defense Policy* (Baltimore: Johns Hopkins University Press, 1974), p. 204.
9. James Schlesinger, *Report of the Secretary of Defense to the Congress on the FY 1975 Defense Budget* (Washington, D.C.: Government Printing Office, March 1974), p. 38.
10. Hans J. Morgenthau, "Four Paradoxes of Nuclear Strategy," *The American Political Science Review* 58 (March 1964): 31.
11. Elizabeth Young, *A Farewell to Arms Control?* (Penguin Books, 1972), pp. 168–69.
12. Philip Noel-Baker, "We Have Been Here Before," in Nigel Calder, ed., *Unless Peace Comes: A Scientific Forecast of New Weapons* (New York: The Viking Press, 1968), p. 230.
13. See examples given in Congressional testimonies by Sen. Albert Gore, Dr. John Foster, Sen. J. William Fulbright, Dr. Jerome Wiesner, and Secretary Melvin Laird, in Ronald L. Tammen, *MIRV and the Arms Race: An Interpretation of Defense Strategy* (New York: Praeger, 1974), pp. 27–28.
14. See, for example, George W. Rathjens, *The Future of the Strategic Arms Race* (New York: Carnegie Endowment for International Peace, 1969), p. 8.
15. *New York Times*, April 23, 1972.
16. *New York Times*, August 5, 1972.

17. George Sherman, "Debate Mounts on Schlesinger Nuclear Policy," *Washington Star-News*, April 15, 1974.
18. Many excellent explanations and defenses of counterforce doctrine have appeared since 1974. One of the best is Lynn Etheridge Davis, "Limited Nuclear Options: Deterrence and the New American Doctrine," *Adelphi Paper*, no. 121 (London: The International Institute for Strategic Studies, Winter 1975/1976). For a more complete list, see this volume's bibliography.
19. Sherman, "Schlesinger Nuclear Policy."
20. Paul H. Nitze, "Atoms, Strategy and Policy," *Foreign Affairs* 34 (January 1956): 187–88.
21. Gerard Smith, *Congressional Record* 110 (May 20, 1974).
22. Leslie Gelb, "Schlesinger for Defense, Defense for *Détente*," *New York Times Magazine*, August 4, 1974.
23. *New York Times*, April 5, 1974.
24. See Tammen, *MIRV and the Arms Race.*
25. *London Times*, March 1, 1974.
26. "Flexibility: The Imminent Debate," *Arms Control Today* 4 (January 1974): 2.
27. Smith, *Congressional Record.*
28. Schlesinger, *FY 1975 Report*, p. 38.
29. Otto Klineberg, "Fears of a Psychologist," in Calder, ed., *Unless Peace Comes*, pp. 208, 212.
30. Stanley Hoffmann, "Weighing the Balance of Power," *Foreign Affairs* 50 (July 1972): 618.
31. See, for example, Schlesinger's *Report*, where he first states that evidence on what the U.S.S.R. is "up to is, to say the least, fragmentary and conflicting" (p. 29), and then goes on to describe Soviet strategic weapons capabilities and programs in some detail (pp. 45 ff.).
32. Dr. Brock Chisholm, before U.S. Senate Committee on Foreign Relations, *Hearing on Psychological Aspects of International Relations*, 89th Cong., 2d sess., May 25, 1966, pp. 59–60.
33. Robert Heilbroner, *An Inquiry into the Human Prospect* (New York: Norton, 1974), pp. 43–44.

4

1963 Nuclear Strategy Revisited

Alain C. Enthoven

This paper is a response to an invitation to review an article on U.S. defense policy, particularly nuclear strategy, that I wrote in early 1963 and to reflect on how its main principles have fared in the subsequent twelve years.

It would be an understatement to say that much has happened in the field of defense policy since that time. The article does, to some extent, reflect the particular controversies of the time. There have proved to be important omissions; for example, there was no discussion of mutual restraint in force levels, as opposed to mutual restraint in the use of force. And the focus was on the nuclear confrontation with the U.S.S.R. and the defense of Europe; it ignored Vietnam.

But the main themes have stood up very well. These were the emphasis on the controlled and limited use of force, the necessity of conventional forces equal in strength to those of our opponents, the feasibility of adequate conventional forces, the necessity of invulnerable nuclear forces and command and control systems, and the limited role of nuclear weapons. Of course, I was not the author of these principles. Their development was shared by President John F. Kennedy and his principal White House advisors —Secretary of Defense Robert McNamara, Charles Hitch, William Kaufmann, John McNaughton, Paul Nitze, Henry Rowen, Maxwell Taylor, Albert Wohlstetter, and others. It is my hope

---

Dr. Enthoven is Marriner S. Eccles Professor of Public and Private Management, Graduate School of Business, Stanford University. He was formerly Assistant Secretary of Defense for Systems Analysis. The earlier article to which Dr. Enthoven refers, "Reason, Morality, and Defense Policy," is reprinted as Appendix D of this volume. Based on an address, "U.S. Defense Policy for the 1960's," before the Loyola University Forum for National Affairs, Chicago, February 10, 1963, it originally appeared in *America* 108 (April 6, 1963 and April 13, 1963): 461–65, and was reprinted in a number of anthologies.

that a brief review of the background and development of some of these principles will be useful to students of defense policy who have entered the field more recently.

THE STRATEGY OF THE 1950s

In the 1950s the United States' policy for the defense of Europe was based on the belief that NATO land and air forces were hopelessly outnumbered by the forces of the Warsaw Pact countries. Therefore, an effective nonnuclear defense was thought to be impossible. Some thought the imbalance could be offset to some extent by NATO's use of tactical or battlefield nuclear weapons. Many weapons were deployed. But no plan for their use was developed, other than as part of a general nuclear war. There was no concept of limited war with the U.S.S.R.; the design of our military response to Soviet aggression was "all or none." The main purpose of U.S. forces in Europe was to demonstrate our commitment and to serve as a "trip wire" so that a Soviet attack (presumably unlimited) would unleash a total response by the Strategic Air Command (SAC). In the first part of the 1950s the United States had a near monopoly of long-range nuclear striking power, so that SAC could destroy the military forces and industry of the U.S.S.R. without the United States being destroyed in retaliation. But by the end of the decade, the U.S.S.R. had substantial retaliatory power.

U.S. strategic airpower was mostly long-range bombers, based soft and concentrated on about sixty bases. This force was to become dangerously vulnerable as the Soviet missile force grew. But for several years this vulnerability was not perceived as a serious problem by U.S. military leaders because the main scenario in terms of which they thought was a Soviet attack on Europe followed by a U.S. strategic response. At the start of the war, all available forces would have to be launched because of the vulnerability of forces on both sides. There was no built-in capability for control or restraint.

KENNEDY AND McNAMARA, 1961

President Kennedy and Secretary McNamara saw very clearly that nuclear weapons were not a substitute for conventional forces. Nuclear weapons were too dangerous and destructive to be used in any but the most desperate circumstances. The threat to use them was not an effective way to counter Soviet threats (for example, threats to deny our access to Berlin). Therefore, NATO must have conventional forces equal to those of the other side, and the United States must limit the role of nuclear weapons in its overall strategy to that of retaliation for a nuclear attack on it or its allies. Because of political sensitivities in this country and Europe, and because our conventional forces were inadequate, we had to be very careful how we said this. But the goal was that "our forces will be adequate if we can never be forced because of weakness to be the first to have to resort to nuclear weapons."

This did not eliminate the moral dilemmas of nuclear strategy. Kennedy, McNamara, and their associates recognized that, even in retaliation, it would be wrong to attack cities and kill millions of innocent civilians. Yet if we did not have a capability to retaliate, and plans to use it, the United States and its allies would be at the mercy of the U.S.S.R. Our response was a policy designed to make the ultimate catastrophe as unlikely as possible by restricting to a minimum our dependence on nuclear weapons. We could do that by having adequate conventional forces (so that we would not have to be the first to use nuclear weapons) and by making our nuclear retaliatory force invulnerable (so that the U.S.S.R. would have no incentive to attack with nuclear weapons). Moreover, we went on to design our strategic retaliatory posture so that it could be used with deliberation and control. Thus, for example, Kennedy and McNamara favored the Polaris submarine-launched missile system even though it had no powerful military lobby behind it. And they phased out the B-47, stopped procurement of B-52s, and arrested development of the B-70, all against the forceful opposition of an extremely powerful military lobby. Their reasoning was that, in the event of a nuclear attack, the Polaris missiles could be safely withheld at sea, for weeks if necessary, while the president assessed the situation and attempted to negotiate a cease-fire; bombers, on the other hand, would have to be launched on warning before their extremely vulnerable bases could be destroyed, and if those bases were destroyed, they would have to be committed to an attack in the first hours of war, or lost. Kennedy and McNamara also directed the deployment of survivable command and control systems, such as airborne command posts. And they directed the development of war plans that would give the president the flexibility to limit his retaliatory attack to the enemy's strategic bases, or to those plus other military targets, avoiding attacks on cities. (However, the radioactive fallout from such attacks would have killed millions.)

THE ROAD TO AND FROM ANN ARBOR

When John Kennedy became president, the link between any armed combat with the U.S.S.R. and unlimited nuclear war seemed perilously close. Therefore he and his associates wanted to build many "firebreaks" between any local conflict and the nuclear destruction of our societies. It was in this spirit that McNamara sought to establish the "no [attacks on] cities" doctrine. In his famous commencement address at Ann Arbor, in June 1962, he said:

> The U.S. has come to the conclusion that to the extent feasible, basic military strategy in a possible general nuclear war should be approached in much the same way that more conventional military operations have been regarded in the past. That is to say, principal military objectives, in the event of a nuclear war stemming from a major attack on the Alliance, should be the destruction of his military forces, not of his civilian population.[1]

It has often been noted that McNamara subsequently backed away from this idea, and I have frequently been asked why. I can offer only my personal interpretation. First, while the Ann Arbor address elicited some thoughtful comment, it also elicited some confused emotional responses. One powerful member of the Senate Armed Services Committee sharply criticized McNamara for showing a lack of resolve. Some thought that weakening the certainty of destruction of Soviet cities would make a nuclear attack on the United States more attractive to the U.S.S.R.—despite our overwhelming nuclear superiority. And it did not appear that there was any useful purpose to be served by arguing the point. Second, the goal of destroying enough of the Soviet strategic forces to make an appreciable difference in the number of Americans surviving a Soviet retaliatory attack generated an open-ended requirement for more strategic weapons. The controversy over the RS-70—a bomber with an alleged capability to reconnoiter the U.S.S.R. and attack surviving missile sites—was particularly intense in the year following June 1962, and the Ann Arbor speech was used in an attempt to give the program a sensible strategic rationale. Third, as one looked ahead to the late 1960s, it became apparent that with the deployment of a large Soviet missile submarine fleet, no amount of U.S. offensive power could destroy enough of the Soviet forces to make an appreciable difference. So procurement of a capability to attack Soviet land-based forces did not appear to enhance our security in any important way.

But the most important reason for abandoning the Ann Arbor theme was that it was confusing the far more important message that *nobody wins a nuclear war.* There was still a great deal of controversy over that, in the Pentagon and on Capitol Hill. For example, General Curtis LeMay was fighting a very effective campaign for the idea that the United States should buy a capability to fight and win a nuclear war with the U.S.S.R. rather than spending the money on an apparently hopelessly expensive build-up of conventional forces. (Recall that in the mid-1960s, it was still widely believed that NATO forces were hopelessly outnumbered on the ground.) Most people in the Pentagon and on the Armed Services Committees, if not the Congress generally (not to mention NATO capitals), still did not understand that the threat to resort to nuclear war was no longer a usable instrument of policy. Technology and forces were changing much more rapidly than the general understanding of their implications. As a practical matter, it was impossible to communicate a clear distinction between McNamara's view of deliberation, control, and "no cities" as a last desperate hope to make the best of a catastrophe, and General LeMay's view that we could fight and win a nuclear war—if only we would buy RS-70s and the like instead of conventional forces. The Ann Arbor theme was too subtle an idea to be effective in the political arena.

THE 1963–1968 STRATEGIC POLICY

Strategic-weapons policy must evolve as forces and technology evolve. Over the next five years, the following ideas became the main principles of U.S. policy:

First, the size and composition of our strategic retaliatory forces would be determined by the "assured destruction mission." Under this policy, we would buy amounts and kinds of forces sufficient to be sure, even under very pessimistic assumptions, that they could survive a deliberate Soviet attack well enough to strike back and destroy 20 to 25 percent of their population. This was a criterion for adequacy of our deterrent; it was not a declaration of how the forces would actually be used in case of war. Since the amount of forces we needed to achieve the assured destruction mission were not very sensitive to the size of the Soviet offensive forces, this policy appeared to put a ceiling on U.S. offensive force requirements.

Second, given the force size determined by the assured destruction criterion, we would enhance their damage limiting (countermilitary) capabilities where this could be done at a low cost. We recognized that it was no longer possible to achieve a first-strike, offensive capability sufficient to destroy enough of the Soviet forces so that our society could not be destroyed in retaliation. Nevertheless, some countermilitary capability appeared useful for two reasons. If we were attacked, it might serve some useful (for example, damage-limiting) purpose to be able to destroy residual Soviet forces. This would be a matter of making the best of a catastrophe, not making the threatened use of nuclear weapons a usable instrument of policy. Additionally, there was the important factor of virtual attrition. In other words, well over half the United States' expenditures for strategic offensive forces were (and still are) for the protection of our forces from a Soviet attack. We could buy many more missiles within the same budget if we did not have to spend so much on silos and submarines. And we chose the Minuteman ICBM with its low payload (compared to that of the large Soviet ICBM) because it was easier to protect. But if our forces had no countermilitary capability, it would be much cheaper and easier for the Soviets to protect their forces, and they could put the freed resources into more offensive power. As it is, the Soviets had to (and still have to) concentrate a great deal of payload in their large ICBMs, which pose a threat to our ICBMs.

Third, in public statements we would emphasize the assured destruction mission and the disastrous consequences of nuclear war, in order to drive home the points that nobody wins a nuclear war, and that nuclear weapons are not a substitute for adequate conventional forces.

Fourth, we would attempt to stabilize force levels on both sides by refraining from deploying an antimissile defense of our cities against Soviet attack (which would have been ineffective in any case), and by emphasizing that when we had enough forces for assured destruction, we had enough forces, regardless of the force ratio (which was very much in our favor in those years). In other words, the declining margin of U.S. numerical superiority was not a threat to our security as long as we maintained an assured retaliatory capability.

NATO TODAY

I have recently written on NATO strategy elsewhere,[2] so I will make only a few summary points here.

First, NATO has more total military manpower than the Warsaw Pact countries, and about equal land forces in the critical center region. However, NATO isn't getting the military power we are paying for. Lack of integration of defense establishments and other factors have cost us major losses in defense effectiveness. The priority goal of the alliance should be to achieve the maximum conventional military power available from the resources we are spending. One important part of doing this would be to bring home and dismantle about 6,000 of the 7,000 nuclear weapons we have deployed in Europe. This would free about 30,000 men, who could then be reassigned to increased conventional forces. Such a program should enable us to maintain conventional forces equal in power to those of the Warsaw Pact countries, in which case we would not need to depend on the threatened first use of nuclear weapons.

Second, the United States must keep substantial (not token) forces in Europe, to help maintain the balance and to hold the alliance together. To pull out our troops and revert to a "trip-wire" strategy would be dangerous, ineffective, and wrong.

NUCLEAR STRATEGY TODAY

There is still no resolution to the moral dilemma of nuclear targeting. A strategy that emphasizes the ability to destroy enemy strategic forces on their bases seems like a dangerous exercise in futility: dangerous because increasing the enemy's perceived vulnerability of his forces might put pressure on him to launch those forces in a crisis before they are destroyed on the ground; futile because even the ability to destroy all the Soviet silos would leave hundreds of their submarine-launched missiles at sea, able to destroy our society many times over. On the other hand, a strategy that emphasizes the destruction of enemy cities means killing millions of innocent civilians. While I think that the efforts of scholars and strategists such as Fred Iklé and Bruce Russett to find a way out of the dilemma are worthwhile and ought to be continued, I am not at all optimistic that a satisfactory resolution will be found.[3] It seems to me that the best approach continues to be based on the twin themes we stressed in the early

1960s. First, we must continue to stress invulnerability as the foundation for the *controlled* and *deliberate* use of our strategic forces, if they should ever have to be used. In some circumstances, countermilitary attacks might have to be executed quickly. But retaliation should not have to be fast. Submarine-launched ballistic missiles continue to be the most appropriate weapon system. Our ICBM silos are gradually becoming vulnerable as accuracies, payloads, and yields improve. And our strategic bomber bases have been extremely vulnerable for years, so that the bombers offer minimal capability for control and deliberation. (The fact that they require defense suppression attacks to be able to assure penetration of enemy airspace makes them even worse.) Second, we should continue seeking to minimize the role of nuclear weapons in our overall strategy. We should threaten enemy cities only in retaliation for deliberate attacks on ours. We should plan to meet all nonnuclear aggression with nonnuclear defenses. These measures should minimize the likelihood of a deliberately started nuclear war.

As for actual targeting plans and capabilities, I think that flexibility, including some capability to attack strategic and other military targets, makes most sense, provided the cost is kept low. I do not accept the view that we should rigorously confine our target destruction capabilities to enemy cities. As Albert Wohlstetter observed, not even Ghengis Khan deliberately avoided attacks on military forces in order to be able to concentrate on destruction of civilian populations.[4] A moderate counterstrategic military capability will continue to pressure the Soviet Union to put more of its strategic budget into protection and less into offensive capabilities. But, given their large force of submarine-launched ballistic missiles (SLBMs) and the size and protection of their ICBM force, a preemptive disarming attack by the United States is out of the question by a very wide margin, so a moderate U.S. capability to attack silos should not be a significantly destabilizing factor.

However, while I sympathize with his desire to wrestle with the dilemmas, I still believe that Secretary of Defense James R. Schlesinger's announcement of a new U.S. strategic-targeting doctrine, in January 1974, was both unnecessary and unwise.[5] It was unnecessary because there had been no real change in policy. I cannot speak for the years since January 1969, but Schlesinger's suggestion that previous strategic-targeting doctrine was limited to massive attacks on cities certainly was not an accurate description of the thinking of the leaders or the plans of the Defense Department from 1961 to 1968. One must distinguish criteria for measuring the adequacy of forces from targeting doctrine. As McNamara and others, including myself, stated repeatedly during that period, assured destruction was a criterion for the adequacy of our strategic retaliatory forces, not a statement of targeting doctrine. For example, in June 1968, I told the Preparedness Investigating Subcommittee of the Senate Committee on Armed Services:

> Our targeting policy, as reflected in the guidance for the preparation of the targeting plan, has not changed. From 1961–62 on, the targeting plan has been based on the principle that we should have different options that target the strategic forces and cities.[6]

The principle of flexible plans and targeting options that avoided cities was established in the early 1960s. If Schlesinger, or his strategic analysts, didn't like the plans he inherited in 1973, he had the authority to change them without involving the Congress or the press.

The statement was also unnecessary because Schlesinger did not need to invoke a new strategic doctrine to justify continued research and development programs for improving U.S. missile accuracy. I believe he could have justified them as pursuit of continued U.S. technological leadership, a goal which we ought to pursue relentlessly, at least in the absence of a reliable agreement to accept mutual limitations.

And the announcement was unwise because, as anyone recalling McNamara's experience after June 1962 might have predicted, it elicited many confused and emotional responses both in Washington and in Moscow. "What is the secretary talking about?" "Why is he saying it now?" In particular, it rekindled the belief, in some quarters, that strategic forces might be substituted for conventional forces. I believe that Schlesinger would agree that no nuclear targeting doctrine can be a substitute for adequate conventional forces, but his statements were open to that interpretation.[7] And that kind of misinterpretation can further confuse and weaken the resolve of our NATO allies.

Moreover, while I believe that any use of nuclear weapons ought to be controlled and deliberate, I do not believe that the concept of limited, strategic nuclear war offers any meaningful policy alternative for the United States. The United States does not have an effective national fallout-shelter program. So a Soviet attack that, for example, detonated thousands of megatons on our ICBM sites would inevitably kill tens of millions of Americans, even if the Soviets tried to avoid attacks on cities. Additionally, if the Soviets were attacking strategic targets in the United States, they would have to consider our bomber and submarine bases to be the most attractive targets—and many of them are in or near populated areas. The pressures for escalation would be enormous. Because of these factors and the inevitable confusion, hysteria, communications breakdowns, and the like, I doubt that nuclear war could be controlled and restrained for long, if at all. Trying to control it is a last desperate hope to limit the catastrophe—no more. So we must not let attempts to limit the damage in a nuclear war confuse the message that nuclear war would be extremely dangerous and destructive. Whatever the difficulties of maintaining adequate conventional forces in Europe might be, nuclear forces do not offer a viable alternative.

NOTES

1. William W. Kaufmann, *The McNamara Strategy* (New York: Harper and Row, 1964), p. 116.
2. "U.S. Forces in Europe: How Many, Doing What?" *Foreign Affairs* 53 (April 1975).
3. Fred C. Iklé, "Can Nuclear Deterrence Last Out the Century?" *Foreign Affairs* 51 (January 1973): 267–85; Bruce Russett, "Assured Destruction of What? A Countercombatant Alternative to Nuclear MADness," *Public Policy*, Spring 1974, pp. 121–38, also reprinted in this volume.
4. Alain C. Enthoven, "Reason, Morality and Defense Policy," *America* 108, (April 6, 1963): 465.
5. James R. Schlesinger, in remarks to the Overseas Writers Association Luncheon, International Club, Washington, D.C., January 10, 1974. For example, "We must be in a position in which the President of the United States, if he's called on to use strategic forces, has an option other than the option that I have referred to which concentrates on cities and which therefore carries in its wake the notion of inevitable destruction of American cities." The theme was reiterated in a news conference at the Pentagon, January 24, 1974.
6. U.S. Congress, Senate Committee on Armed Services, Preparedness Investigating Subcommittee, *Status of U.S. Strategic Power*, 90th Cong., 2d sess., April 26, 1968, part 1, p. 138.
7. For example, Ray Cromley's nationally syndicated column, as it appeared in the *Palo Alto Times*, February 25, 1974, said: "For one, the 'retargeting' is not primarily involved with a Russian first strike on the United States, which Schlesinger discounts heavily. It is rather that Schlesinger tends to regard nuclear missiles more as conventional weapons to be used when necessary in foreign local wars when Soviet victories would strongly threaten U.S. security. . . . This strategy is Schlesinger's alternative to developing the dreadfully expensive conventional forces and weapons required to deal with an all-out Russian drive into Western Europe. . . . Nuclear weapons therefore will substitute for a shortage of Western conventional forces in the crunch."

5

An "Outsider's" View of the Arms Race

Alva Myrdal

Ethics and nuclear strategy? The question itself is paradoxical, even if first asked only in the accustomed American context: namely, that of the conflict between nuclear superpowers in the fields of technology and diplomacy. While designing and testing weapons systems calculated to gain unilateral advantage over their adversary, the United States and the Soviet Union simultaneously wrestle in the diplomatic arena to control the pace and cost of the arms race without yielding any of the political or military advantages the two of them, as superpowers, possess in relation to all other nations. Ethics, it seems, is forgotten in this double-tiered drive for supremacy.

A handful of the citizens of these superpowers, including the contributors to this volume, seek, largely in vain, to recall to the competitors the story of Pyrrhus. To observers who are citizens of neither superpower, the current apocalyptic arms race also seems better described in terms of this ancient Greek myth of futile victory than in the conventional concepts of political dynamics. Therefore, as an outsider to great-power politics who has watched the East-West arms race from a number of perspectives—as a citizen of a country, Sweden, which has renounced such weapons; as an ambassador stationed in India, a nation which has now entered the "nuclear club"; as a participant in years of international efforts to negotiate the control of nuclear weapons—I

Dr. Myrdal is Ambassador at Large and Minister without Portfolio in the government of Sweden. She has long been Chief Swedish Delegate to the U.N. Disarmament Committee and has held a number of distinguished international offices. This essay is a summary of Dr. Myrdal's paper as presented at the seminars. A great deal of the material contained in the original essay has since been incorporated in *The Game of Disarmament* (New York: Pantheon Books, 1975).

wish to speak candidly about the superpowers' insensitivity to the interests and concerns of the rest of the world.

These interests and concerns can conveniently be grouped under three headings: (1) the advent of new, ever more sophisticated generations of nuclear weapons and precision guidance systems, applicable to both strategic and tactical nuclear weapons, including so-called mininukes; (2) the "defense" of Europe, which currently rests on a NATO military doctrine calculated rather to deter aggression than to defend against it, and which would surely result in the destruction of Europe if deterrence failed; and (3) the dilemma of nuclear proliferation, which must be understood to have two dimensions: the "horizontal" spread of nuclear weapons to nonnuclear powers and the "vertical" increase and sophistication in warheads and delivery systems on the part of the superpowers—a dilemma which can be resolved only by linking these two dimensions in a solution that is marked by mutual costs and benefits to both the "haves" and "have nots" of the "nuclear development gap."

I discern (perhaps because of my particular situation and experience) several pending conflicts on the armament agenda which are insufficiently appreciated in Washington and Moscow. My remarks are intended to heighten the paradox of ethics and nuclear strategy by underlining the inadequacy of *bilateral* solutions to *multilateral* problems.

THE SUPERPOWERS' ARMS RACE

An obvious benefit of détente is that the style of the superpowers' exchange of views has become less ideologically strident. Still, the perception of each other as "the enemy" has remained prevalent; see, for instance, former Secretary of Defense James Schlesinger's report to Congress on the Budget for FY 1976. But SALT and the subsequent summits, talks, and agreements show that the bilateral negotiations have rather served to create a new model of institutionalizing the arms race, conducting the competition in contractual form, as it were. The superpowers are consolidating a certain mutual parity or "essential equivalence," regrettably at higher rather than lowered levels.

That this deterrence is retained at such an unnecessarily high level of overkill and that the two competitor nations carry a tremendous cost on that account is primarily for their own legislators and taxpayers to judge. Yet the waste that is implied cannot correspond with true human interests. Even as outsiders, we are quite persuaded by the arguments proffered by critics that a small fraction of the arms—let us say 400 of the permitted 2,400 intercontinental missiles—would be enough, both for deterrence and defense. The game of *quantities* of strategic arms—and only of their delivery vehicles, not their warheads—evokes very little interest outside of Moscow and Washington whose experts are fascinated by numerical exercises as to missiles, throw-weight, and so on. In the rest of the world it is generally understood to be of immediate concern only to the two nations involved, regarded from the outside as a kind of feud between two rivals. The motivating force is the assertion of each nation that it must be "second to none." Such an ambition of maximation can, of course, never be realized more than momentarily, and then not safely held.

What is of concern to all of us, however, is that the balance be kept. Even the bilateral arrangements heralded in the 1974 Vladivostok communiques fail to insure us against the threatening destabilization of the balance which is implicit in the continued, open-ended competition for improved *quality* of weaponry, even in the strategic arms category (i.e., the permissibility of opting for turnover, modernization, and new generations, even whole new systems, of weapons). If the United States proceeds to develop maneuverable reentry vehicles (MaRVs), the Soviet Union will not be far behind; its prestigious Strategic Rockets Division will not allow itself to be laid off. The question of concern to the world is whether the two can safely keep each other down to a position of mutual deterrence; the great risk to the whole world is that one or both might proceed to first-strike capability (in other words, make themselves ready for actual war-fighting). Much strength should be attached to the words of the U.S. Senate in ratifying the Vladivostok agreement: that the two powers should "make every effort to halt the continuing competition."[1] To pursue such a costly race, and for no rational purpose, is, of course, outright unethical.

This is particularly painfully clear to an observant European, one whose voice is not tied by considerations to either of the two military blocs dominating that continent.

THE ANXIETY OF EUROPE

As the very name SALT modestly admits, the bilateral negotiations have so far been restricted to controlling and matching *strategic* arms. It is, of course, the *tactical* forces, especially tactical nuclear weapons, that become of most immediate interest to all those who are not superpowers or even nuclear-weapon powers.

On that very urgent agenda, there have apparently not been any constructive solutions advanced as yet—at the bilateral SALT negotiations, the multinational European Security Conference, the negotiations for Mutual and Balanced Force Reduction, or the Conference of the Committee on Disarmament (CCD). The wishes of the lesser powers are clearly expressed, particularly at the CCD and the U.N. But they go unheeded. And we have now learned the bitter lesson that the two superpowers are in deep, albeit hidden, agreement that they do not want to disarm.

The fact that the worldview of the superpowers has become so fixed on their own position vis-à-vis each other reveals that their dominant interest is to safeguard their own homelands from destruction and, therefore, to balance each other in strategic weaponry. Insofar as this balancing holds down the risks of a shooting war, it *does* serve the interests of other lands, even if it is a balance of terror. But it also represents what has been called "the sanctuary" doctrine of strategy. To Europe this is, of course, unnerving, to say the least. As Europe has been and is the major field of joint crisis-management, it means that the superpowers have reached a consensus to respect each others' delimitation of the boundary between alliance territories and are also inclining toward an agreed view that a military confrontation between them be fought out as a limited war in Europe. Unlike World War I and World War II, the origin of such a war, the *causa belli*, would this time hardly be of European making.

The eminent German scholar, Carl Friedrich von Weizsäcker, has published a 700-page treatise with detailed analyses by experts on the consequences for Europe of different war scenarios. In one place he concludes that even limited war can mean total devastation of Central Europe, and that its probable escalation would entail the extinction of its people (*alles Leben*).[2] Other experts give the same general estimates. The peoples of Europe, both allied and neutral, should be aware of what is in store for them if the superpower rivalry leads to a military confrontation.

There is in Europe a deep disbelief in any protection by the nuclear umbrellas of the superpowers, and a growing concern about the bilateral agreements on intercontinental weaponry and the "new" U.S. strategic doctrines, announced by former Secretary Schlesinger, which seem to fortify the position of sanctuaries for the two great powers themselves. This is a basic inequality, which cannot be interpreted as anything but unfairness by other nations. When they are assured of "defense" it rather sounds like cynicism.

To conclude on this sensitive point: There is a deep anguish on the part of the people of Europe, both allied and neutral, which is evidently not understood on this side of the Atlantic. There is a fear that European security is being jeopardized, perhaps sacrificed, in the superpowers' gaming with each other. The voices expressing this fear are not all European. A study from the Brookings Institution has this to say:

> The idea that tactical nuclear weapons furnish a plausible "option" for *defending* Western Europe (as distinguished from their escalatory role) has had a lingering half-life. In fact, the use of hundreds of atomic weapons could cause so much collateral damage to the area being "defended" that the inhabitants might prefer surrender as a lesser evil. This would be less true of certain low-yield or "clean" weapons; but even if NATO so limited its weaponry, an enemy might not.[3]

The changes imminent in strategic doctrines and weapons development have here been viewed from the European angle, certain as one can now be that a war in that theater would be a war of superpower-making. The actual risks for starting a shooting war lie mostly outside Europe, particularly in the Middle East. But any superpower confrontation—so far avoided—would have ominous consequences for all countries.

These deep, potential conflicts have been hardly brought on to the agenda at any negotiation table, either at the European Security Conference in Helsinki, or the Mutual and Balanced Force Reduction Talks in Vienna. The allies of the superpowers are a silent majority. It is perhaps understandable why somebody from a neutral country like Sweden speaks more openly (as, of course, do academics in many lands).

THE IMMINENT RISK OF PROLIFERATION

The third, and presently most unsettling, item on the arms agenda is the threat of proliferation: the impending probability that a continuation of the vertical nuclear arms race between the United States and the U.S.S.R. for unilateral qualitative and quantitative advantage will beget in some of the remaining 142 nations a determination to break the nuclear monopoly by building their own nuclear weapons.

The enticement to emulation, offered by the superpowers' incessant competition for more nuclear weapons also in the tactical category, constitutes an ethical responsibility which the superpowers are not sufficiently reminded of. If these weapons are of value to them for battlefield use, why not to others? The continuous possession by Britain, France, and China of independent nuclear forces, defended as of "deterrent" value, also sets precedents and provides allurement to other nations. What is the rationale for considering tactical nuclear weapons militarily useful to some countries and not to others? The conviction held by some nations, such as Canada and Sweden, from early on, that the possession of nuclear weapons is counterproductive for lesser powers, is not given any prominent display.

The "club" of nuclear-weapon powers was closed by the present powers in the Non-Proliferation Treaty (NPT), concluded on December 31, 1967, which allowed for a membership of five and resolutely refused the option for all other nations to join. But the Indian nuclear explosion of 1974 has served as an eye-opener that the expectations of the superpowers had been mistaken. With its underground test India demonstrated its possession of the device which is *per se* an atomic bomb, whether it is so used—or intended.

The treaty devised to assure acceptance of nonproliferation is now in jeopardy. It came up for mandatory scrutiny in May 1975, in a meeting that proved a failure from a disarmament point of view. No suggestion was approved for strengthening the NPT and making it more acceptable to the very important countries that have, as yet, refused to join. Instead, the conference was turned into a promotion vehicle for the spread of installations for producing nuclear energy. Thus, at the same time as grave political uncertainties about proliferation persist, the rapid spread of reactors for producing nuclear energy is leading to a world-wide multiplication of stocks of fissile material. As technological knowledge is also spreading, the prerequisites are created in a great number of countries for independently manufacturing atomic bombs, even if of the primitive Hiroshima-type, able to kill some 100,000 people at one blow. For a more precise forecast, the following may be quoted from SIPRI:

The total nuclear electrical capacity in 1980 (taking this year as an example) will be about 300 GWe (gigawatts of electricity) and this will produce about 80,000 kilograms (265x300) or 80 tons of Pu-239. This plutonium will become available in 1983—the three-year delay being the time during which the fuel is kept in the reactor and the time needed for the extraction of the plutonium from the spent reactor fuel elements. About one-third of this plutonium will be produced in the present non-nuclear-weapon countries. This could, in theory, correspond to the production of about 50 bombs of nominal size (20 kilotons) per week in these countries. [And that is about the size of the Nagasaki bomb!][4]

What could and what should be done? Most appropriate to meet the risk of proliferation would be renunciation by the nuclear-weapon powers of further advances in the *quality* of their weapons, for modernization or even whole new generations of nuclear weaponry. Most urgent of all, not least for the sake of nonproliferation, is the cancellation of plans for the development of tactical mininukes and terminal guidance systems with high accuracy for local theaters of war, heralded as being of superior value for defense; these are the very weapons lesser powers may be tempted to find useful.

There is one, and only one, international measure that could function as a legal padlock against proliferation of nuclear weapons: a duly implemented treaty involving a comprehensive ban on testing nuclear devices. But is there any longer a hope of attaining that disarmament goal, verbally given the highest priority since 1954?

The new alibi is now being constituted in the attempt to provide possibilities for conducting nuclear explosions for so-called peaceful purposes. But this opens a loophole.

As India has been the cause of the present alarm by exploding a nuclear device, indistinguishable from a nuclear bomb, I will cite how that country now formulates the conditions for a nondiscriminatory solution (to which it would presumably adhere, thus cutting out the ambiguous explosions "for peaceful purposes"):

We can make a beginning in controlling the nuclear arms race by agreeing on a comprehensive test ban. Only in the context of a complete cessation of all nuclear-weapon tests could consideration be given to the possibility of concluding an agreement on the regulation of underground nuclear explosions for peaceful purposes to be signed by all States. The accompanying system of international safeguards which will have to be devised should be based on objective, functional and non-discriminatory criteria. It should be universal in application.[5]

As early as 1968, the nonaligned members of the Geneva Committee had recommended such a solution. However, the superpowers have hitherto not been inclined to agree to a rational view, not even at the risk of proliferation offered by the "peaceful explosion." Rather, through their bilateral 1974 agreement, the so-called Threshold Test Ban, they have indicated that they want to keep their options open for producing new nuclear-weapon systems and, therefore, are evidently ready to let other nations also explode nuclear "devices" (i.e., test nuclear bombs) if it is done only underground.

Considerations of this ominous reality, in the light of practical possibilities, have led the Swedish delegation to the CCD to present a draft treaty on a comprehensive test ban with two special features: (1) verification by challenge (i.e., a series of queries and responses, including local inspection by invitation, whereby an accused party has the responsibility to free itself from charges of violation); and (2) three protocols which would allow different time lapses before various proscriptions enter into force. One of these protocols deals with peaceful nuclear explosions and envisages a comprehensive sequence of an international licensing authority and a managing agency, both placing all nations under the same, nondiscriminatory rule.[6]

There are a number of other specific measures that should be undertaken, most of them serving to reduce the discrimination between haves and have-nots in the application of NPT rules and International Atomic Energy Agency (IAEA) safeguards. Any honest analysis should have forewarned the superpower architects that the NPT could not be a reliable or even workable instrument, because it did not entail any mutuality of benefits.

The political aspects of the proliferation problem have been grossly neglected by the superpowers. When the NPT was being actively negotiated, from 1965 to 1968, warnings were issued and improvements suggested by nonaligned nations. But they were met by stubborn refusal. In the end they were able to extract only the promise that the superpowers should "in good faith" negotiate the cessation of the nuclear arms race. But, as we all know, that promise has been turned into its opposite, a spiralling arms race.

The nonnuclear-weapon powers must now be given more assurance as to their own national security, to take the place of the "security guarantees" of 1968, which have proven to be a most misbegotten device. At that time—in order to satisfy the clamor for some security assurances to nuclear-weapon-free nations—the superpowers moved a resolution in the U.N. Security Council whereby they promised immediate assistance to any nonnuclear-weapon nation, party to the NPT, "that is a victim of an act or an object of a threat of aggression in which nuclear weapons are used." But with the veto powers of the five nuclear-weapon members of the Security Council, no U.N.-sponsored action against nuclear attack or blackmail is now conceivable. As a protection for nonnuclear-weapon countries, the resolution is, according to common judgment, valueless.

I have, therefore, suggested that a political move should now be made by the superpowers to "pay the price" for the NPT, a price they should have been ready to pay at the outset. It would be a grand gesture of historical significance if the nuclear-weapon powers—jointly, bilaterally, or even unilaterally—gave a pledge never to attack nonnuclear-weapon powers with such weapons. The pledge could be included in an additional protocol to the NPT. It may verbatim follow the one already in force for the Tlatelolco Treaty (ratified by the United States on May 12, 1971): "Article 3. The Governments represented by the undersigned Plenipotentiaries also undertake not to use or threaten to use nuclear weapons against the Contracting Parties to the Treaty for the Proliferation of Nuclear Weapons in Latin America"—the last phrase to be changed to "the Contracting Parties to the Treaty on the Non-Proliferation of Nuclear Weapons."

This would be a highly appropriate and very urgent subject for talks between the superpowers in order, if possible, to synchronize such a pledge. (Some exception must, of course, be made for cases where nonnuclear-weapon powers cooperate with nuclear weapon powers in actual nuclear warfare.)

MORE ARMS RACES

To these notes, which have concentrated on the evil of nuclear weapons, should be added some reminders as to dangers appearing in other arsenals. The increase in the production and sophistication of conventional weapons is reflected in the enormous increase of the economic burden of armaments costs—totaling close to $300 billion annually. This represents a tragic denial of possibilities for satisfying the crying basic needs of the poor multitudes of humankind. It is also reflected in a rapid upsurge in the trade of arms, significantly changing its pattern by more than doubling the purchases by the Third World between 1970 and 1975. The new oil-rich countries are demanding and receiving large quantities of highly sophisticated weaponry. But everywhere, the political aspect is undeniable: The militarization of the world is progressing fast. Military regimes are having their heyday in our era.

Sophisticated weapons are more "effective" weapons: i.e., they are more effective in killing people, as recent wars have testified, and also more effective in causing pain. Modern fine-caliber, high-velocity arms are, for instance, more "effective" in tearing gaping wounds in the human body. Their use goes contrary to the principles of humanitarian laws of war, adopted by the Hague Conventions of 1897 and 1907. At present, efforts are being made through negotiations inaugurated by the Red Cross, in Geneva, to outlaw the use of a number of such cruel weapons, as well as indiscriminate area bombing, which kills more civilians than soldiers. This is the apex of the ethical dilemmas raised by our weapons culture.

A significant feature of all modern developments in the armaments field is that they heighten the factor of discrimination between the haves and the have-nots in all respects, and most potently between the superpowers and all lesser powers. This makes disarmament such a burning political and ethical problem. It calls for thoroughgoing and urgent international (*multilateral*) negotiations. But they are at a virtual standstill. Of course, people in all countries are familiar with the notion and the necessity of bilateral negotiations and agreements. We are, however, unable to understand the notion of bilateral ethics which seems to animate even learned discussion in the United States. Negotiations which ignore the vital interests of most of the world's population are discriminatory. For this reason they are also undiplomatic and dangerous. It is to this danger that the ethical critic, even (or perhaps especially) from a nonnuclear nation, seeks to draw attention.

NOTES

1. U.S., Senate, 94th Cong., 1st sess., resolution 20, 1975.
2. Carl Friedrich von Weizsäcker, ed., *Kriegsfolgen und Kriegsverhütung* (Munich: Carl Hanser Verlag, 1971).
3. John Newhouse et al., *U.S. Troops in Europe* (Washington, D.C.: The Brookings Institution, 1971), p. 45.
4. Stockholm International Peace Research Institute, *World Armaments and Disarmament: SIPRI Yearbook* [*1976*] (Stockholm: Almqvist & Wiksell, 1976), p. 60.
5. U.N., General Assembly, First Committee, November 11, 1974. A/C.1/PV. 2016.
6. CCD 348, 1971. For easy reference, see *SIPRI Yearbook* [*1972*] (Stockholm, Almqvist-Wiksell).

6

Deterrence and the Defense of Europe

Robert A. Gessert

Other papers in this volume have considered the current strategic debate in the United States in its broad political context and in its ethical context, especially in relation to just-war theory. Most of these papers have focused rather sharply, though by no means exclusively, on the strategic relationship between the United States and the Soviet Union. The purpose of my paper, however, is to consider the U.S. strategic debate in the wider context of the North Atlantic Treaty Organization (NATO), and, in particular, to examine some of the domestic debate's implications for the defense of Europe, and the impact of the requirements for deterrence and defense in Europe on the issues in debate here.

Accordingly, I have set three broad, interrelated objectives for this paper: (1) to review briefly some of the central themes in the U.S. strategic debate, with a view to evaluating how they bear on the problems of European security, as compared to U.S. security; (2) to review some of the dominant military and political problems of providing for deterrence in and the forward defense of Europe, problems that may shed new light on the U.S. strategic debate; (3) to deal with these subjects in a way that is sensitive to the ethical issues involved.

CENTRAL THEMES IN THE U.S. DEBATE

If one takes Secretary of Defense James Schlesinger's March 1974 report to the Congress on the 1975 defense budget and the 1975–79 defense program as the touchstone for the debate,[1] three

---

Mr. Gessert is a Principal Scientist at the General Research Corporation. He was formerly a member of the Institute for Defense Analysis and of the President's Science Advisory Committee.

closely related strategic themes or issues appear to lie at the center of the programs he announced and the national debate he invited. The first of these themes deals with what should be done in the unlikely event that deterrence fails and to what degree this action should be prepared for in advance and made known to our allies and adversaries. The second deals with how deterrence should be shored up across the broad spectrum of threats, how the strategic balance should be maintained over the long haul, and the extent to which our strategic programs should match or anticipate those of the Soviet Union in order to maintain "essential equivalence" with or without firm agreements on arms limitations. The third theme (less well developed in the report) deals with the political significance of relative strategic power—its visibility and credibility to our adversaries, to ourselves, to disinterested third parties, and to our allies.

These themes are hardly new in the history of the U.S. debate about the utility of nuclear weapons, a debate which stretches back into the 1950s. What is new is the emphasis and some of the accents Schlesinger and his colleagues have given to these themes through criticism of the strategic/military posture that had evolved over the years; the extent to which he, as secretary of defense, has made them national issues requiring serious public debate beyond the confines of the national security community and the handful of academic and research analysts who normally participate in such debates; and the particular mix of military, political, economic, and ethical concerns that lie behind the stress given to these themes and issues at this particular point in history.

I do not expect that everyone will agree that these themes are or should be the dominant themes in the current U.S. debate or even that I have correctly identified the broad terms that James Schlesinger's annual report set for a national debate. I cannot develop all the arguments for my interpretation within the confines of this paper, so I prefer to ask the reader to accept them as given for my purposes and use my space to comment a little more on each of these themes and their importance for the defense of Europe.

If Deterrence Fails

For at least the past decade, while rough parity in strategic forces between the Soviet Union and the United States was evolving and assured destruction gained the ascendancy over damage limitation in our strategic calculations and programs, deterrence of nuclear war in any form has been the predominant goal of U.S. strategic nuclear policies and forces. One could argue that these policies and forces have been successful in averting nuclear war and that they have been successful because of the way we designed our forces to emphasize deterrence by primary—if not sole—reliance on assured destruction. In fact, so the argument runs, the situation of *mutual* assured destruction (in which we, by choice, have granted the Soviet Union a capability to retaliate massively against our unprotected cities while we retained an invulnerable capability to retaliate against their cities) is best since it denies either side any basis for believing it could profitably undertake a nuclear strike or for fearing that the other side would contemplate such an initiative.

One of the dominant arguments for the new emphasis on flexible response, however, derives from concern with the possibility—however small—that deterrence could fail and that a miscalculation, a political crisis, escalation from a conventional war, an accident, or some unimagined event could lead to a first use of nuclear weapons. As Schlesinger said, "Flexibility of response is also essential because, despite our best efforts, we cannot guarantee that deterrence will never fail; nor can we foresee the situations that would cause it to fail."[2]

This theme in the new debate is well known and requires little elaboration here. It had been adumbrated in Mr. Nixon's first annual report to the Congress on foreign policy in 1970,[3] amply developed by Fred Iklé in the January 1973 issue of *Foreign Affairs*,[4] stressed by Robert Ellsworth and others in a public television debate in February 1974,[5] and fully developed in Schlesinger's annual report, particularly with reference to the retargeting of existing forces so as to provide selective and limited nuclear response options which would avoid high civilian casualties and other collateral damage.[6]

In the context of this paper, the point to emphasize is that clearly one of the not inconceivable ways deterrence of nuclear war could fail would be through an attack on our allies. Again to quote Schlesinger, "Threats against allied forces, to the extent that they could be deterred by the prospect of nuclear retaliation, demand both more limited responses than destroying cities and advanced planning tailored to such lesser responses."[7]

Shoring Up Deterrence

A statement such as Schlesinger's directly connects the first theme of the debate to the second. If the United States and the Soviet Union are mutually deterred from any direct first use of nuclear weapons against each other by the threat of mutual assured destruction, then deterrence as we have broadly conceived it in the past (encompassing deterrence of attack—conventional or nuclear—on our allies) is in jeopardy. Our European allies, who still feel quite dependent on the U.S. nuclear guarantee, are haunted by this possibility. Their response is either to take comfort in the fact that the Soviet Union cannot be sufficiently certain that an attack on Europe would not lead to general nuclear war, even under present circumstances, or to seek ways to maintain or strengthen the coupling of the U.S. strategic arsenal to the U.S. conventional and theater nuclear forces deployed in Europe.

This issue is very complex indeed[8] and again not very new—only newly complicated both by the strategic nuclear parity (if not superiority) with the United States that the Soviet Union has evidently sought, and by the continued (and in some ways qualitatively improved) offensive conventional capabilities that the Soviet Union maintains in East Germany, Poland, and Czechoslovakia. West Europeans who worry about such things confront a serious dilemma. If the United States does not have flexible and selective nuclear options for response against a nuclear attack limited to West Europe or a conventional attack against West Europe, the credibility of the involvement of the U.S. strategic arsenal in deterrence of attack against them is in doubt. On the other hand, if the United States appears to be seeking options that would enable it to limit response entirely within Europe, then that same credibility is equally in doubt.

Europe cannot afford to be too logically rigorous about this dilemma—especially those countries who are denied or who deny themselves an independent nuclear option that could appear to provide an independent deterrent or present the implicit possibility (certainty is not required) of triggering a U.S. strategic involvement. Real, diverging national interests are at stake, and our European allies may have to content themselves with denying the Soviet Union a high degree of confidence that the U.S. strategic arsenal could be decoupled, rather than with an absolute certainty that it would automatically be involved in response to any conventional or nuclear attack on them. If I understand Schlesinger correctly, he was determined to reinforce European confidence that the United States has nuclear options (as well as others) that contain implicit, if not inherent, linkages between conventional, theater nuclear, and strategic nuclear capabilities that should deny the Soviet Union any possibility of believing it could threaten Europe without seriously risking strategic nuclear war.

The Political Utility of Nuclear Weapons

Shoring up deterrence with respect to threats to our allies is very closely related to the political significance of strategic nuclear power.

We have come a long way since Secretary of State John Foster Dulles enunciated the doctrine of massive retaliation in 1954. It is useful to remember that the original version of this doctrine was formulated when the United States was recovering from a protracted and frustrating war in Korea and confronting (but shunning, at the time) a possible new engagement of its ground forces in Asia—this time in Vietnam. The doctrine was intended to deter Communist aggression anywhere in the world by indicating that we would deal with such aggression at places and times of our own choosing, rather than being sucked into another protracted conflict. The doctrine was a declaratory political doctrine, more than an action policy with military plans to back it up. Although many people were troubled by it from the beginning, it had some credibility because of the overwhelming superiority of the U.S. atomic arsenal; it also appeared to provide an economic means of averting having our national interests nibbled away on the fringes or in the central area of our concern, Europe. Despite the fact that the Lisbon goals for NATO ("fifty divisions, four thousand aircraft and strong naval forces by the end of 1952"[9]), and the rearmament of West Germany acknowledged the existence of a massive conventional threat in Central Europe that required some offsetting conventional capability, there was an assumption of the basic utility of nuclear weapons for deterring all threats against Europe and for providing a means for dealing with a war should it occur there.

Advocates of primary or sole reliance on the threat of assured destruction for deterrence share with proponents of the original doctrine of massive retaliation reliance on a threat of retribution rather than a capability to defeat military forces in detail. The primary difference is that the former have narrowed the threat for which this response is relevant almost solely to the threat of a major first strike against the continental United States. In doing so they—especially those who advocate *mutual* assured destruction—have, not unknowingly or unwillingly, denied any political utility to nuclear weapons. As Edward Luttwak has put it, "As we have seen, the basic axiom of the 'mutual' version of the doctrine is that strategic power cannot be applied usefully to political purposes."[10]

A concern for the political value of nuclear weapons and posture ran throughout Schlesinger's annual report. Laurence Martin, in a very thoughtful article on the recent changes in U.S. strategic doctrine, has correctly pointed out that a desire to re-establish a clear relation between strategic power and political purpose in any broad sense was one of the most problematic themes of the Schlesinger emphases.[11] Schlesinger was evidently not nostalgic for the dubious and transitory political utility of massive retaliation. What he appeared to be most concerned with (as other public statements have confirmed) was not abandoning the political significance of nuclear weapons to the Soviet Union, especially in the Middle East or in Central Europe.

EUROPEAN INTEREST IN THE U.S. STRATEGIC DEBATE

I cannot claim to have watched the European press with comprehensiveness or consistency for general opinion on the U.S. strategic debate or some of the innovations Schlesinger has introduced. What I say in this section is drawn principally from conferences and interviews with a rather small sample of informed Europeans. It is thus derivative, impressionistic, and subject to correction by experts on European opinion.

Varieties of European Opinion

My first impression of European views on the U.S. strategic debate is that they are about as varied as interests and opinions in the United States itself.

There are those in the extragovernmental and academic communities who focus on some of the research and new weapons-procurement programs announced by Schlesinger and see these as representing little more than the continuing influence of a military-industrial complex; they view many of the doctrinal statements as simply a rationale to justify spending for these programs. On the whole, Europeans who react this way are probably a little less censorious of the new U.S. programs than are their U.S. counterparts, perhaps because they do not share the immediate competition for natural resources.

Other critics—found particularly in the European arms-control community (inside and outside the governments)—see arms-control negotiation and détente as the priority issues; again like their U.S. counterparts, they focus on the new weapons programs and view most of the new strategic emphases as stimulants to further arms competition and a threat to détente. For this group, as well as for the first, the new U.S. strategic debate is unwelcome not only for its possible consequences for East-West relations but also for its implications of division and vacillation within the society and government of their dominant partner.

The existence of indifferent European opinion about the U.S. strategic debate should surprise no one. Many Europeans do not believe its existence or its outcome makes much difference. Either they have accommodated themselves to the existence of military/strategic asymmetries that they feel cannot be solved by defense programs within the political and economic reach of the Atlantic alliance, or they have assessed the intentions and ambitions of the Soviet Union and other Warsaw Pact countries vis-à-vis the West in a way that does not include military initiatives and conquest. Many of these Europeans are preoccupied by other national issues—especially the dangers of further war in the Middle East and the unforeseeable consequences this could have for Europe, European dependence on Arab oil, divergencies between the United States and Europe on Middle-East policy in general, the strain of defense budgets at a time of severe inflation in all NATO countries, and so on. To these Europeans and many others it would be far better to leave well enough alone insofar as defense programs specifically related to the presumptive threat from the Warsaw Pact countries against Western Europe are concerned. They would prefer to concentrate on efforts to reduce that threat by a mixture of arms-control negotiations, diplomacy, and economic and cultural interchange and interdependence, rather than see their dominant partner undertake new programs to shore up either deterrence or defense against a threat they believe very unlikely to materialize.

While such European opinions obviously present inertia, if not resistance, to U.S. strategic innovations, the direct concern of this paper is the opinion and interests of those Europeans who do perceive a real military threat from the Warsaw Pact countries (and its political consequences, including those for further détente, arms-control negotiations, the Middle East crisis, and so on).

European Security Interests

A discussion of serious European security interests in the U.S. strategic debate can profitably focus on West German concerns since, by geographical and political necessity, the defense of West Germany is at the heart of the defense of Western Europe.

When the first intimations of changes in U.S. strategic doctrine were reported in Europe (on the basis of Schlesinger's comments following a speech in January 1974), reactions among West Germans concerned with defense were rather jittery. In the first place, the pending U.S. changes seemed to be another unilateral U.S. initiative, one bound to affect NATO, but for which adequate groundwork of advance consultation had not taken place.

Beyond this normal—and probably not totally avoidable —reaction, Europeans were initially alarmed at talk of limited or limiting nuclear war. They have never had the same interest in the concepts of limited nuclear war that has always been present in the U.S. defense community. To them any such concept raises the specter of a nuclear war limited to their immediate battlefield, or even the European theater in general, leaving U.S. and U.S.S.R. territories as sanctuaries. Almost no matter what U.S. spokesmen say, the fear remains that it could be in our interest to raise the threshold at which the U.S. strategic arsenal would become engaged in Europe to a point so high that U.S. strategic forces would become effectively decoupled from the defense of Europe.

There has already been enough in what U.S. spokesmen have said and urged on Europeans to give some basis to this fear. The concerted push in the early years of the Kennedy administration to raise the conventional capabilities of NATO in the forward area was strongly motivated by a desire to raise the nuclear threshold. Little matter that Americans conceived providing a credible deterrent to conventional attack against Europe to be in the best interest of Europeans; most of the latter felt that, for a complex of political, economic, and military reasons, conventional parity was not within reach, and, even if it were, they would not welcome the possibility of a major conventional war in Europe. To them, the ultimate security against such a war remained the implicit or imminent threat that the U.S. strategic arsenal would become engaged, rather than the assurance that a conventional potential existed to hold for a few days or weeks—or even to regain lost territory after months or years of conventional warfare. To imply escalation to the nuclear level was more important than to guard against its necessity.

Europeans, and particularly West Germans, have now generally come to recognize that if the U.S. strategic deterrent is based solely on mutual assured destruction, it loses some credibility for the defense of Europe. In this respect the initial jitteriness about U.S. innovations that tend to emphasize limited strategic nuclear options has now been assuaged, and they accept the idea that such innovations may strengthen, rather than weaken, deterrence of conventional or nuclear attacks initially aimed at Western Europe. The retargeting aspects of the Schlesinger emphases are thus tending to become accepted, if still not enthusiastically embraced. However, judgment is more reserved on new weapons programs that still seem potentially inimical to prospects of maintaining a superpower stability sufficient to prevent the interests of Europeans from becoming lost in the United States' preoccupation with bilateral deterrence/détente interaction.

Schlesinger's visit to Germany in November 1974 and the announcement that the United States was increasing the combat-to-support ratio of its ground forces in West Germany seemed to improve that country's acceptance of current U.S. innovations as aimed at strengthening, rather than weakening, commitment to NATO. The two-brigade increase in deployed U.S. strength —among other things—appears to have helped the West Germans sustain and improve their own conventional contribution to NATO, although there is still strong doubt as to whether conventional comparability with the Warsaw Pact countries is possible. (Even the desirability of full conventional comparability is still very much in question; fears of decoupling always lurk in the background, whether they arise from talk of limited nuclear war or from talk of achieving conventional balance with the Pact countries.) The West Germans, in particular, have become staunch advocates of flexibility of response, seeing it as a means by which to confront the Soviet Union and other Warsaw Pact countries with the real possibility that a NATO response to an attack on Western Europe might be either conventional or nuclear, depending on the circumstances. Perhaps their feeling can be stated more precisely: The Soviet Union must be confronted with real uncertainty about the nature of a NATO response to either a conventional or a nuclear attack on Western Europe. (This accounts for West German reticence about doing as much detailed public debating on strategy as Americans are wont to do.)

During the past ten years even the existing conventional balance with the Warsaw Pact countries has periodically seemed to be threatened by U.S. worries, public and Congressional, over the balance-of-payments and other problems associated with our maintaining sizable forces in Europe. At the same time, the credibility of the U.S. strategic deterrent for Europe appeared to be eroding by the emergence of strategic parity. In this context West Germans, in particular, took comfort in the thought that the presence of some 7,000 theater/tactical nuclear weapons in Europe (about 5,000 in West Germany) would confront the Soviet Union with the uncertainty discussed above.

Although these theater/tactical weapons have presented many privately acknowledged problems of command and control, of security, of reduction of vulnerability, and of reducing the temptation for the Pact countries to preempt in wartime, they have served two purposes in the minds of West Germans. First, they have appeared to compensate in part for deficiencies in the conventional forward defense that could disrupt a massed Pact attack. However, this purpose has been as much a source of friction and military uncertainty (about when to introduce nuclear weapons and on what scale) as it has been a genuine comfort to the West Germans. But the weapons' second, almost more important purpose has been to serve as the critical link coupling the forward defense of Europe with the U.S. strategic arsenal.

Because of the importance of this second purpose, the West Germans have heretofore been extremely reluctant—in public at any rate—about contemplating serious revisions or reductions in the theater/tactical nuclear posture. Now, however, in the light of new technologies, strategic/nuclear parity, and new concern with the conventional posture, there are indications that they, as well as other Europeans, are willing to re-examine the extent to which the theater/tactical nuclear posture of NATO meets the optimal requirements for deterrence and defense in the central region.

ELEMENTS OF THE DEFENSE OF EUROPE

The U.S. strategic debate has been accompanied, in the last year or two, by two other re-examinations of the U.S. military posture, especially vis-à-vis the defense of Europe. It is my impression that these topics have attracted somewhat less attention than the strategic debate in the general U.S. consciousness and very little attention from ethicists in particular. Yet in the long run, they may be more important for deterrence and defense against attack in Europe and will probably significantly affect the extent to which any strategic retargeting doctrines and new weapons procurements can genuinely contribute to the security of Europe.

From the vantage point of Europeans—and especially the West Germans, who occupy the most exposed position—security rests on a triad of strategic nuclear capabilities, theater/tactical nuclear capabilities, and immediately available (forward) conventional capabilities. These three must supplement each other; one cannot substitute for another or compensate for another's weaknesses. Full conventional capabilities cannot significantly reduce ultimate reliance on U.S. strategic capabilities, especially in the deterrence role. On the other hand, no amount of flexibility in the U.S. strategic posture would prove credible as the initial response to an attack that was confined to Europe. Tactical nuclear weapons cannot be used successfully to keep a war at the border, nor can they be used to regain territory that has been lost to *blitzkrieg* assaults with conventional weapons. They also cannot adequately replace the possibility (or guarantee) that U.S. strategic weapons would become engaged in countering an initial or sustained attack against Western Europe.

NATO's Conventional Capabilities

There is a growing school of thought within U.S. defense circles that something approaching comparability with the Warsaw Pact countries in conventional capabilitites is within reach. In the 1960s and early 1970s Alain Enthoven was the principal spokesman for this point of view.[12] More recently Steven L. Canby has become the most noted advocate of conventional comparability.[13] Other authors, more restrained in their optimism, such as Richard D. Lawrence and Jeffrey Record, have argued for changes in U.S. and NATO force structure that would, according to their view, significantly reduce the present imbalance between the Warsaw Pact countries and NATO in conventional capabilities.[14]

Such authors have not yet convinced Europeans (or the U.S. Defense Department) that conventional comparability is within reach, or even that it would be an unequivocal blessing. Enthoven's arguments rested heavily on his attempts to reduce Soviet capabilities to size and on his comparisons of NATO's and the Pact countries' collective resources (emphasizing proportions of populations and GNPs committed to defense efforts). As Canby has pointed out, there were significant weaknesses in that argument which ignored differences in force structure and the kind of war each force was designed to fight.[15] Moreover, Enthoven's arguments were formulated at a time when Europeans still firmly believed that NATO's best deterrent depended on an early and perhaps massive first use of nuclear weapons. Finally, most contemporary military analyses and war games tended to show that, with current capabilities in the forward area, NATO forces could well be overrun in the first few days or weeks of an attack by the Pact countries, before all the resources Enthoven counted in his equations could be brought to bear.

The Canby and Lawrence/Record arguments addressed the last point directly. Canby argued that the Pact countries' forces are designed for a short, *blitzkrieg* war with an apparent aim of overrunning NATO forces before reinforcements could arrive and long before the heavy support forces designed for a long war could serve many useful purposes to NATO combat forces. U.S. Army forces in particular, he argues, are structured as general purpose, expeditionary forces, requiring a high support-to-combat ratio. Such forces would be useful to NATO only if they could screen, delay, fall back, and regroup with reinforcements to conduct offensive operations for regaining lost territory. In short, in Canby's view, presently deployed U.S. forces almost appear to be designed to make introduction of nuclear weapons necessary either to prevent being overrun (which would not be in the best interests of the United States and probably not in those of Europe) or to make a protracted counteroffensive campaign possible (which would not be in the interests of Europe and probably not in those of the United States).

The Lawrence/Record argument, although not so detailed or so emphatic, rested on similar grounds. It also proposed restructuring U.S. and other NATO forces with a much higher combat-to-support ratio, taking advantage of recent advances in the technology of nonnuclear weapons, placing greater emphasis on immediate availability in the forward area, and emphasizing tactics and doctrine tailored to counter armored and motorized *blitzkrieg* tactics.

Such arguments are based on both military and political grounds. Militarily, redesigned forces could provide stiffer forward resistance to a conventional attack, even a major one. With adjustments in the theater/tactical nuclear posture, conventional operations based on such redesigned forces might be made more compatible with the introduction of tactical nuclear weapons, should that alternative appear necessary or desirable. Politically a strengthened, combat-heavy and support-light conventional capability might lend credence to the implied link among strategic nuclear, theater/tactical nuclear, and conventional forces—especially if accompanied by alterations in the U.S. strategic posture that would provide limited strategic options, including the possibility, but not the necessity, of first use. Movement in this direction might be welcomed by Europeans and by the West Germans in particular.

The U.S. defense community finds such arguments controversial, mostly for reasons dealing with their appraisal of the Pact countries' threat. They should, however, be welcomed for their balanced focus on military, political, and economic considerations that affect the Atlantic alliance as a whole. There can be little question that the conventional capabilities of NATO could be improved, even within the constrained budgets of its partners. Accepting the idea that they should be improved (in a manner that would emphasize immediate defense in the forward area more than a capability to fight a protracted conventional war) would give proper weight to European security interests and to the close integration of strategic nuclear, theater/nuclear, and conventional capabilities; it would also seem to be in keeping with U.S. emphasis on flexibility of response and extension of deterrence into the wartime period.

Such a change is not merely a pipedream on the part of Defense Department critics and their European counterparts. Recent actions in the U.S. Congress have indicated dissatisfaction with NATO's conventional posture and some willingness to move in the direction of the Canby and Lawrence/Record proposals. The most obvious example of this growing reaction is the Nunn Amendment to the Defense Appropriation Authorization Act of 1975 (PL

93-365), requiring an increased combat-to-support ratio for U.S forces in the forward area and mandating the two-brigade increase in deployed combat potential which was mentioned above.

Theater/Tactical Nuclear Posture

The passage of the Nunn Amendment also confirmed the existence of widespread dissatisfaction with the theater/tactical nuclear posture of NATO and a growing debate about the posture and its rationale. Two recent contributions to the public literature on this subject have attracted attention in both Europe and the United States and seem to be moving in the right directions militarily and politically to shore up the deterrent/defense posture in Europe in a way that is compatible with U.S. interests while reinforcing our allies' support of the Schlesinger changes in strategic posture and doctrine.

The first was another monograph by Jeffrey Record in which he identified and reviewed what he considers the principal weaknesses in the present deployment of 7,000 theater/tactical nuclear weapons in Europe.[16] That deployment, in his view, serves neither the interests of deterrence nor the interest of defense. With respect to deterrence, he said, the stockpile is excessive and contains many weapons that are vulnerable, on Quick Reaction Alert (QRA), or both (all tending to invite preemption). As for defense, he judged the large number of weapons, including, for example, many artillery-delivered warheads, to be extremely difficult to command and control.

In his study, Record examined four broad alternatives to the present posture: (1) a more-or-less arbitrary reduction in deployment to about 2,000 weapons; (2) a reduction similar in size but with a focus on reducing or eliminating those weapons that are particularly vulnerable, targets for preemption, or excessively hard to control; (3) a posture using recent technology (particularly miniaturization of tactical nuclear weapons) to develop a better war-fighting capability; and (4) elimination of the forward deployment. Basing his conclusion heavily on "the great political importance of deployed U.S. tactical nuclear weapons to Europeans, for whom the U.S. nuclear presence on the continent (although not necessarily the current deployment) represents the most visible proof of the U.S. strategic guarantee,"[17] Record favored the second option: a reduced deployment that would rely heavily on battlefield and long-range missiles, terminate the

QRA, eliminate artillery-delivered weapons, and limit yields to the 0.5 to 10 kiloton range.

The size of the reduction Record proposed, however, is somewhat unconvincing and premature. His arguments rest principally on the worthy objectives of reducing occasions for preemption by the Warsaw Pact countries and improving political control of NATO weapons while maintaining the political utility of their presence but appear to have no well thought-out rationale for the weapons' political/military use.

Laurence Martin, in a recent review of our theater/tactical nuclear posture, examined two principal alternatives and did appear to present thought-out rationales.[18] He noted the manner in which the current posture evolved without benefit of a coherent doctrine for the weapons' use but with growing political importance to Europeans, and he considered the military and the political constraints to alterations now, as well as reasons for making them. Both the alternatives he examined would have rational coherence from a military point of view. The options he suggested were (1) a posture that would give a nuclear orientation to in-theater or battlefield defense by emphasizing miniaturized nuclear weapons; and (2) a nuclear covering force that, in contrast to the first alternative, would respond to the overall military situation rather than to local tactical circumstances. Both postures would emphasize the role of theater nuclear weapons in containing or defeating an attack, including a conventional attack. Both would also attempt to restrict damage by focusing on military targets, restricting yields, emphasizing target identification, and using precision guidance.

Despite their similarities, Martin's alternatives are quite different. The principal military difference was noted above: One would be oriented to defeating the enemy in detail, the other to responding to the overall military situation (for example, by undertaking relatively close interdiction missions). The two also have rather radically different political significances. The first alternative would be politically unacceptable to Europeans; they would see it as an attempt to decouple theater nuclear war from strategic nuclear war and thus undermine the U.S. strategic guarantee. The second alternative, which Martin recommended, would provide about the same defense orientation as the first—perhaps even better—but would also be in keeping with a strategy that emphasizes deterrence and the linkage between conventional, theater nuclear, and strategic capabilities. The military advantage of a nuclear covering force would be that it clearly would supplement (and not replace) conventional capabilities, either immediately (as the miniaturized nuclear alternative would tend to do), or after conventional forces had been defeated (as the current posture would tend to do). The political advantages of such a posture would not be confined to reassuring allies; it would also convey to the Soviet Union both NATO's determination and the restraint with which it was prepared to respond to an attack on Western Europe.

Résumé

The new emphases in the strategic posture and doctrine presented in Schlesinger's annual report of early 1974 appear to provide both thought-out plans for using nuclear weapons to limit and end war in the unlikely event that deterrence fails and a means for shoring up deterrence over the long haul and for our allies, while conveying politically to both allies and adversaries the determination and the restraint with which we intend to protect our own and our allies' vital interests. To be effective, these emphases will require concerted efforts similarly to restructure or reorient the other two elements in the triad on which Europe depends—the conventional capabilities and the theater/tactical nuclear posture. In all three cases the objective should not be to supplant deterrence with a so-called war-fighting capability, but rather to strengthen deterrence and extend it into any war by providing a war-limiting capability.

ETHICAL CONSIDERATIONS

Many individuals have insisted that one should attempt to be explicit in ethical-theoretical terms about the U.S. strategic debate and the side or sides one takes in that debate. In one sense, such insistence can only be applauded, since it represents an effort to insure that the debate is not settled—or even conducted—only on technical or strategic grounds. Great human issues of life and death for millions of people may be at stake in the decision to continue to rely solely on mutual assured destruction or to modify our strategy so as to be prepared for limited and selective nuclear options.

In another sense, however, insistence on being explicit about ethical considerations is frustrating. In the first place, any serious debate about strategy is implicitly and inescapably a debate about the ethics of what a nation does with its strategic nuclear power. Hence an attempt to "be explicit" may be redundant; worse, it can get in the way of disciplined and rigorous development of arguments if the appeal to ethical categories begins to take on the flavor of merely adding to the legitimation or authority of one's arguments. Finally, there is less common vocabulary when it comes to ethical considerations and ethical methodology than when strategic issues are being considered.

Nonetheless, I accept the charge to be explicit and to try to show where and how my strategic concerns relate to any coherent ethical theory. I will attempt to do this by glosses on the ethical theories proposed by other contributors to this volume rather than by any systematic statement of my own ethic.

Frequently—and generally in defense of sole reliance on mutual assured destruction—it is argued that we confront an ultimate ethical dilemma. Most commonly, that dilemma is posed in something like the following terms: "The nuclear strategic dilemma is that we must be prepared to do and threaten to do what we know is totally unacceptable to do in any moral sense."

That to employ nuclear weapons—particularly strategic ones—in war would be tragic can hardly be denied. But that it would be unacceptable or wrong under any and all circumstances is a moral judgment, not a given fact of nature. It is a judgment based on *estimates* of the possible or likely consequences of detonating nuclear weapons in war. Moreover, for advocates of mutual assured destruction it is a judgment tied to embracing tragic and inhuman consequences—namely, *assured destruction* of a large fraction of the enemy's population. Thus the ethical dilemma may be a chosen dilemma rather than a given one.

The argument is made, however, that we know enough about the destructive power of nuclear weapons to assume that any consequences of their employment in war would almost certainly be dire and that, since each side would fear being devastated by the other and fear losing its retaliatory power, the temptation or compulsion to employ all nuclear weapons quickly would be so great as to make nuclear war virtually uncontrollable. All of this lends plausibility to the consequentialist argument that the sole utility of nuclear weapons which is morally admissible is to render nuclear war totally dysfunctional and unacceptable by a posture of mutual assured destruction.

The greatest methodological difficulty I have with this version of the consequentialist argument is that it is circular and ultimately reduces ethics to a gamble. The circularity derives from the desire to say that nuclear weapons are uncontrollable or unsuitable to any limited employment (i.e., mutual assured destruction is affirmed as the appropriate posture and strategy) in order to make nuclear war totally unacceptable because nuclear weapons are uncontrollable and unsuitable to any limited employment. This is finally also an ultimate gamble because the strategy it backs may not always work.

It strikes me as ironic and slightly perverse that this argument for mutual assured destruction should be made by appeal to a consequentialist tradition in ethics. In many ways I have always been drawn to the consequentialist tradition, largely because I saw it as a tradition that forced one to think through all the possible consequences of one's policies or actions and to take into account even the possibility that one's preferred policy or action might fail. But in some modern versions of consequentialism, ethics almost seems to have been reduced, at best, to a game-theory or systems-analysis choice of a strategy that is intended to maximize some expected payoff or minimize some chance that an untoward outcome will result. Worthy—in their context—as these objectives may be, consequentialist ethics must provide more guidance to the policymaker than merely offer a gamble. It must also reckon with the possibility that unexpected and untoward consequences may result and that there may not be second chances.

Occasionally the possibility of the strategy of sole reliance on mutual assured destruction failing has been dealt with by an appeal to a different ethical tradition. If deterrence of nuclear war fails, it is argued, resort to the fighting use of nuclear weapons would still be wrong on deontological grounds. Specifically, in the theory and doctrines of the just war, the use of nuclear weapons would violate both the principle of proportionality and the principle of discrimination; hence their use in war cannot be justified. But the threat of their use as a deterrent to war may be provisionally justified on consequentialist (gaming) rather than deontological grounds.[19]

That particular use of the deontological argument is also a bit circular. Efforts to design nuclear weapons and to plan for uses that could be more proportional and discriminating are rejected as abhorrent or inadmissible in order to maintain the belief that under no circumstances could they be admissible for selective, discriminating, and proportional uses.

Perhaps I belabor the point. It seems to me, however, that both the consequentialist and deontological traditions impel us to look beyond deterrence of war to what Herman Kahn called, a long time ago, the "unthinkable" prospect that deterrence could fail.[20] At least the policymaker or the responsible official—as James Schlesinger, as well as Max Weber, knows—must think of the possible wartime uses of nuclear weapons. Neither ethically nor strategically does this require us to plan for or convey to our opponents that we are seeking splendid ways to win a nuclear war or even make it more palatable. All we may be allowed to think of, ethically or strategically, is how to design weapons and plan for uses that will give us the best means of containing destruction, limiting and controlling the danger of escalation, and providing some deterrence even in a war that would give all sides the greatest incentive to terminate war and return to other ways of resolving conflicts.

In the immediate context of this paper, however, there is a more fundamental way in which such ethical discussions are frustrating. Most of these discussions imply that all we are talking about is bilateral relations between the two superpowers. In that context distortions of consequentialism and deontology only question how to avoid using nuclear weapons under any and all circumstances. However, by the North Atlantic Treaty and by the Non-Proliferation Treaty the United States has proposed that its strategic deterrent will somehow provide for the security of many other nations, as well as its own, and attempted to dissuade them from seeking an independent nuclear deterrent of their own.

If we really believe that nuclear weapons are totally dysfunctional for any purpose except making nuclear weapons dysfunctional, then how can we continue to try to get nonnuclear NATO partners and others to rely on our nuclear deterrent and to prevent them and others from seeking a nuclear deterrent of their own?

It is not very fashionable in the post-Dean Rusk and the post-Vietnam era to speak dramatically about "our commitments." However, there is an ethical tradition besides the consequentialist and the deontological traditions that ought to enter into and inform the debate about our strategic posture and doctrine. That is, for want of a better term, what one might call a "covenantal tradition." Fundamental ethical responsibilities in this tradition derive primarily from relationships that are entered into and commitments undertaken, not primarily from the nature of things or from calculations of the consequences of specific actions.

The differences among consequentialist, deontological, and "covenantal" ethics may seem subtle and semantic. To be sure, in my view, their differences are nuanced more than radical differences, and it is possible to be a consequentialist on deontological grounds and vice versa. However, what the "covenantal tradition" (perhaps more biblical than the others) does remind us of is that there is a creative and responsive character to ethics.

Both biblical ethics and the ethics of liberal democracy found the idea of the covenant or the relation of responsibility and commitment entered into to be something of a touchstone. In entering into a covenant or contract or treaty we create and affirm certain commitments and responsibilities to and with the other parties. With this view, the U.S. alliance system becomes central to the U.S. strategic debate. Either we should take this commitment seriously and insure against reasonable doubt that the U.S. strategic posture and doctrine are relevant to the security of our NATO partners for deterrence of aggression against them as well as for deterrence of direct attack on ourselves, or we should be encouraging them to develop an adequate deterrent of their own.

NOTES

1. James R. Schlesinger, *Report of the Secretary of Defense to the Congress on the FY 1975 Defense Budget and FY 1975–1979 Defense Program* (Washington, D.C.: U.S. Government Printing Office, March 4, 1974).
2. Ibid., p. 38.
3. *U.S. Foreign Policy of the 1970s: A New Strategy for Peace.* A report to Congress by Richard Nixon, president of U.S. (Washington, D.C.: Government Printing Office, February 18, 1970).
4. Fred Charles Iklé, "Can Nuclear Deterrence Last Out the Century?" *Foreign Affairs* 51 (January 1973): 267–85.
5. Robert Ellsworth et al., "Should We Develop Highly Accurate Missiles and Emphasize Military Targets Rather Than Cities?" *The Advocates* (Public Broadcasting Service, taped February 12, 1974). Reprinted as "Nuclear Policy Debate" in *Congressional Record,* March 28, 1974, S4663–4668.
6. Schlesinger, *Report on the FY 1975 Defense Budget,* passim.
7. Ibid., p. 38.
8. There are many other issues involved in shoring up the deterrence across a broad spectrum of threats and over the long haul. Most of the new weapons programs proposed by Schlesinger relate more to these other issues and respond to U.S.S.R. strategic programs that have long-haul implications and implications about "essential equivalence" in arms-limitations negotiations. Since these have less immediate bearing on the security of Europe (though they do have long-term

importance), I must pass over most of them in this discussion.

9. *NATO Facts and Figures* (Brussels: NATO Information Service, 1969), p. 34.

10. Edward N. Luttwak, "Nuclear Strategy: The New Debate," *Commentary* 57 (April 1974): 58.

11. Laurence Martin, "Changes in American Strategic Doctrine—An Initial Interpretation," *Survival* 16 (July/August 1974): 163, 164.

12. See Alain C. Enthoven and K. Wayne Smith, *How Much Is Enough? Shaping the Defense Program, 1961–1969* (New York: Harper & Row, 1971); Alain C. Enthoven, "U.S. Forces in Europe: How Many, Doing What?" *Foreign Affairs* 53 (April 1975); and Alain C. Enthoven, "Reason, Morality, and Defense Policy," *America* 108 (April 6, 1963, and April 13, 1963): 461–65. The last has been reprinted in several anthologies, including the appendix of this book, and is reviewed and updated by the author in chapter 4 of this volume.

13. See Steven L. Canby, *NATO Military Policy: Obtaining Conventional Comparability with the Warsaw Pact*, a report prepared for the Defense Advance Research Projects Agency (Santa Monica: RAND Corporation, June 1, 1973); and "Damping Nuclear Counterforce Incentives: Correcting NATO's Inferiority in Conventional Military Strength," *Orbis* 19 (Spring 1975): 47–72.

14. Richard D. Lawrence and Jeffrey Record, *U.S. Force Structure in NATO: An Alternative* (Washington, D.C.: The Brookings Institution, 1974).

15. Canby, *NATO Military Policy*, pp. 4–15.

16. Jeffrey Record, with the assistance of Major Thomas I. Anderson, *U.S. Nuclear Weapons in Europe: Issues and Alternatives* (Washington, D.C.: The Brookings Institution, 1974).

17. Ibid., p. 68.

18. Laurence Martin, "Theatre Nuclear Weapons and Europe," *Survival* 16 (November/December 1974): 268–76.

19. Cf., for example, J. Bryan Hehir, "Political and Ethical Considerations," in Robert A. Gessert and J. Bryan Hehir, *The New Nuclear Debate* (New York: The Council on Religion and International Affairs, 1976), pp. 35–73.

20. Herman Kahn, *Thinking About the Unthinkable* (New York: Avon Books, 1962).

7

Flexible MADness? The Case Against Counterforce

Herbert Scoville, Jr.

On January 10, 1974, Secretary of Defense James R. Schlesinger announced that "there has taken place . . . a change in the strategies of the U.S. with regard to the hypothetical employment of central strategic forces." A goal voiced since 1970 in President Nixon's annual foreign policy statements is now apparently an accomplished fact: "flexible response" has replaced "deterrence of nuclear war by assured destruction" as the cornerstone of our strategic policy. We now propose to respond to Soviet nuclear aggression by attacking a variety of military targets instead of by massive retaliation against cities. As Schlesinger made clear, this flexibility can be obtained by revised targeting doctrine and improved command and control procedures, and does not necessarily require additional weapons; on the other hand, new specialized weapons with higher accuracies, greater explosive powers, and more warheads will also increase our efficiency for destroying military targets. However, the repercussions on our security and on the arms race from these approaches toward increased flexibility can be quite different. The consequences of this move away from mutual assured destruction (known as MAD by its detractors)—by which nuclear war has so far been avoided—are profound, and vitally affect our survival. The new strategy and the alternate ways it can be implemented should be carefully examined before we are irretrievably launched on this new path.

Mr. Scoville is presently associated with the Federation of American Scientists. He was formerly Senior Scientist with the Atomic Energy Commission; Deputy Director for Science and Technology, Central Intelligence Agency; and Assistant Director for Science and Technology, U.S. Arms Control and Disarmament Agency.

This article was previously published as "Flexible MADness?" in *Foreign Policy* no. 14 (Spring 1974), pp. 164–77.

The catastrophic effects of the explosion of even a few nuclear weapons on this country have made the avoidance of strategic war the overriding objective of our strategic policies for twenty years. Since defense was impossible against an all-out Soviet nuclear attack, we have been forced to rely on deterrence based on an ability to produce unacceptable damage in retaliation.

THE ABM TREATY

The Anti-Ballistic Missile (ABM) Treaty signed in Moscow on May 26, 1972, formally established deterrence as the basic strategic policy of both the United States and the Soviet Union. Both countries agreed to forego the acquisition of a capability for defending their territories and thus guaranteed, for the foreseeable future, a state of mutual deterrence. With all missile warheads, once launched, having an assured arrival on target, even the most exaggerated fears over the security of our retaliatory capability of thousands of warheads became groundless. The basic goal of our strategic policy for twenty years finally had a stable, more permanent foundation.

With this success, our strategic policies might have been expected to remain fixed for at least a short time, but the ink was hardly dry on the treaty before the administration raised questions about the desirability of a strategic policy based solely on deterrence. It sought to achieve the additional strategic objective of "flexibility" when Secretary of Defense Melvin Laird, with White House support, requested funds for the development of a "hard target" multiple independently-targetable reentry vehicle (MIRV), i.e., multiple warheads with sufficient accuracy and yield for each warhead to have a high probability of destroying enemy missile sites and command centers. These weapons were supposed to provide a "flexible response" in the event of a limited Soviet nuclear attack. That this would look to the Russians like an attempt to develop a first-strike capability on our part, and would erode the mutual deterrent posture so recently agreed to by the treaty, was ignored. However, the Senate, which even during the SALT negotiations had expressed concern over the destabilizing nature of such weapons, refused to authorize funds for this development in the aftermath of SALT. Thus, the program was driven underground. In all probability it was continued under the program for the development of advanced ballistic reentry systems (ABRES). Now Schlesinger admits this and openly endorses proceeding with attempts to improve the accuracy of our MIRV—and giving it a more efficient silo-destroying capability. A confrontation between Congress and the executive could come when specific funds are sought for missiles with new and potentially more accurate guidance systems.

The concept of flexible response in which military installations, not cities, would be the targets of a retaliatory attack, did not of course arise full blown in the immediate aftermath of the SALT-I agreements. Secretary of Defense Robert McNamara had proclaimed a "city-avoiding" strategy in 1962 at a NATO conference, but this strategy was rapidly discarded. On February 18, 1970, President Nixon, in his first report to the Congress on U.S. foreign policy for the 1970s, posed the question: "Should a President, in the event of a nuclear attack, be left with the single option of ordering the mass destruction of enemy civilians, in the face of the certainty that it would be followed by the mass slaughter of Americans?" It is from these questions that the concept of flexible response flows. In the immediate years following, there was little public elaboration of what the president had in mind, but he repeated these generalitites in later foreign policy reports. It was not until after Moscow that we saw a specific weapons program defended on the basis of this policy goal.

Since May 1972, many national security analysts have publicly questioned the desirability of our deterrent policy. Some, such as Donald Brennan, had long felt that a defense-oriented strategy—one that relied on extensive defenses to protect populations and to permit a nation to survive—was far superior to one relying on deterrence through offense, and used the occasion of the Moscow summit to restate their views. They decried the current state of mutual assured destruction, sanctified by the ABM Treaty, as MAD. These arguments, which have not been widely accepted by either the military or arms controllers, do not provide support for a policy of flexible response and should be differentiated therefrom. A defense-oriented policy does not provide flexibility; quite the contrary, extensive defenses on both sides preclude a flexible response because large-scale retaliation is needed to overwhelm enemy defenses in order to achieve even a limited goal. Thus, the restrictions on ABMs agreed to in Moscow in May 1972 provided opportunities for increased flexibility previously unavailable. Paradoxically, those most opposed to ABM limitations are the strongest supporters of increased flexibility.

DETERRENCE UNDER ATTACK

The deterrent policy has, however, come under fire on a number of other counts which have been persuasive to some on all sides of the strategic debate. Fred Iklé, who was later appointed the head of the Arms Control and Disarmament Agency, attacked the "balance of terror" approach as a morally repugnant national policy.[1] Instead, retaliation should be aimed at the assured destruction of military, industrial, and transportation assets. Iklé also condemned deterrence as directed entirely to the rational mind and pointed out that nuclear war will only occur as a result of accident or an irrational decision. Other writers have argued that a wider range of retaliatory options is needed in response to military or political provocations more limited than an all-out first strike. They argue that massive retaliation may be a less effective deterrent than a selective one because its implementation lacks credibility.

Certainly the strategic policy of deterrence under which peace is maintained by holding hostage tens or even hundreds of millions of people, and by putting modern civilization in jeopardy, is psychologically unsatisfying. According to this concept, the more inevitable the devastation, the more stable the peace. We are right to seek some alternative, but we must not discard a policy that has worked until all the implications are evaluated.

To be successful, any alternative must decrease the risks of a nuclear conflagration. If, in the process of moving out from under the umbrella of mutual deterrence, we were to increase significantly the probability that nuclear warfare, no matter how limited, will start, then the new policy will be self-defeating. Therefore, the primary criterion for any new strategic policy must be *the assurance that it will in no way increase the likelihood that nuclear warfare will be unleashed.* A limited nuclear conflict presents a major risk of uncontrollable escalation to widespread nuclear devastation so that almost no gain is worth risking an increase in the probability that it will occur.

The ideal goal for a flexible response would be to have the weapons, together with their command and control, which could provide an appropriate response or variety of responses to any potential provocation. A small attack could be followed by a limited response. A purely military conflict could involve a retaliation against military targets alone. Ideally, one might like to be able to destroy a missile launcher, a command post, or even an artillery piece without causing any damage to the civilian sector. In practice, however, such surgical nuclear strikes would be hard or impossible to achieve. The controlling factor in determining civil destruction is the distance from the target, not the accuracy of the missile.

Because we have adopted a policy of deterrence through assured destruction and because in evaluating the effectiveness of our deterrent force we normally test it in the extreme case of all-out retaliation following a massive Soviet first strike, it is often assumed that we have no flexibility today and have no recourse in the event of aggression but to retaliate with our entire strategic force. The plaintive note in President Nixon's statements and the tenor of Schlesinger's remarks would seem to support this. Of course, this is not true, as Wolfgang Panofsky has shown in his response to Iklé.[2] We are not limited to the single option of full-scale strategic retaliation to deter any aggression; we never have been. We have large conventional forces in both Europe and the Far East; escalation to nuclear weapons is not required as an early response to a conventional attack.

On the other hand, the deployment, in exposed locations near frontiers, of many of our nuclear weapons could needlessly lead to nuclear conflict. This decreases our flexibility to deal with the situation at the nonnuclear level and greatly enhances the risk of nuclear war. The 7,000 tactical nuclear weapons in Europe and appreciable numbers in Korea should, even if moved to rear areas, be a sufficient deterrent against the introduction of nuclear weapons by the other side. We need not rely on our strategic stockpile for this purpose.

Even at the strategic level, President Nixon is not forced, with the weapons now available, to launch an all-out attack against Soviet cities knowing that our society might be similarly destroyed in response. A variety of less cataclysmic strategic retaliatory options has always been available, provided that appropriate command and control procedures were adopted. The United States now has the weapons to respond at lower levels if it so desires, although not always with optimum effectiveness. Although it is not obvious why such a capability is needed, some—but by no means all—Russian ICBM sites can with high confidence be put out of action. We can destroy military command centers, but as long as they are located near population centers, not without collateral damage to the civilian sector. Even if we improve the accuracy of our nuclear weapons, there will always be serious side effects.

INCREASED DETERRENCE OR RISK?

The topical question, therefore, is not whether one wishes to have a flexible response, but whether additional capabilities will increase deterrence or instead increase the risk that nuclear war will actually break out. Enhanced flexibility from improved command and control is probably on balance a positive step since it does not threaten a significant portion of the deterrent force and could reduce the risk of accidents. Furthermore, it provides more flexibility *not* to be forced to undertake certain responses. Deterrence provided by fear of possible massive retaliation would remain unaffected. On the other hand, the desire for more flexible weapons can become an open-ended justification for new, expensive programs and will certainly push the arms race further along the road.

No matter how often we disclaim it, the development of improved silo-killing missiles must inevitably look to the Russians like an attempt to acquire a first-strike counterforce capability against their ICBMs. Similar Soviet programs for getting high-yield MIRVs have been viewed here in exactly such alarming terms. One response to the increased threat to military forces provided by improved counterforce capabilities could be expensive programs by the other side to reduce their vulnerability. New missiles in superhardened silos or mobile ICBMs are two that have been proposed in the United States. The Russians will almost certainly react to our moves in some manner. A cheaper way is to shorten the time fuse on the nuclear missiles by adopting "launch-on-warning" operational procedures with all the increased risks of accidental war that this would provide. False alarms are difficult to completely rule out. While we may not wish to give up the option for an early response to an attack, we certainly do not wish to be in a position where we have no other choice than retaliation before any weapons have been exploded. Nor do we wish to force the Soviet Union, China, or any other nuclear power to place their missiles on a hair trigger alert. Thus, weapons programs designed for improved flexibility have the potentiality to greatly increase the risk of nuclear war.

An extreme, albeit much discussed, scenario in which increased flexibility is considered desirable has been put forth by leading military planners. It involves a Russian attack on our land-based ICBMs and intercontinental bombers after which they would dictate terms of our surrender. A U.S. response which required devastation of Soviet populations is, according to this scenario, not credible since it, in turn, could trigger Russian annihilation of urban centers in the United States. We might have a greater deterrent against such a Soviet action if we had the alternative of knocking out those Soviet missiles which had not yet been launched.

Is this scenario at all credible, and if so, what would increased flexible response buy? In order to have high confidence of knocking out the U.S. force of more than 1,000 U.S. ICBM launchers, the Russians would have to fire, at a minimum, two to three megaton warheads at each launcher. In order to have a high probability of destroying hard targets, such as missile silos, the weapons would have to be detonated very close to the surface of the earth, producing heavy radioactive fallout directly downwind. A single 15 megaton explosion at Eniwetok in 1954 covered an area of 5,000 square miles, extending 200 miles downwind, with fallout which would have been lethal to exposed populations. Even larger areas were covered with very serious contamination. Yet in this scenario an attack would produce fallout 200 or more times as great. If an attack against our bombers is added to that against the missiles, the devastation would be still worse. Millions of people would be killed and large sectors of our society completely disorganized, even though the attack was directed with surgical precision at military targets.

Even if completely successful, what would the Russians have accomplished? True, they might have destroyed a large part of the land-based missile and bomber elements of our deterrent triad; but our submarine missile force of forty-one Polaris-Poseidon submarines, with more than 5,000 nuclear warheads and yields several times that of the Hiroshima bomb, would still be untouched. We would still have an overwhelming strategic force which would not only be a threat to the survival of the Soviet Union as a civilized society, but which would have a capability of destroying hundreds of military targets as well. Without the necessity of overpowering a large ABM, now foreclosed by the ABM Treaty, command centers and an appreciable number of (but not all) missile silos can be destroyed by Poseidon with its present accuracy by allocating sufficient warheads to each target. Does such an attack, even if completely successful, leave the Soviet Union in a position to dictate terms to the U.S. government? Are any possible gains commensurate with the risks that any U.S. government might retaliate against Soviet population centers and devastate the Soviet Union, even though such an action might mean a similar devastation in the United States from those Soviet weapons not used in the first strike? Any Soviet leader in contemplating such a "limited attack" would have to take into consideration that even with the firmest intentions of exercising restraint, the U.S. leaders might be stampeded into a retaliation which would kill millions of Russians in exchange for the millions of Americans already killed. Democratic leaders have more difficulty than dictators in remaining wholly rational since they must frequently respond to popular passions.

Moreover, would an improved capability for a flexible response have any important effect under such a scenario? Procuring ICBMs with greater accuracy and, consequently, a higher single-shot probability for destroying an ICBM silo would be of little value and a waste of money, since most of our ICBMs, according to this scenario, would have been destroyed. Giving a larger payload to some Minuteman missiles would be similarly ineffective. Increased accuracy for our invulnerable submarine missiles might more effectively destroy any Soviet ICBMs that had not been used in the initial salvo, and the collateral damage in areas surrounding the Soviet missile sites would be reduced. But even if we destroyed all leftover ICBMs, the Russians would still have hundreds of submarine-launched ballistic missiles with which to threaten our undefended cities. How would the existence of such an improved hard-target capability affect a Soviet decision to launch such an attack in the first place? It is hard to see why they would be more deterred because the United States could retaliate in a limited way. If the Russians were willing to launch an attack of this scale, they would certainly be prepared to have all their remaining land-based missiles destroyed. They would be thankful that they had gotten off so cheaply. If any aggressor were so irrational as to contemplate such an extreme action, he might be more prone to risk it if he thought that the United States would be more likely to respond in a limited way than with a devastating attack. In sum, aggression on this scale provides no gains even marginally commensurate with the risks; greater potential flexibility in response would probably not improve deterrence and might instead increase the danger that such an attack would occur.

A SECOND EXAMPLE

Since this extreme case is so unreal, some less extensive form of nuclear aggression should be examined. Suppose, for example, the Soviet Union decided to destroy one Minuteman complex of 100 missiles as a muscle-flexing exercise and a demonstration of the superiority of its missiles. Under such circumstances, it could be argued that the United States might wish to respond with less than massive destruction; we might want a capability for a retaliation in kind. In the absence of a Soviet ABM, we could do this today with our present forces by expending several of the undamaged Minuteman warheads per Soviet silo. An improved U.S. hard-target capability would make such graduated retaliation easier but is unlikely to affect a Soviet decision to adopt such a strategy in the first place. The political gains from such a conflict even for the winner are hard to imagine and are certainly out of all proportion to the risks.

This is not the kind of contest which we should wish to enter or even encourage. This limited scenario is one which is probably considered only by players of war games who have lost touch with the meaning of nuclear war. Such irrational leaders would more likely be deterred by the consequences of all-out retaliation than by the thought that we might try to play in this game—a game in which they might always hope to come out ahead. The gains from being able to fight this type of battle more effectively are far outweighed by increased risks that it might actually be fought.

A central question which arises in any scenario is whether a better capability to respond to aggression at a variety of levels enhances deterrence through greater credibility of a response, or whether the possibility that retaliation will be limited in scope reduces the inhibitions against aggression through decreased fear of the consequences. A second and perhaps more critical question is whether the improved ability to respond at lower levels of violence increases the risk that nuclear war will erupt. The latter cannot be tolerated.

The deterrent must be made credible to rational and, insofar as possible, to irrational decision-makers alike. Since nuclear aggression on any scale is today almost always irrational, greater attention should probably be directed toward the less rational leaders and toward those situations where rational decision-making might be more difficult. Deterrence would probably be more effective if fewer opportunities were provided in which a leader might believe, or be lead to believe, that he could fight a nuclear war, survive, and perhaps even win.

The initiation of nuclear war at any level is a disaster that is more likely to occur if national leaders can fool themselves into believing that it might be kept small and that they might come out the victors. This is less likely to occur in any specific crisis if the military have not prepared plans long in advance and acquired specially designed weapons to fight a limited nuclear war.

Nuclear war might be made less likely if the decision to initiate it can be made more difficult rather than easier. Over the past twenty-five years, strong firebreaks have been built between conventional and nuclear war. Even when overwhelming nuclear superiority existed, no nation seriously contemplated using nuclear weapons in even the most limited way. Korea and Vietnam, both large-scale conventional conflicts, have passed without their use. Despite many rumors of their intention, the Russians have never initiated a nuclear strike to eliminate the emerging Chinese nuclear force. The soundest and most moral policy would maintain, and if possible strengthen, all the firebreaks that exist, not only between conventional and nuclear weapons, but also between tactical and strategic weapons. The development of improved capabilities for fighting strategic nuclear war at a lower level, thereby fusing tactical and strategic nuclear conflict, is only a step in the wrong direction. It is misguided thinking to believe that deterrence against nuclear war can be improved by increasing the likelihood that strategic nuclear weapons will be used.

SAFETY AND CONTROL

Instead of procuring new weapons with improved nuclear-war-fighting characteristics, efforts should be directed toward improving the safety and the command and control over the weapons now available. The several agreements with the Soviet Union designed to improve communication and to prevent nuclear warfare are useful steps. Tremendous advances have been made over the past ten years with the incorporation of devices in many nuclear weapons to prevent unauthorized firing. However, there is still a long way to go. Particular attention should be paid to control procedures for our missile submarines. Operationally oriented officers have inordinate fears that more rigid safety and control procedures would make it more difficult to use nuclear weapons in the event that war breaks out. Such inverted thinking must be rooted out; the overriding objective is to prevent nuclear wars, not fight them. Our deterrent is not improved by looser controls; no nation will risk a holocaust on the slim hope that our command system will break down.

The dangers of inadvertent nuclear war do not arise solely from a U.S.-Soviet confrontation. The smaller Chinese force presents even more explosive potentialities than do the much larger U.S. and Russian forces. Because of its limited size, it could be vulnerable to a U.S. or Soviet first strike since concealment or hardening can never be relied on completely. As a consequence, its leaders could feel forced to place a hair trigger on their weapons and adopt a launch-on-warning operational tactic. Thus, it is in our national interest to try to insure that the Chinese have a deterrent in which they can be confident without requiring rapid response. Such confidence may be difficult to attain as long as the Soviet Union and the United States have their present overwhelming superiority. When the Chinese acquire their first ICBMs we should not, at the very least, take any steps which might look like an attempt to maintain a first-strike threat against them.

Does increased flexibility alleviate the understandable concerns of those who find a peace maintained by threats of annihilation morally repugnant? Making it easier to fight nuclear wars, even on a limited scale, is hardly a psychologically more attractive policy. It is probably more moral to prevent slaughter by threatening disaster than to facilitate limited death and destruction. True moral satisfaction will come only when we succeed in moving away from nuclear conflict as a means of settling international differences.

In conclusion, the objective of improving the flexibility of our strategic weapons to provide the president with additional strategic options beyond those now available is a goal which sounds superficially attractive, but which, in practice, can only decrease our security. Making it easier to fight strategic nuclear war does not truly enhance deterrence and only increases the risk that fears of nuclear devastation will turn into reality. Instead of buying new weapons with more sophisticated war-fighting capabilities, efforts should be concentrated on increasing the control over, and the safety of, the weapons we now have.

NOTES

1. Fred Charles Iklé, "Can Nuclear Deterrence Last Out The Century?" *Foreign Affairs* 51 (January 1973): 267–85.
2. Wolfgang K. H. Panofsky, "The Mutual-Hostage Relationship Between America and Russia," *Foreign Affairs* 51 (October 1973): 109–118.

8

A Countercombatant Alternative to Nuclear MADness

Bruce M. Russett

IS THERE REALLY NO CHOICE?

Writing in *Foreign Affairs* in January 1973, Fred C. Iklé asked, "Can Nuclear Deterrence Last Out the Century?" and replied with an unfashionably pessimistic judgment.[1] For most of us, our fears of mass destruction have eased since the Cuban missile crisis of 1962 and the heyday of arms-control writing that was so influential about that time. We have come to regard nuclear deterrence as stable—an awesome threat but one so very unlikely to be executed that we can carry on, in reasonable security, under its shadow. Iklé reminded us, however, that the stability is not secure. It could be upset by any of the following, singly or in combination: a nuclear accident, which, despite all precautions, will forever have some possibility of occurring; crisis desperation by some otherwise "rational" leader; deliberate firing by an overzealous subordinate or deranged leader (yes, there was a Hitler); or catalytic nuclear war initiated by a "have-not" smaller power with far less to lose and, at least in the mind of its leader with some perverted value, more to gain than a superpower could imagine. Most plausible is the interaction of several of these factors at an

---

Dr. Russett, Professor of Political Science, Yale University, has written widely on matters of ethics and international affairs. The major part of this article was previously published as "Assured Destruction of What? A Countercombatant Alternative to Nuclear MADness" in *Public Policy* 22 (Spring 1974): 121–38. Mr. Russett has written the last section, marked "Postscript," especially for this volume.

inopportune moment. Smaller powers, for example, will not be able to afford all the highly sophisticated "fail-safe" precautions of the superpowers, and regional antipathies may be more likely to plunge them into war.

At the moment all these dread possibilities really do seem distant. We have learned a great deal about how to deal with the bomb and have spent enormous sums to avoid accidents. Technology has been kind, and its practitioners shrewd. Most of the developments of the last decade have favored the defense, providing confidence in a second-strike posture, able to ride out an attack or other threatening events so as not mistakenly to initiate a "retaliation" that would bring cataclysm. The Polaris-Poseidon submarine missile system is at the heart of this security, but bombers and land-based missiles still retain a great measure of invulnerability. Yet while this security may be with us now and may even be reasonably assured for the next decade or so, only a very rash prophet would be sure it will last for several decades or a couple of generations—for example, for the lifetime of our children. It is possible that we may look back on this era with some nostalgia, as a period of virtually unique stability whose underlying conditions were lost.

The balance is built precisely on terror, the terror of death to the civilian populations of the United States and the Soviet Union. As phrased by Secretary of Defense Robert McNamara in his last posture statement in 1968, this means an American-assured destruction capability of one-fifth to one-fourth of the population and one-half of the industrial capability of the Soviet Union. Because of the greater urbanization and smaller land area of the United States, it is widely assumed that the corresponding damage this country would sustain from a Soviet strike would be greater. Furthermore, these estimates are acknowledged to be "conservative": They include only the immediate casualties from the blast and heat of nuclear explosions and not the deaths from fallout, secondary fire, sickness, and starvation that would surely follow. And again, the threat is posed primarily against civilian noncombatants—men and women who in the Soviet Union do not choose their government nor direct its actions, and wholly innocent children. No one who feels there is any possibility that deterrence just might fail, sometime, can avoid a sense of horror.

If we had no alternative, then by definition we would have to live this way. Many sophisticated observers act as though this were indeed the case. It is hard to be optimistic about radical disarmament proposals. The obstacles are enormous. Misconceived disarmament could weaken deterrence in an asymmetrical way, bringing on the war it was supposed to avoid. Even if the weapons were destroyed, the knowledge of how to build them can never be. How could the superpowers disarm without a multilateral agreement that included other major states? And the bureaucratic-political hurdles, the complex of arms interests in both this country and the Soviet Union, are hardly about to fold. As for bold unilateral disarmament initiatives, pacifism may appeal to some of us on an individual basis, but few are ready to raise personal preferences to the level of national policy. If you lived on the San Andreas Fault, and a job you could not leave required you to be there, it would be pointless for me to warn you of the dangers of earthquakes. Since you could neither control the natural forces nor remove yourself from them, it would be cruel, and perhaps counterproductive, for me to worry you. In the realm of nuclear strategy, reading even such a brilliant and moving statement as Iklé's could lead to despair or quite irrational behavior.

I contend, however, that we are not necessarily living on the equivalent of the San Andreas Fault; that there may be an acceptable alternative, short of unachievable radical disarmament or unacceptable radical pacifism, that deserves the closest and most open-minded scrutiny we can muster. It requires that we recognize the ambiguity in the term "assured destruction"—destruction of *what?*—and ask whether the necessary target must in fact be civilian population centers. A failure to do this would make a policy of Mutual Assured Destruction deserve its acronym. Presumably the threat of destruction ought to be centered upon whatever it is that the enemy leadership holds most dear. Given some of the folklore that all Bolsheviks are as callous toward their people as Stalin seemed to be, the insistence on assuring destruction of civilians seems a bit curious, especially since the top leaders themselves will be well protected and very likely to survive. Instead, might we not focus the threat upon the leaders' power, on their ability to control and defend the state? I have proposed elsewhere,[2] and will expand on the idea here, that we consider substituting a strategy of assured destruction of the military and police powers of the Soviet state, rather than of population and civilian industry. I call the strategy a "countercombatant strategy," to distinguish it from the familiar counterforce on the one hand, and countercity or counterpopulation strategies on the other. The term emphasizes an intention to strike against those kinds of targets traditionally, in the laws and ethics of warfare, regarded as permissible targets, while taking pains to minimize the death of noncombatants.

THE SEVERITY AND LIKELIHOOD OF WAR

Any proposal for arms control or a change in nuclear strategy must provide satisfactory answers to three crucial questions:

1. If the proposal were implemented, would it offer prospects that war would be less destructive, or at least not more destructive, than if it were not implemented?
2. Does the proposal offer prospects that war would be less likely, or at least not more likely, than if it were not implemented?
3. Is the proposal consistent with arms-race stability; that is, does it imply less, or at least not additional, armament expenditure?

In logic, the proposal must obtain an affirmative answer to the strong form of at least one of the preceding questions; that is, it must offer a prospect of less damaging or less likely war, or fewer expenditures. If it also produces an affirmative answer to at least the weak form of the remaining two questions (no increment in war damage or war likelihood, and no increment in spending) then the proposal will be dominant over the status quo, and presumably it should be implemented unless a better proposal came along. But if it produces an unfavorable answer to one or two of the questions, then some hard tradeoffs have to be made. Would a diminution in the expected damage from war compensate for some increase in the likelihood of war, or vice versa? Or how much additional spending are we willing to undertake for the prospect of diminishing the expected damage or probability of war?

The proposal for a countercombatant strategy is directed at the first question and does offer good prospects of a diminution in the total amount of damage, especially to civilians. Since no one can *know* how a nuclear war might be fought, it does not answer the strong form of the question with certainty, but the probabilities seem good and in any case the amount of civilian destruction certainly would not be increased. The proposal does not offer much chance of affirmative answers to the strong forms of the second and third questions, but I will try to present some reasons why at least it does not worsen the situation for either. That argumentation is unavoidably speculative and in some degree requires, for greater certainty, a detailed examination of information on weapons availability and development that is not publicly available. But I contend that the arguments are at least sufficiently plausible to demand careful, extended analysis. And even should one of these questions be answered negatively in some moderate degree, the tradeoffs in potential war-destruction may still make the proposal attractive. That decision would require very full debate—but we probably have time and should use this period of strategic stability for the discussion of alternatives, not squander it under the illusion that the conditions of relative security will last forever.

A strategy of countercombatant targeting would certainly include those basic enemy nuclear striking forces and immediate support facilities that are subject to attack under current strategy: military airbases, nuclear storage sites and perhaps missile silos, air-defense and ABM systems, submarine bases and nuclear submarines in port, and weapons-oriented atomic energy plants. It would *not* involve, however, any effort to extend antisubmarine warfare to effective attack on missile-launching submarines at sea, nor any incremental effort to attack land-based missiles. The reasons should be obvious—this strategy should be consistent with strategic stability, the confidence of Soviet leaders that they have an invulnerable second-strike force capable of surviving any hypothetical American first strike. Any degradation of this capability, or apparent degradation, might raise the risk of a possible "preemptive" Soviet first strike in a crisis, or stimulate the arms race into a new round of procurement of offensive and defensive systems. A countercombatant capability should not be, nor appear to be, nor appear capable of becoming, a first-strike capability in the usual sense of counterforce.

But it need not be such a capability, simply because it depends for its effectiveness primarily on a threat not to enemy nuclear retaliatory capabilities, but to the enemy's ability to maintain internal security and to control its borders and neighbors by tactical means. Thus the special targets would be concentrations of troops and materiel for tactical military forces (nuclear and conventional), particularly those of sufficient size and isolation to be destroyed with minimum residual damage to the civilian population. Particular attention would be given to Soviet divisions in Eastern Europe and along the Chinese border, and to KGB units, often of substantial size, intended for deployment against civilian unrest. Troops of China and the Soviets' East European allies would be carefully spared. Furthermore, some military equipment and weapons-manufacturing plants would be targeted, as would selected tactical military headquarters, ammunition and supply centers, marshalling yards and repair facilities, transportation centers, pipelines and fuel-distribution centers, and power plants. The purpose of all this is not simply to destroy the entire Red Army; that would be impossible and, in any case, quite unnecessary. Rather, it is to destroy the effectiveness of Soviet conventional forces—in essence to destroy the Soviet government's ability to *use* troops. After a substantial number of the kinds of targets listed had been destroyed, the Soviet government would lack assurance that it could repress civil dissent, control its East European allies, or maintain its borders in Eastern Europe and, especially, with China. This would apply both immediately and, with the destruction of war industry, over the longer run.

This strategy, then, would be directed against targets deliberately chosen for their political significance and tailored to the particular domestic and international conditions of the Soviet Union. Domestic dissent, especially in the metropolitan centers, such as Moscow and Leningrad, is a problem for the leadership, even if we do not credit the notion that the government is wildly unpopular. Moderate and slowly escalating damage to the power of the state, as occurred in World War II or more recently to the Hanoi government, is frequently associated with an ability to retain or even strengthen popular loyalty. No such assumption can be readily made about the effects of sudden, massive damage to the state that would both cripple police control and disrupt the flow of essential goods and services. The civilian population, escaping the direct personal losses that spawn political apathy, is likely to respond to indirect deprivation with active dissent against the weakened government. More serious is the continued existence of separatist sentiment in many of the republics, such as the Ukraine, Byelorussia, Georgia, and the former Baltic states. A crippling of central authority would certainly revive such aspirations. The popularity of Soviet control in Eastern Europe also remains limited, and virtually every one of the U.S.S.R.'s European neighbors has a long-standing boundary dispute with it. Irredentist sentiment in Finland, Poland, East Germany, Czechoslovakia, and Rumania would surely seek to exploit opportunities. The fact that Soviet troops are generally bivouacked in areas removed from East European forces and the local populations makes it easier to attack them while sparing East European capabilities. And the profound, perhaps even excessive, Soviet fear of China hardly needs emphasis.

As a result of this kind of strike, the Soviet government could find itself virtually helpless against a variety of forces which initially might have been quite weak. While it might retain substantial strategic nuclear capabilities, such forces would be useless against internal dissent and of only marginal utility in holding Eastern Europe, where ground troops would be needed for occupation. In a world where China or other third powers had significant nuclear and conventional capabilities, the political potential of nuclear weapons alone would be sharply circumscribed.

I find it hard to imagine that the threat of such a counter-combatant retaliation could fail to constitute a very great deterrent to a Soviet attack on the United States or its major allies —very likely fully as much of a deterrent as is constituted by the threat of destruction to one-fifth to one-fourth of the Soviet population and one-half of the industry. The latter are, in great degree, mere "magic numbers" anyway, not arrived at by any careful computation of what would in fact constitute the lowest level of psychologically "unacceptable damage" to the Soviet government. Rather, these figures represent points on the "cost curve" of American capability, beyond which marginal increments in the damage inflicted could be purchased only by very great increments to American striking power. There is no compelling *political* rationale why they should be set there. Indeed, McNamara's earlier formulations, such as the one in his posture statement of 1965, set the requirement of assured destruction even higher, at one-fourth to one-third of the Soviet population and two-thirds of the Soviet industrial capacity. The downward revision of these estimates seems to have been the result far less of any reassessment of the psychological criteria for deterrence than of changes in the cost curves.

Recognition that the criteria for assured destruction come as much from mythology as from science, and that what matters is not how much is damaged but how much that damage hurts, is essential to any consideration of whether a change in declared and intended targeting strategy would diminish deterrence. Furthermore—and I do not mean this to be a weasel way of having the best of both sides, but merely wish to state what is a fact—there is no definitive way to bury the threat of destruction of population centers. Whatever the peace-time intent of this or any succeeding American government, no one can be sure how it would react in the actuality of nuclear war and in the face of millions or tens of millions of American casualties. Especially the

Soviet government cannot be sure. I most assuredly do not want to exploit this fear. For a variety of reasons I would like to see the American government have the capabilities and the real intention of sparing civilians so far as it possibly can. But there simply are no means by which a stake can be driven through the heart of the counterpopulation specter, killing it beyond any possible revival. For all these reasons I cannot see how this suggested change in the content of an assured-destruction strategy would make nuclear war more likely through weakening deterrence.

There remains another version of the second question ("would a countercombatant deterrent posture make war more likely?") which must be dealt with, but first we must satisfy ourselves that the first condition is truly met. Would a nuclear war fought under this strategy stand real prospects of being less destructive than one fought under current strategy? I have urged that the targets be military or quasi-military ones, and that no efforts be made deliberately to hit civilian population centers. Certainly no one could imagine that *no* civilians would be killed by execution of such a strategy. Some civilians, very possibly millions, would be in or so near the target areas that they would die in the initial strikes. Perhaps millions more would die from radioactive fallout and the civil disruption that would follow any large-scale nuclear war. Nuclear war would not lose its horror-provoking capacity. But if we are talking about an attempt to limit civilian casualties rather than to seek them, the difference in the Soviet Union might be great indeed, very possibly an order of magnitude. This becomes true if nuclear weapons are chosen and employed so as to minimize fallout (relatively "clean" weapons, exploded in the air rather than on the surface), and if they are of a size no greater than is necessary to destroy their military targets. So-called "bonus effects" would not be sought, and would be minimized. The American government could tolerate even greatly expanded Soviet civil-defense efforts without fearing that the American deterrent were thereby being degraded. With relatively small warheads and high delivery-accuracies, collateral damage to civilians in the neighborhood can generally be kept low.

Small warheads would generally be feasible because most of the targets listed are relatively soft, unlike modern missile silos, whose destruction would require large, dirty explosions. Even accuracies of a quarter of a mile would permit a great deal of target discrimination. For example, a target hardened to 60 psi in overpressure will be destroyed by a 20-kiloton Hiroshima-sized bomb striking within a quarter of a mile of it. The same bomb would destroy frame houses up to about one-and-three-quarters miles away, but not much further. Continued improvement in accuracies to be expected in coming years would enable the use of still smaller warheads and consequent further reduction of the damage area. One authority recently put his estimate of achievable ICBM accuracy at 100 feet.[3] The combination of small warheads and high accuracies, even with the latter nearer the current than the hypothetical end of the scale, would make it possible to strike, with a minimum of civilian casualties, military targets that were quite near urban centers. And for cases where such discrimination is not possible, one could simply refrain from striking at the military targets. After all, as I have emphasized, the purpose of a countercombatant strategy need not be to destroy *all* military targets, but only enough to make the surviving military units essentially valueless. That level can be reached well below the level of 100-percent destruction. (A careful examination of the United States Strategic Bombing Survey of World War II supports this. While the Bombing Survey is frequently cited for support on all sides of questions like these, detailed study of it concerning the potential for countercombatant targeting is instructive.)[4]

We have said that civilian casualties in the Soviet Union could be greatly reduced by American execution of such a strategy should nuclear war occur. I assume that this ought to be a serious consideration for us, that we are not so brutalized by decades of cold war and ideological conflict that we do not care. Legal, ethical, and moral recommendations vary widely; men reason from a variety of normative premises. But virtually all require warriors to spare noncombatants wherever possible, to avoid needless civilian deaths. Should it be needless to threaten such killing, we ought to care about what would happen to Soviet civilians *even if the Soviet government did not care about ours*. But, in fact, there is reason to think the Soviet government might reciprocate and be willing to limit American and European civilian casualties as well.

Soviet military doctrine is frequently ambiguous on these matters but, according to one expert, "Soviet targeting doctrine does not seem to reflect a basic preoccupation with population hostages for deterrence or with the deliberate destruction of population targets in war. However, the targeting doctrine includes an approach which generally mixes counterforce, counter-industry, and counter-administration. Soviet strategists have tended to emphasize the effect of attacks upon the social organization and the control net of the adversary, an approach which reflects, perhaps, their own emphasis on administration and control."[5] Soviet leaders have repeatedly declared they are in a struggle with the American government and capitalism, not the American people. They consistently picture antiballistic-missile (ABM) systems as desirable for preserving human lives, and Soviet abandonment of ABMs in the SALT-I agreements does not necessarily mean repudiation of this view; their abandonment may equally well be due to the system's cost and/or apparent infeasibility. We cannot expect the Soviets to embrace all of the rather unflattering implications of a countercombatant doctrine. But we can, over time, try to educate them about its virtues. The goal of achieving some form of reciprocation demands the effort—and that we not try to keep a countercombatant intention as part of some secret plan.

If, accepting these precedents in their doctrine, the Soviets did attempt to reciprocate an American initiative of declaratory countercombatant strategy, what might they consider to be appropriate targets for them? The political and military situation of the United States is not precisely symmetrical to Russia's. Americans like to think that domestic tolerance of the government depends less on police and military force than it does in the Soviet Union, and their country lacks powerful and hostile neighbors or neighbors with recent territorial grievances. Destruction of American tactical military power might thus seem not a very strong deterrent threat. Very possibly the Soviet equivalent of a countercombatant targeting system would include a wider definition of war-related industry than the one I have suggested the United States government employ, additionally incorporating heavy manufacturing and other important bases of economic strength. Even so, that still is not quite the same as pure counterpopulation strikes. Better for them to hit the River Rouge Ford plant than to hit Detroit.

Soviet reciprocation of the American initiative might come as an overt doctrinal acceptance or, in the absence of that, at least in the form of city-avoiding behavior. The latter might be almost as advantageous as the former, and the pressures impelling it could be heavy. After all, American city-avoidance during the course of a war could, and in practice almost certainly would, be made contingent on Soviet reciprocation.[6] Soviet cities would, therefore, remain as hostages to the Soviet government's continued restraint even after the outbreak of a war. There would be moral as well as practical grounds to recommend initial American city-avoidance, since U.S. retaliation against cities, if it should ultimately occur, would then be in retaliation for attacks against cities, not just for *any* large-scale attack on the United States or its allies. We could at least withdraw the threat that any large-scale strike, whether or not initially city-avoiding, might be met with a counterpopulation retaliation.

Of course it is possible that the Soviet government might refuse to reciprocate an American countercombatant policy, forcing the Washington government to decide whether or not to maintain the policy. At the minimum, the real moral onus would be forced back on Moscow, since we would have tried. Anyway, only a rather thoroughgoing Soviet effort at noncompliance would constitute a real defeat for an American initiative. If the Soviet government deliberately put its military targets right into the midst of heavily populated areas so as to make discrimination impossible, or if it spent vast sums to harden and disperse its military forces beyond the point at which they presented a manageable number of targets, we would know the initiative had failed. Any less massive effort at frustrating a countercombatant strategy might actually prove helpful. Dispersion, after all, compounds the demands on transportation facilities, fuel, materiel and ammunition supply, and command and control. The Soviet Union is not a country with a surplus of transportation equipment. (The 1968 intervention in Czechoslovakia produced a massive logistics problem for the Red Army, necessitating the requisition of many civilian vehicles.) Finally, it is hard to imagine why the Soviet government would engage in such a thoroughgoing nonreciprocation. The effort would surely be observed (especially by U.S. reconaissance satellites), and met with a return to an American policy of retaliation against weapons *and* cities, not by abandonment of reliance on the nuclear deterrent.

WOULD A COUNTERCOMBATANT STRATEGY BE TOO THREATENING?

If a countercombatant strategy could result in a meaningful reduction in the horror of nuclear war—leaving it still horrible but measurably less so if war ever should, despite our best efforts, occur—we have satisfied the first requirement. One aspect of our second question, whether it might make war more probable, has already been dealt with. I have tried to show that the assured destruction of Soviet military and internal-security forces would, in the special context of that country's relationships, still provide an extremely powerful deterrent, possibly even a more politically relevant and therefore effective one than a threat posed primarily against cities. No one would imagine that the United States was growing soft in its deterrent resolve or that the damage level would be so low that any rational opponent would willingly accept it. But there remains another version of the second question: Would the size and nature of the American deterrent force be such as to look like, or perhaps even be, a force capable of executing a "damage-limiting" first strike against the Soviet Union, in the sense of a capability for limiting the strategic nuclear damage the Soviet Union could inflict in retaliation? If so, I noted that the result might be to disrupt strategic stability by tempting the Soviet Union into a "preemptive" attack in a time of crisis. Or another consequence, instead of or in addition to that, could affect the third question. Would this lead to major acquisitions of new defensive and/or offensive systems, thus destroying any precarious arms-race stability?

These questions are frequently raised by members of the liberal arms-control community who worked so hard and successfully to secure the two kinds of stability we now have. Those who fought for the principle of mutual assured destruction, with its undoubted benefits as well as its long-term risks, ought not to want it lightly abandoned. The pressures, domestic as well as international, for a new round of strategic arms acquisition are not imaginary.

The risk of inadvertently posing a first-strike threat depends upon what steps each side takes to protect its own nuclear retaliatory force or to make more vulnerable that of its opponent. There is nothing in the targeting system proposed above that would provide either side with new damage-limiting capabilities. The primary targets explicitly are not intended to be strategic delivery vehicles. Nevertheless, it is possible that major qualitative improvements in striking power or major new acquisitions in numbers of weapons could degrade some kinds of retaliatory forces. The most vulnerable, of course, are the land-based fixed-site intercontinental ballistic missiles (ICBMs) on either side. They would become more vulnerable to warheads of greatly improved accuracy (which would otherwise be desirable for their potential to limit collateral damage to civilians) or to a very great increase in the number of potential attacking warheads, especially as a result of using multiple independently targetable reentry vehicles (MIRVs).

Major improvements in accuracy probably are *not* necessary to make very great reductions in the probable level of civilian casualties. Yet it is hard to imagine how present-day accuracy levels can be frozen anyway; development improvements continue on both sides, and inspection to enforce any agreement would be extraordinarily difficult. Nor does there seem to be much prospect for any agreement to prevent the MIRVing of existing missiles or their replacements. There is some consolation in the fact that MIRV is not compatible, at least given the size of most American launch vehicles, with very large warheads. The MIRVed Poseidon missiles, for example, are expected to have warheads in the 50-kiloton range. Even with increased accuracy, their limited explosive power offers some degree of protection to well-hardened missile sites. Finally, we must recognize that the day of land-based immobile missile systems is passing in any case. While their demise will not come tomorrow, in the long run a secure deterrent must rest on submarine-based missiles or some exotic new technology, and perhaps to a lesser degree on alert aircraft and mobile land-based missiles. To forego a countercombatant strategy just because it might seem to pose a threat to fixed-site missiles would be a purely quixotic gesture.

Thus the third question: Would new pressures from the weaponeers, both the military and their civilian allies, on both sides, be released by adoption of a countercombatant strategy? My answer to this question is the least confident, though I see no reason why it has to be unacceptable. First, although I have presented a rather long shopping list of target types for a countercombatant strategy, that does not mean that an enormous number of each type would have to be struck. I have repeatedly emphasized that destroying the utility of a military machine need not require the physical destruction of all of it. It is quite possible to produce military chaos and to open opportunities for the domestic and neighboring enemies of the Soviet regime without killing anything like every last Russian soldier or destroying every last Red Army tank. The strategy instead requires concentrating on the facilities for commanding, supplying, and transporting those troops and tanks. Second, no one should underestimate the numerical strength of existing or already projected American retaliatory forces. With MIRVs on

Poseidon, Polaris, and Minuteman, plus the bombers in the Strategic Air Command, the United States will have about 8,000 warheads targeted on the Soviet Union at any one time. The majority of these will be on vehicles, primarily submarines, with a very high probability of surviving any Soviet first strike, and probably will not have to face an effective Soviet ABM system. Nor does this figure include shorter-range land-based or sea-based aircraft and missiles, which could play a significant role in executing a countercombatant retaliation along the periphery of the Soviet Union. Without indulging in the rhetoric of overkill, is that not enough of a force utterly to cripple, at any desired level of assurance, Soviet military power and leave that country almost naked to its enemies?

I grant that this last question cannot be answered definitively from the unclassified literature, though I think a very strong presumption for a favorable answer does exist. At the very least, it would be utterly irresponsible to dismiss the countercombatant proposal on these grounds without the most careful and dispassionate study of its implications for weapons acquisition.

I should grant, too, that a very great virtue of present strategic doctrine is that it does provide a reasonably clear answer to the question of how much is enough. Defined in terms of percentages of population and industry, which are themselves a function of the cost curves, one has a ready and plausible brake to the ambitions of the arms hucksters. Doubtless this very fact recommended the doctrine to its original proponents, and the brake should not lightly be cast aside. It does seem unlikely that the cost curves for military targets, as proposed for a countercombatant strategy, would give quite such a neat solution. Some demands for new arms acquisitions would be forthcoming, using the new strategy as an excuse if not as a reason. We would need to maintain constant vigilance against such ambitions, not least because a new spiral to the arms race could feed back into raising the chance of war. But there are important counterpressures that did not exist ten years ago. The SALT agreements provide some constraint. Furthermore, opinion, both in government and in the public at large, is much more skeptical toward military spending than it has been at any time since the beginning of World War II.

Public-opinion data can illustrate the point. In a September 1973 Gallup poll on this topic, 46 percent of the people declared that the United States ought to be spending less for defense and only 13 percent thought it should spend more. Considering that the immediate irritant of the Vietnam War had passed, this is not markedly lower than what was found from 1969 to 1971, when repeated pollings turned up a steady 50 percent of the populace saying that military spending ought to go down. It contrasts sharply with the earlier era, when for three decades virtually every poll found fewer than 20 percent of the population desiring a cut in military spending. Moreover, the new skepticism about military spending is strongest among the more attentive, highly educated, and professional portions of the population. Typically the percentage of business and professional people saying that too much is being spent on defense is 10 points higher than that of the rest of the population. And in my own survey of almost 600 major corporation vice presidents in April 1973, 51 percent wanted to see the defense budget cut, and only 20 percent wanted an increase. Thus, antimilitary feeling is concentrated precisely in that part of the populace most likely to vote, to express opinions, to make campaign contributions, and to participate in some form of organized political activity. It should pose a powerful restraint on overzealous activities by the arms merchants.

And ultimately we should face the matter of tradeoffs squarely. Of course we should be concerned with avoiding wasteful spending on strategic weapons systems. Of course the competing priorities in this country have very strong claims to resources. I think I have, in my previous writings of the past few years, established my own credentials as one concerned with holding down and reducing Pentagon spending. But if it comes to that, shouldn't we be willing to spend *something* to get out from under the current awful threat to civilian populations throughout the northern hemisphere? Is prudence, is morality, of interest only if it costs us nothing?

THE DOMESTIC POLITICS OF STRATEGY

It is not enough that a countercombatant strategy make strategic good sense. It also must make political sense within the domestic systems of the superpowers, most notably within the United States. The preceding discussion has covered some of these points, especially the pressures and counterpressures for new weapons purchases. But there is more to it. Is there a potential political base for such a proposal in the United States and, if so, how is it composed?

The idea of a countercombatant strategy is not uniformly popular in circles traditionally concerned with arms control. In part this results from a lack of clarity about some of its implications, primarily from what I believe to be the misconception that the strategy change would lead to strategic or arms-race instabilities. Its acceptability will be enhanced to the degree its proponents can demonstrate its feasibility without major quantitative or qualitative additions to existing capabilities. Another problem, however, stems from the correct perception that the countercombatant proposal would not, for the foreseeable future, lead to major reductions in the level or rate of acquisition of strategic weapons. Under the exigencies of a countercombatant strategy the number of weapons would have to remain high for some time. Those who place a very great value on cuts in force or expenditure, therefore, may not be pleased. But, as noted, there are other goals, and that of a major arms reduction should not by itself override powerful strategic and moral considerations. In the longer run the United States and the Soviet Union may be able to negotiate a drop to a much lower assured destruction capability on both sides. Efforts in that direction should continue. Meanwhile a countercombatant strategy could well lead to phasing out the big, multimegaton warheads that currently hang over civilization—no small gain.

Opposition may also come from quite another source. Implementation of a countercombatant strategy would require very close attention to controlled response, flexibility, and an extremely well articulated command and control system, with special concern for control by the top civilian leadership. In principle such control exists, and the current administration has repeatedly stated the need for flexibility. It is not apparent, however, that the doctrinal capability in fact exists. That is, the physical communications capabilities may be present, but if there is not substantial thought and planning well in advance of a crisis, a president might nevertheless find himself confronted with making a choice from the very limited range of options the military command is really prepared to carry out. One thinks, for example, of the elaborate French, German, and Russian mobilization plans of 1914, and the inability of civilian authorities to execute partial or localized mobilizations that did not immediately threaten their opponents' security. Actually providing the needed flexibility in the nuclear-age Single Integrated Operational Plan (SIOP) might require intervention by the president and his immediate advisers in areas of strategic planning normally considered the responsibility of military officers. A clash about questions of military professionalism and civilian-military relations over the issue is conceivable.

On the other hand, several potential sources of support for an emphasis on countercombatant deterrence exist. There is a widespread, if virtually silent, sense of moral revulsion against counterpopulation deterrence. It remains largely silent so long as no viable alternative seems to exist, but presentation of a seemingly feasible countercombatant alternative could cause much of this latent feeling to become manifest. At least passive support could be found among groups whose interests might seem threatened by disarmament proposals. A countercombatant strategy would not involve any major reductions in strategic force levels. Moreover, some who worry about the continued effectiveness of counterpopulation deterrence in light of Soviet countermeasures, such as civil defense and evacuation plans, might actually feel reassured by a shift in strategy that emphasized military targets. The passive support of such groups must not become an excuse for enormous new weapons procurement, but it is simply a fact that any new strategic consensus will have to be broadly based. Finally, there is something about a posture of mutual massive counterpopulation destruction that is subtly but profoundly subversive of the authority of the modern state. In the event of a failure, it would not only admit but would exploit the state's failure to secure the most fundamental interest of its subjects—their lives. Long-term appreciation of this fact may produce some surprising advocates of change.

At the moment there is no broadly based political constituency for a countercombatant deterrent strategy. It lacks the kind of popularity that greeted such administration moves as the opening to China or the SALT treaty, and would stimulate searching and perhaps acrimonious discussion. Nevertheless there are important precedents for concern with the issue. It was hotly discussed in the B-36 vs. aircraft-carrier debate of 1949, when the Navy insisted that counterpopulation bombing would be immoral as well as ineffective. While much of this argument may have been self-serving, its impact should not be forgotten. A similar initiative is associated with Secretary McNamara in 1962, particularly his famous Ann Arbor speech calling for graduated response. That initiative failed, in large part because it came at a time of American nuclear superiority and was linked with counterforce doctrines of damage limitation. Such a strategy and capability was seen as destabilizing and was widely criticized. But the countercombatant strategy I have suggested here comes at a time of essential Soviet-American parity and explicitly renounces the notion of seeking a damage-limiting capability. It should not be rejected with arguments that do not apply.

There are some signs that the administration is trying to shift in this direction, albeit while perhaps still toying dangerously with the notion of damage limitation. One certainly should not infer too much from Fred Iklé's nomination to head the Arms Control and Disarmament Agency. There are a number of possible good reasons for that appointment. Yet his *cri de coeur* about assured destruction surely came at a significant moment. And President Nixon himself declared, in his annual report on foreign policy for 1973, "If war occurs—and there is no way we can absolutely guarantee that it will not—we should have means of preventing escalation while convincing an opponent of the futility of continued aggression." Still more pointedly, "While the specter of an unacceptable response is fundamental to deterrence, the ability to kill tens of millions of people is not the only or necessarily the most effective deterrent to every challenge. . . . Moreover, the measure of the effectiveness of our strategic forces in terms of numbers of dead is inconsistent with American values."[7] That remains a point to remember.

POSTSCRIPT

As mentioned in note 6, the foregoing was written before former Defense Secretary Schlesinger's January 1974 statements about flexible response and the subsequent beginnings of debate on the purpose and instruments of nuclear strategy. Without entering into an extensive discussion of those events, a few brief points may be worth making at the current time (April 1976).

1. The new concern with flexible response is more a shift in emphasis than a radical departure from past policy. As Alain Enthoven and others have made clear, even in the 1960s assured destruction was a criterion for the adequacy of U.S. strategic retaliatory forces, and not necessarily a statement of targeting doctrine. Recent developments give much more attention —especially in public statements—to the idea of city avoidance, but some such capability and intention has long existed. If this is understood, recent efforts may, because less novel than they may have appeared, also seem less threatening.

2. Much of the subsequent critical reaction to the Schlesinger statements assumed that the new strategy would be counterforce in the sense of being directed against enemy nuclear retaliatory forces. While the statements in question were ambiguous, it is probable that a wide variety of such targets, extending well into the realm of targets included in the definition of countercombatant in this article, is intended. Of course nuclear retaliatory forces may also be included in the intention, and that is not the recommendation of this article.

3. As emphasized in the text, a countercombatant strategy need not require a massive strike. An Air Force Colonel once remarked to me that the U.S. tactical war-fighting capability in Western Europe could effectively be eliminated with thirty relatively low-yield, high-accuracy warheads. That figure may be an underestimate, and in any case the comparable figure for destroying the much larger Soviet capability, dispersed across all of Eastern Europe and the U.S.S.R., would be much higher. Nevertheless it is two orders of magnitude below the number of U.S. strategic warheads (3600) estimated, even under very conservative calculations, as able to survive any Soviet attack against them.[8]

4. My assumption in the text that the physical (though not doctrinal) aspects of command and control might already be adequate to the demands of a countercombatant strategy was premature. This needs attention, on a high-priority basis.

5. Finally, it should be emphasized that, whatever the intention of some U.S. government spokesmen may be, this article does *not* recommend the first-use of nuclear weapons by the United States, even in "demonstrative" or other small-scale modes. We know much too little—and can know much too little in the absence of direct experience—about the readiness with which various "firebreaks" can be maintained if nuclear weapons are actually used. The prospects for preserving limitations on their use during wartime seem far too unpromising to make deliberate first-use desirable.[9] The recommendations of this paper are intended precisely—and only—in the same way as are recommendations to develop and use better passenger restraints (e.g., seatbelts) in motor vehicles. "Accidents" can occur, and we ought to take appropriate steps to minimize the carnage in the event they do occur. But having taken those steps would not, therefore, give us a license to drive more recklessly.

NOTES

1. Fred C. Iklé, "Can Nuclear Deterrence Last Out the Century," *Foreign Affairs* 51 (January 1973): 267–85.

2. See my "A Countercombatant Deterrent? Feasibility, Morality, and Arms Control," in Sam Sarkesian, ed., *The Military Industrial Complex: A Reassessment* (Beverly Hills: Sage, 1972), reprinted with slight modifications as chapter 14 of my *Power and Community in World Politics* (San Francisco: W. H. Freeman, 1974).

3. D. G. Hoag, "Ballistic Missile Guidance," in B. T. Feld et al., eds., *Impact of New Technologies on the Arms Race* (Cambridge: The M.I.T. Press, 1971), p. 100.

4. See John Lauder, "Lessons of the Strategic Bombing Survey for Contemporary Defense Policy" (New Haven: Yale University, 1973), unpublished.

5. Johan Jorgen Holst, "Comparative U.S. and Soviet Deployments, Doctrines, and Arms Limitations," in Morton A. Kaplan, ed., *SALT: Problems and Prospects* (Morristown, N.J.: General Learning Press, 1973), pp. 72–73.

6. Wolfgang K. H. Panovsky has replied to Iklé, offering small-scale, controlled, limited response as the only alternative to counterpopulation or destabilizing counterforce ("The Mutual Hostage Relationship Between America and Russia," *Foreign Affairs* 51 [October 1973]: 109–18). In this article Panovsky did not consider the option proposed here. If the aim of controlled *response* were to be countercombatant, our proposals might be compatible. Nevertheless, I greet suggestions for "small-scale" strikes with great trepidation. If the nuclear threshold were to be crossed by an attacker we could still try to make some reply short of counterpopulation—but neither they, *nor we*, could cross the threshold with anything like impunity. Similar reservations apply to Defense Secretary James R. Schlesinger's statements of January 1974, which appeared after this article originally went to press (news conferences at the Pentagon, January 24, 1974, March 28, 1974; and *Annual Defense Department Report FY 1975* [Washington: GPO, 1974]).

7. U.S., President of, *U.S. Foreign Policy for the 1970's: Shaping a Durable Peace*, A Report to the Congress (Washington, D.C.: Government Printing Office, May 3, 1973), pp. 84, 83.

8. John D. Steinbruner and Thomas M. Garwin, "Strategic Vulnerability: The Balance Between Prudence and Paranoia," *International Security* 1 (Summer 1976): 155–96.

9. For an argument that a "no first use" policy is feasible and desirable, see my "No First Use of Nuclear Weapons: To Stay the Fateful Lightning," *Worldview* 19 (November 1976): 9–11.

9

The Nuclear Arms Race: Machine Versus Man

Francis X. Winters, S.J.

While reading Herbert Butterfield's *Christianity, Diplomacy and War* recently, I was struck as much by a marginal notation left by a previous reader as by the masterful text itself.[1] The notation was the word "Vietnam" scribbled in the margin next to Butterfield's treatment of the Korean War. The original text and its marginal updating recalled an experience I had had during the period of the Korean War itself when I was helping to care for an elderly gentleman. Listening to radio broadcasts from the battlefield, the old man, whose capacity to differentiate between past and present had failed him, used to ask me for further news on the war: "And how are the Central Powers doing?" For him, World War I and the Korean War had collapsed into a single struggle.

Perhaps in these two experiences there rests an important insight; from a note left in a margin and from a failing memory we may be prodded into the realization that war is an enduring reality. We are left, too, with the realization that the moral questions raised by war are always the same: the protection of civilians, and the calculation of costs and benefits.[2] Neither war nor the effort to control it has passed away. Only the victims are gone and some of those who, in their own time and place, wondered what could be done to control the conflict. *Plus ça change...*

Yet the advent of nuclear weapons *has* changed the pattern of recurring violence and the ever-renewed efforts to limit war and the spread of weapons. War has changed at a much faster pace than human understanding has, so far, been able to match. War is winning its race against the human effort to control it. So uneven is the match between the advances in military technology and the progress in political efforts to make use of the newer weapons that man now runs the risk of accepting terms of war dictated by the military machinery itself, rather than by his traditional enemies, other human beings.

Hans Morgenthau pointed to this disturbing anomaly in 1974 when he remarked that, for the first time in history, the principal military antagonists—the United States and the Soviet Union—enjoy a superfluity of weapons over targets.[3] For example, the United States will soon be able to deploy about 18,000 nuclear warheads. Yet in the Soviet Union there are only 219 cities with populations of over 100,000 people. Even supposing that there are four times as many targets other than cities, the ratio of weapons to targets would be a staggering 16:1.[4] Reflecting on this unprecendented and unnerving development, Morgenthau warned that to go on using the words "weapon" and "war" of a possible nuclear confrontation is a dangerous exercise in semantic confusion since the reality of such violent conflict would bear no relation to any previous historical event.[5]

The warning issued by Dr. Morgenthau was underscored the following Fall by a report published by the United States Arms Control and Disarmament Agency (ACDA) entitled "Worldwide Effects of Nuclear War . . . Some Perspectives." One alarming passage said:

> Another unexpected effect of high-altitude bursts was the blackout of high-frequency radio communications. Disruption of the ionosphere (which reflects radio signals back to the earth) by nuclear bursts over the Pacific has wiped out long-distance radio communications for hours at distances of up to 600 miles from the burst point.
>
> Yet another surprise was the discovery that electromagnetic pulses can play havoc with electrical equipment itself, including some in command systems that control the nuclear arms themselves.
>
> Much of our knowledge was thus gained by chance—a fact which should imbue us with humility as we contemplate the remaining uncertainties (as well as the certainties) about nuclear warfare.[6]

I believe this is the first time an official United States government document has described the eerie possibility that these machines of war may escape the grasp of their designers and deployers and themselves begin to determine the course of the war.

It is against these somber warnings that I would like to undertake a moral reassessment of warfare in the light of nuclear weapons developments.

CAN NUCLEAR WARFARE BE JUSTIFIED MORALLY?

The most disturbing transformation in the nature of warfare has occurred because of the unpredictability of the pattern of fighting which would ensue upon the commencement of nuclear hostilities. Literally no one knows what a nuclear war would be like. There is, then, no reliable way to predict the damage that would be done in such a conflict. From this incalculability of damage which might result from nuclear war, there results the most intractable obstacle to the traditional effort to limit war on the grounds of morality. The unknowability of the potential damage precludes any effort to ask one of the essential moral questions about a prospective war: What is the proportion between loss and gain to be expected from the hostilities? If the losses are unpredictable, no calculation of their proportionality to political gains is feasible; hence, policy planners and political leaders are unable to certify the preponderance of gain over loss.

The starting point of a modern moral reassessment of the arms race must be an awareness that the frequently discussed international race for nuclear advantage is not, in fact, the most dangerous aspect of the present military crisis. It is rather the race for survival between men (Soviet and/or American) and their respective war machines. The ACDA report sounded a warning that the machines are currently ahead.

In the present technological and military situation, even the military commanders themselves do not claim that they can exercise "command and control" over the level of hostilities once a nuclear weapon has been used. Such a profound change in the nature of warfare appears to demand the abandonment of moral efforts to control the level of violence, efforts which have always sought to subordinate the military question of the use of force to the political question of the purpose of force. Since the nation's military professionals cannot guarantee their control of the instruments of violence in nuclear war, the political acceptance of such intrinsically uncontrollable weaponry is equivalent to the citizenry abdicating any further efforts to set limits to warfare. Thus, one might argue, it is futile to speak of moral limits on nuclear war.

From this premise of the incompatibility of morality and nuclear warfare, directly contradictory conclusions can, of course, be drawn. As suggested, the first conclusion, embraced by the majority of analysts, is to forego the useless discussion of limiting war.

Others, however, including myself, have reluctantly come to an opposite conclusion: Since one must apparently abandon either ethics or the intention to use nuclear weapons and since life without ethics would be incomprehensible and intolerable, it is necessary to abandon the weapons that have proven to be incompatible with the tradition of civilized warfare. Traumatic as this conclusion must be to a U.S. moralist who rejects the pacifist approach to politics, it seems inescapable because the presupposition of an ethical endorsement of the use of violence is the capacity to compare the costs and benefits of war. When no such calculation is allowed by the weapons themselves, no moral argument for the acceptability of such weapons is plausible. Until military professionals can offer a reasonable certitude of being able to control their weapons, the moralist is forced to re-examine nonnuclear options for defense policy.

To some this moral insistence on the issue of the calculability of the effects of nuclear war may seem too theoretical a consideration to merit discussion or to figure in the moral judgment about such wars. The just-war theorist would disagree with this opinion, but he might, nevertheless, suggest that even without accepting the significance of the *capacity* to make such a calculation, a morally sensitive person could still reject the option for nuclear war simply on an estimate of the *predictable* results of a thermonuclear exchange which escapes human control and ends only with the exhaustion of current and projected weapons stockpiles. In the ACDA report it is estimated that an all-out nuclear war (one in which 10,000 warheads or bombs were detonated) would result in more than 200 million fatalities. Furthermore, such a war would destroy 30 to 70 percent of the ozone layer in the entire northern hemisphere and between 20 to 40 percent of it in the southern hemisphere as well. The destruction of the ozone would have truly apocalyptic consequences, such as a two- to three-year destruction of agriculture (because of a change of even one degree in the average temperature), disabling sunburn or snow blindness, and disruption of communications.[7]

Other relevant considerations were submitted by Harold and Margaret Sprout in a recent essay on geography and politics.[8] In their article they accept Harrison Brown's contention that if the present industrial world economy, built on the exploitation of nonrenewable minerals and other resources, were to be destroyed in a nuclear war, there are simply not enough physical resources remaining in the earth's crust to rebuild it. A postholocaust world will be a preindustrial world inhabited by a postindustrial civilization.[9] Thus, they say:

If Brown's thesis is accepted, the conclusion follows that our conquest of nature, of which twentieth-century man is so proud and boastful, is viable only in a universe from which total war fought with nuclear weapons is permanently excluded. A further implication latent in Brown's thesis is that nuclear war would disable countries in proportion roughly to their level of industrialization and to the geographical concentration of their industrial conurbations. In plain English, a reasonable inference from Brown's thesis is that a future general war would wipe out the densely inhabited industrial countries of Western Europe, damaging the United States and the Soviet Union probably beyond recovery.[10]

Consequently, whether one argues from the uncontrollability of nuclear war or from the predictable results of an actually uncontrolled war, the moral conclusion is the same: No conceivable political goal could justify such a use of violence.

If, however, some future technological or diplomatic breakthrough were to enable the military to offer some reasonable assurance of control, then the traditional moral criteria governing the use of violence would once more be applicable to the political and military decisions concerning war. So let us now examine the moral acceptability of the threat and/or use of nuclear weapons in the circumstance of their controllability, even though that is presently inconceivable.

The first question to be asked about the morality of using such weapons would concern the *purpose* of their use. The enormity of the potential damage to be expected from the tactical or strategic use of such weapons requires that the purpose be nothing less than the defense of the ultimate political values: life and/or sovereignty. Since nuclear arsenals are only marginally capable of defending lives (by denying the enemy the use of some of his offensive weapons and thereby limiting the potential damage which his weapons can do) their hypothetical *controlled* use would be justifiable only by a calculation that such use would protect more lives (not excluding the lives of the hostile populace) than their nonuse. Such a calculation of saving lives by "damage-limiting" use of nuclear weapons in response to a nuclear threat seems highly improbable, at least at present, because the superpowers possess mutually invulnerable submarine fleets which could respond against the enemy's cities following any conceivable counterattack.

However, even one who admits that a nuclear second-strike would not on balance save lives might make a tenuous case that there could still remain a political utility in a retaliatory strike. That political purpose, in the case of the United States, would be the vindication of the values of free institutions against the threat of totalitarian control of the world. This view would morally justify the act of retaliation by arguing that the political value of democractic ideals and institutions would be enhanced by the resolute effort to defend them, even to the death. Such an argument has an initial appeal, perhaps, but yields finally to the realization that such liberal ideals and institutions could never survive a nuclear holocaust nor flourish in a postapocalyptic world, which would be characterized by chaos and by the political/military tyranny required to cope with such unimaginable destruction and disruption. There is then no political purpose that could be defended by a nuclear second-strike.

In order to complete the argument against the moral acceptability of using nuclear weapons, however, let us for the moment bracket the conclusion that there are no moral legitimizing purposes for any nuclear threat or use and ask the second set of traditional questions—those about the *means* of warfare. If, in other words, there were some (not yet discovered) defensible political purpose for the use of nuclear weapons, would such weapons be a morally acceptable means of achieving this goal?

Here we turn to the questions about *discrimination* and *proportionality* in the use of military violence. Recalling the double hypothesis under which these questions about means can even be asked in this case—namely that nuclear weapons could be controlled and that some political purpose could be achieved by their use—let us first examine such use according to the criterion of discrimination. The principle of discrimination in the use of military force forbids all intentional attacks on noncombatants.[11] The application of this principle immediately disallows the nuclear strategy called countervalue (the exclusive targeting of hostile cities and societal requirements, such as economic essentials). The same criterion rules out as well the counterforce strategy, articulated in 1974 by former Secretary of Defense James Schlesinger, which would, under certain circumstances, respond to a Soviet attack by targeting military objectives in the Soviet Union with an announced willingness to escalate the attack, after a suitable chronological firebreak, to an attack on nonmilitary targets such as cities. Since the counterforce strategy as proposed by the Department of Defense explicitly includes the intention merely to postpone, and not to eschew, the targeting of civilians, the strategy *as a whole* is morally unacceptable.

Could other plans for strategic response be deemed morally acceptable under the principle of discrimination? It seems that—exclusive of the effect of radioactive fallout—some countermilitary targeting might be in keeping with the principle of civilian immunity. For example, a counterstrategic defense might be technologically feasible and morally acceptable if the principle of discrimination alone were applied. ("Counterstrategic" is used here to mean an attack limited to the following targets: strategic forces, including ICBMs, submarine support facilities, ABM sites, air fields, fuel depots, missile depots, rail lines serving ICBMs, and whatever targets could be established to be contributing, or about to contribute, to the strategic attack on the United States.)

The moral unacceptability even of such a strategy is seen, however, once the analyst applies the other indispensable criterion of *proportionality*, which requires that the political values to be obtained by the use of force outweigh the evils to be inflicted, including collateral (foreseen but unintended) civilian damage.

A study commissioned by the Arms Control Sub-committee of the United States Senate Committee on Foreign Relations detailed the proportions of the damage which could be expected from even a counterforce attack by the U.S.S.R. against U.S. military installations. This study was undertaken to obtain an independent estimate of the levels of unintended or collateral civilian casualties which might be expected by U.S. citizens if the sort of counterforce exchange discussed by Schlesinger were to occur, and its conclusions were disconcerting. For example, on a typical March day, a comprehensive Soviet attack using two 550-kiloton warheads against each of the 1,102 military sites in the United States (1,054 missile silos, 46 SAC bases, and 2 nuclear submarine bases) would be likely to kill 6.7 million people despite every precaution to avoid civilian damage. If the attack were to target two three-megaton warheads against each of the same targets, estimated civilian fatalities would be 16.3 million. Even if the Soviets were to single out only one ICBM base near a populous area, for example Whiteman Air Force Base in Missouri, and to employ two three-megaton warheads against each of the 150 silos there, the probable civilian casualties would total 10.3 million fatalities.[12]

It seems unnecessary to belabor the conclusion that such collateral civilian damage is *out of all proportion* to any conceivable political goal. (Although there is no precise consensus on the amount of collateral civilian damage that would suffice to make discriminate military strategy morally unacceptable because of the principle of proportionality, surely most critics would accept a figure approximating the number of lives lost in the holocaust of the Jews—six million. It is then worthy of note that the predicted collateral civilian damage from a comprehensive counterforce attack on the United States would be approximately the same figure under the rather favorable circumstances projected in the subcommittee report.) Hence, the hypothetical option of a controlled counterforce attack in response is morally excluded by the criterion of proportionality.

These arguments lead ineluctably, I believe, to the conclusion that *any* serious threat or use of nuclear weapons is immoral. The most critical reason for this is their intrinsic uncontrollability. Furthermore, because of the consequences of their use, no political utility can be discovered for such use, at least by a free society. Even if nuclear weapons could somehow be brought under human control, and even if some political utility for their employment could be demonstrated, their use would still be immoral because of the predicted damage to civilians, even from a strictly countermilitary attack.

THE TRUE DANGER OF NUCLEAR WEAPONS

War, then, has changed. Hans Morgenthau was right in insisting that we abandon the words "weapon" and "war" when speaking of nuclear conflict because the development of military technology in the last thirty years has so transformed the instruments of war that they require new names to represent their new reality. Using the expressions "nuclear weapons" and "nuclear war" creates the impression that such weapons systems and strategies are rational instruments to achieve a political purpose. This, as we have seen, is not the case. The crucial fact to be understood about nuclear conflict is its uncontrollability. Whereas in previous wars we had to be concerned about the runaway momentum of violence because human passions and vindictiveness can escape control, now we are faced with an era in which the weapons themselves, with their computers and communication networks, might escape even the direction of militarist leaders bent on vengeance and set their own mechanical terms for war.

Two passages from the recent ACDA publication cited above underline this dangerous situation:

New discoveries have been made, yet much uncertainty inevitably persists. Our knowledge of nuclear warfare rests largely on theory and hypothesis, fortunately untested by the usual processes of trial and error; the paramount goal of statesmanship is that we should never learn from the experience of nuclear war.

The uncertainties that remain are of such magnitude that of themselves they must serve as a further deterrent to the use of nuclear weapons. . . . Uncertainty is one of the major conclusions in our studies, as the haphazard and unpredicted derivation of many of our discoveries emphasizes.[13]

We have come to realize that nuclear weapons can be as unpredictable as they are deadly in their effects. Despite some 30 years of development and study, there is still much that we do not know. This is particularly true when we consider the global effects of a large-scale nuclear war.[14]

Thus, in the sober pages of recent U.S government reports we finally recognize the reality of a mechanical Prometheus which has stolen the fire of technology and now defies its human maker. It is time to stop, heeding the warning of Fred Iklé, who remarked shortly before his appointment as director of ACDA:

The jargon of American strategic analysis works like a narcotic. It dulls our sense of moral outrage about the tragic confrontation of nuclear arsenals, primed and constantly perfected to unleash widespread genocide. It fosters the current smug complacence regarding the soundness and stability of mutual deterrence. It blinds us to the fact that our method for preventing nuclear war rests on a form of warfare universally condemned since the Dark Ages—the mass killing of hostages.[15]

We must awaken from our hypnotic trance and realize that we live in a state of military emergency, vulnerable at any moment to military challenges to which we could respond only at the risk of terminating the human experiment.

AN ALTERNATIVE TO A NUCLEAR-BASED DEFENSE POLICY

It is not possible, and perhaps not even desirable, for the entire U.S. citizenry to awaken at once to the peril in which we live. Yet the security of the human race depends on the rousing of a few leaders to the imperative of finding an alternative to a nuclear defense policy.

We need adequate military strength to defend the human, cultural, and political values that have been achieved thus far in the process of human development. Yet we cannot any longer afford the illusion that nuclear "weapons" provide such security. We need to develop a conventional alternative to the present nuclear defense policies of the United States; we need a way to protect western interests in a hostile international environment without relying on nuclear weapons. We need, in short, a credible capacity for conventional defense and deterrence.

Is such conventional military posture feasible? Even to ask this question requires an awakening, a snapping out of the hypnotic state described by Iklé. To break the deterrence slumber requires, however, only the work of imagination, the capacity to think through the foreseeable consequences of using our nuclear arsenal. Once the predictable dynamics of a nuclear exchange are contemplated, the question of conventional military posture becomes thinkable once more. Once such a thought has been admitted, the monumental task of reconstruction—ethical, political, military, and economic—has begun. With an awakening to the need for reconstruction, the opportunity and burden of leadership in U.S. political affairs becomes comprehensible.

Such fundamental reconstruction cannot even be adequately imagined at the present moment. Yet some of the challenges to be faced by the architects of such a global renewal are clear. They will have to ask some traditional political questions about military affairs. From these questions will emerge other questions, perhaps more precise and more penetrating. Eventually, perhaps, to the right question there will be found an answer. Then the task of reconstruction will be under way.

What are some of the traditional political questions which might initiate this process of reconstruction? Let me suggest that a constructive beginning has already been made by Arthur L. Burns. In "Ethics and Deterrence: A Nuclear Balance without Hostage Cities?" which appeared simultaneously with similar suggestions from other creative minds, such as Bruce Russett and Paul Ramsey, Burns asked the proper political question: What are the vital interests of the U.S.S.R. which can be denied to them without resorting to the genocidal attack on Soviet cities?[16] While Burns' own answer (the recommendation that the United States target the one million Soviet troops stationed on the Sino-Soviet border, thereby disrupting the U.S.S.R.'s capacity to deal simultaneously with the external security needs of their western and eastern frontiers and their internal security problems) is not persuasive to many analysts, his question itself remains valid and illuminating.

Reflection on Burns's question (identical in content, I believe, with the question posed by the just-war tradition) may reveal the possibility that there are indeed some vital Soviet interests which could be denied without reliance on nuclear "weapons" at all. For example, it might be possible, in response to a Soviet nuclear strike on the United States, to threaten Soviet industry and transportation centers with conventional warheads delivered by ICBMs which have been made more precise through the technological advance called maneuverable reentry vehicles (MaRVs).[17] Despite severe political and military obstacles, it might be possible to oppose aggression in Western Europe by the Soviet Union and the Warsaw Pact countries with greatly augmented conventional NATO forces, capable of threatening, if necessary, the security of some of the U.S.S.R.'s Eastern European satellites. In response to attempts to deny Western nations access to needed supplies or markets, it might be possible to create similar problems for the Soviet economy.

These particular possible responses to potential Soviet acts of aggression may turn out, for various reasons, to be either impractical or unwise. Yet simply posing the question of which Soviet vital interests can be threatened in response to aggression without threatening or using nuclear weapons may eventually reveal a feasible political and military doctrine that is neither genocidal nor suicidal, as our present doctrine surely is.[18]

I submit that we have no alternative to asking this question most earnestly. Rather, we have only the alternative of allowing technology to triumph over man. We now know that nuclear weapons might escape human control, but we do not yet know whether we can escape their control.

NOTES

1. Herbert Butterfield, *Christianity, Diplomacy and War* (London: The Epworth Press, 1953).

2. For an able treatment of the principal issues, see Theodore R. Weber, *Modern War and the Pursuit of Peace* (New York: Council on Religion and International Affairs, 1968). See also my other essay in this volume, "Ethics, Diplomacy, and Defense."

3. Hans J. Morgenthau, "The Question of Détente," *Worldview*, March 1976, p. 10.

4. See F. X. Winters, "Morality in the War Room," *America* 132 (February 15, 1975): 106–10.

5. Morgenthau, remarks made in a seminar session at Georgetown University in October 1974.

6. U.S. Arms Control and Disarmament Agency, "Worldwide Effects of Nuclear War . . . Some Perspectives," report no. 81 (Washington, D.C.: U.S. Government Printing Office, 1975), p. 5.

7. ACDA, "Worldwide Effects of Nuclear War," pp. 3, 4.

8. Harold and Margaret Sprout, "Geography and International Politics in an Era of Revolutionary Change," in *The International Political System*, ed. Romano Romani (New York: John Wiley and Sons, 1972), p. 471.

9. See Harrison Brown, *The Challenge of Man's Future* (New York: The Viking Press, 1954).

10. Sprout and Sprout, "Geography and International Politics," p. 471.

11. Sidney Bailey, "Protecting Civilians in War," *Survival* 14 (November/December 1972) pointed out that the principle of discrimination is almost universally recognized as valid by scholars who maintain the Christian version of the just-war doctrine. He noted that two U.S. scholars, W. O'Brien and R. Hartigan, dissent from this near unanimity (p. 267, n. 3). An answer to their arguments can be found in Weber, *Modern War*, p. 33.

12. U.S. Congress, Senate Committee on Foreign Relations, Subcommittee on Arms Control, *Analyses of Effects of Limited Nuclear Warfare*, 94th Congress, 1st session, September 1975, pp. 18, 19, 46. [These independent estimates were submitted by an Ad Hoc Panel, under the chairmanship of Jerome B. Wiesner, convened by the Technology Assessment Board of the U.S. Congress.]

13. ACDA, "Worldwide Effects of Nuclear War," p. 1.

14. Ibid., p. 24.

15. Fred Iklé, "Can Nuclear Deterrence Last Out the Century?" *Foreign Affairs* 51 (January 1973): 281.

16. Arthur L. Burns, "Ethics and Deterrence: A Nuclear Balance without Hostage Cities?" *Adelphi Papers* no. 69 (London: The Institute for Strategic Studies, July 1970), p. 11. Cf. also Bruce Russett, "Assured Destruction of What? A Countercombatant Alternative to Nuclear MADness," *Public Policy* 22 (Spring 1974): 121–38, which is reprinted with a postscript in this volume, and Russett's exposition of the same theme in "A Countercombatant Deterrent: Feasibility, Morality, and Arms Control," *Power and Community in World Politics* (San Francisco: W. H. Freeman, 1974), and Paul Ramsey, "The MAD Nuclear Policy," *Worldview* (November 1972): 16–20.

17. The Circular Error Probable (CEP) of U.S. ICBMs is now approaching ninety feet over a trajectory of eight thousand miles, which means that half the missiles launched will land within ninety feet of the target. Such accuracy is adequate to do extensive damage with conventional explosives. (The source for these figures is *World Armaments and Disarmament, SIPRI Yearbook* [Stockholm: Stockholm International Peace Research Institute, 1971]. Others question the attainability of such low CEPs.)

18. A related consideration concerns the moral acceptability of maintaining the present U.S. nuclear arsenal even after declaring that these weapons will not be used even in retaliation. The issue has ethical, political, military, and technological dimensions. A possible answer is that a democratic society might be morally justified in leaving such an arsenal intact so as to allow subsequent administrations and Congresses to return to a policy of nuclear use. To dismantle the arsenal and to cease research and development would foreclose options to which a future government probably has a political right. Thus the issues of the threat or use of, and the possession of, nuclear weapons are separate moral issues. A decision against use and in favor of possession would have clear implications for the total pattern of deterrence in the international system.

10

Ethics and Deterrence: Moving Beyond the Just-War Tradition

Pierce S. Corden

INTRODUCTION

Thirty-one years after the end of World War II, the globe is divided into some 150 theoretically independent and sovereign nations; their people live in a situation of profound danger. The danger lies in the fact that at least five of these nations possess arsenals of nuclear weapons (and other weapons of mass destruction) and have promised each other—in varying combinations—that if sufficiently provoked they will use them to cause damage and destruction of nearly unimaginable scope.

By some indices, such as the yet increasing number of nuclear warheads on strategic missiles, this situation is worsening. By others, such as the outlawing of biological weapons by the Biological Weapons Convention, it is far from hopeless. On balance, this is not a very comfortable period of history in which to contemplate man's future tenure of the planet.

The existence of nuclear and other kinds of weapons that can be used for mass destruction has prompted three questions of fundamental importance and urgency:

1. Can the possession of such weapons be justified?

The author is a Physical Science Officer of the United States Arms Control and Disarmament Agency. The views expressed in this paper are his own and do not necessarily represent those of the United States government.

2. If so, what is a proper declaratory policy regarding their use?
3. What actual use might be justified?

The answers to these questions clearly play a central role in the struggle to build a world order less susceptible to, and less in need of, the violent resolution of interstate conflicts. The search for these answers should be no utopian or languid exercise; humanity's advances in the natural sciences and its resultant acquisition of a technological base together have produced the capability to build weapons of a character and in sufficient quantity to end civilized life, if not to eradicate the race entirely.

This paper is an attempt to show that new elements should be included in the ethical considerations involved in attempts to answer these questions, and to pose again the broader question of the ethics of using violence *at all* in international relations. My discussion presumes those ethical elements that have, in the past, usually been labeled as the "just-war tradition," particularly the principles of discrimination and proportionality;[1] it goes on to introduce certain elements which have not previously been included in this traditional evaluation, but which I believe have become necessary for an adequate ethical assessment.

In presenting this broader ethical inquiry, I have found it useful to survey both the development of weapons capable of mass destruction over the past half century and the simultaneous efforts to control them through arms-control and disarmament agreements, and to trace the rationales for their possession, declaratory policy concerning them, and policy for their actual use. Then I discuss the ethical elements—old and new—which, I believe, must determine contemporary value judgments on the use of force in international relations. The paper ends with some comments, in light of my expanded theoretical structure, on the concept of a deterrence which relies on a capability for assured destruction.

THE EVOLUTION OF WEAPONS CAPABLE OF MASS DESTRUCTION

The advent of "weapons of mass destruction" or "weapons adaptable to mass destruction" (to use the terms current in diplomatic parlance)[2] occurred during World War I. During that conflict, chemical warfare agents such as chlorine, phosgene, and mustard gas were introduced by Germany and then adopted by

France and the United Kingdom. These weapons were capable of killing or wounding large numbers of troops in a short period of time; their effects could be countered only by wearing bulky protective clothing and/or gas masks.

The insidiousness of chemical agents lies in their ability to penetrate fortifications and in their widespread and uncontrollable effects. Unlike rifle or machine gun fire, they cannot be avoided by recourse to fortified positions, and when applied they affect an area of uncertain size. There is a certain question of degree here, since other weapons, such as high explosive shells, also affect an entire area, but in such a case this area is fairly well defined by the radius of the explosive charge's effect. The area affected by chemical weapons, however, is not only large, but also unpredictable (even to the detriment of their user if the wind shifts).

Although chemical agents were used only against military personnel in World War I, their pervasive and areal properties lend themselves equally well, if not better, to use against unprotected civilians, especially in areas of concentrated population—cities. This threat immediately leads to the concept of deterrence. The argument is as follows: If one's adversary has the capability to effect such use, the defender must deter this use by himself possessing the same capability, in terms of both technological knowhow and the actual possession of stocks of agents, in order to be able to respond in kind in the event that chemicals were used against him. This argument is of course similar to that often cited to justify the acquisition or retention of nuclear weapons. There appears, unhappily, even to be a perverse logic connecting the nature of weapons of mass destruction and the argument that a capability to retaliate in kind is a necessary deterrent to use of such weapons. Perhaps the fear generated by the perception of being essentially powerless to stop vast destruction prompts the conclusion that the power to cause such destruction in response is the only feasible counterbalance.

This argument was used to justify the acquisition of chemical agent stockpiles by states prior to World War II, for use in battle and to deter threatened use directly against civilian populations. And the United States and the United Kingdom were both adamant in their promises to retaliate in kind, *and more*, if Germany or Japan initiated any use of chemical agents during the war.[3]

Chemical weapons were not, however, used in World War II.

Indeed, it is important to note that states had been sufficiently alarmed by the use of chemical agents in World War I that the single arms-control agreement negotiated or attempted following the end of those hostilities to stand the test of time and remain a vital force today is the Geneva Protocol of 1925, outlawing the use of chemical and bacteriological methods of warfare.[4]

Another technological development that began to take on significance for use in war during the first decades of the century was not controlled, despite efforts to do so after World War I and even before. This was the aircraft, in particular the airplane carrying bombs and machine guns.[5] More than any other single technological change, the airplane has led to the blurring of the distinction between soldier and civilian which has been a central concern of the just-war tradition. Although sea-going vessels have, since prehistoric times, brought war to civilian populations, the aircraft introduced true mobility and flexibility to the military forces of a nation wishing to strike behind the front lines, and thus has provided the potential for bringing the physical violence of war to every citizen of the state against which the war is being waged. An aircraft employed to release bombs or to fire guns can be directed to military targets only, but its mobility and flexibility add an enormous degree of power (and temptation) that must be dealt with by the decision maker.

During World War II, since prior efforts to negotiate an arms-control agreement respecting the use of aircraft had failed, the availability of large airplanes and Germany's developments in rocket technology made possible the direct bombing of large numbers of civilians by both sides. In addition, an ancient weapon—fire—was coupled to the aircraft in the form of incendiary bombs; when these were applied in sufficient numbers over a very short period to Dresden and Hamburg, they caused the entire city centers to be consumed in fire storms as many small, localized fires merged into areal fires, which fed on all combustible material available and sucked in oxygen from the surrounding areas for support.[6] The resultant devastation was so great that it must be concluded that the term "weapon of mass destruction" should be applied to incendiary bombs when used in such a manner. The same term should probably also be applied to the saturation bombing of urban areas, such as occurred against the civilian center of London during the Blitz. Regardless of terminology, it seems almost impossible to argue that such applications of force were discriminate, although it may be possible to justify them on grounds of proportionality.

The seeds of these technical "advances" in aircraft, rocketry, and incendiary bombs bore fruit in the initial development and use of nuclear weapons and in their subsequent refinements. From the primitive fission bombs used against Hiroshima and Nagasaki at the end of World War II, we have "progressed" to today's vastly more powerful thermonuclear weapons, which add the explosive release of the energy of the fusion of the heavy isotopes of hydrogen to that of nuclear fission. Such explosives are deliverable by intercontinental-range ballistic missiles (ICBMs) and their submarine-launched counterparts (SLBMs) as well as by the shorter-range missiles and gravity bombs which constitute the payload of aircraft.

The indiscriminate use of incendiary bombs against cities required an attack using many individual weapons delivered by many individual bombers; a *single* nuclear weapon, even of the primitive kinds that were used against Hiroshima and Nagasaki, is sufficient to cause a like amount of indiscriminate destruction. And there is an additional consideration: besides blast and heat, any nuclear explosion produces radioactivity, whose effects on the people exposed to it can endure a lifetime and perhaps even into future generations. As with chemical agents, this radioactivity predictably but uncontrollably moves outside the target area. It can, therefore, even affect the attacker; indeed, to some extent it ultimately is distributed in the global environment. (While the question of the effects of radioactivity at very low levels is still open to dispute, most current calculations are based on the assumption that exposure to any radiation in addition to that resulting from the natural background radioactivity may have harmful effects.)

In sum, the nuclear weapon must be considered a weapon of mass destruction, or a weapon capable of being used to cause mass destruction.[7] Although one might argue that *very* low-yield nuclear weapons which might produce *very* small amounts of fallout are "precision" weapons,[8] most of the nuclear weapons in the arsenals of the nuclear powers today undoubtedly have destructive power equal to, if not many times greater than, those which caused such great devastation at Hiroshima and Nagasaki.[9] Moreover, it can be predicted that the effects of a nuclear weapon will be experienced over an uncertainly large area. The employment of nuclear weapons, at least in any considerable numbers, thus directly raises the issue of proportionality, which the just-war tradition requires as a necessary criterion for use. Clearly, any use of nuclear weapons to destroy urban population centers must also be enormously difficult, if not impossible, to justify in terms of the criterion of discrimination.

The development of all these weapons of mass destruction—chemical and biological agents, incendiary and saturation bombing, and nuclear weapons—has clearly changed the destructive power available to both military and political leaders. This additional power is sufficient to suggest that a difference in kind as well as degree has been introduced. That is, the new capability for destruction is so different from what was possible before that it must be treated under a new set of moral categories, a situation like that which required a new set of physical laws to explain the behavior of subatomic particles when the laws describing the motions of the planets were found to be insufficient.

THE GROWTH OF ARMS CONTROL AND DISARMAMENT MEASURES

More or less concurrent with the evolution of weapons of mass destruction have been a number of efforts to restrain qualitative and quantitative additions to the destructive capabilities of man. Recent successful examples include (1) the Anti-Ballistic Missile (ABM) Treaty, bilaterally negotiated between the United States and the Soviet Union in 1972, which prohibits the deployment of more than two hundred (now one hundred by terms of the 1975 Protocol to the Treaty) ABMs by each side, and which also prohibits the development, testing, and deployment of air-, space-, and sea-based ABMs; and (2) the 1974 "Threshold" Test Ban Treaty between the same two states, which will limit the underground testing of nuclear weapons to yields no greater than 150 kilotons when it enters into force.[10]

A different approach has been successful in limiting the possession of biological weapons. The Geneva Protocol of 1925, mentioned in the previous section, prohibits their use. In 1969, the United States took a unilateral decision to renounce both its stockpiles of such weapons and its intention to develop them any further; subsequently, there was successful negotiation, in 1971, of the Biological Weapons Convention, which prohibits the development, production, and stockpiling of biological agents or toxins and weapons designed to use them. More than sixty states are now parties to the Convention, which thereby enjoys wide adherence.

Other important formal agreements also aim at controlling the level of destructive capability in the world. In addition to the four agreements previously discussed, there are treaties prohibiting nuclear weapons in the Antarctic (1959) (more precisely, in this treaty, any measures of a military nature), in Latin America (1967), in outer space (1967), and on the seabed (1972), the Limited Test Ban Treaty (1963), the 1972 Interim Agreement resulting from the first set of Strategic Arms Limitation Talks (SALT), and the Nuclear Non-Proliferation Treaty (1970).[11] With the conclusion of SALT II, the world may see "the beginning of the end" in a more definitive sense than before if, at this stage of the SALT process, there is a meaningful limitation on total numbers of strategic nuclear weapon systems. If there is a SALT III in the coming years, it would presumably bring about further qualitative constraints and an actual reduction in the numbers of nuclear weapons. A comprehensive ban on underground nuclear explosions, to complete the limitations imposed by the Limited and the "Threshold" Test Ban Treaties, would provide a further qualitative restraint on the evolution of nuclear weapons.

All these agreements—completed and contemplated—point in the direction of reversing the world's course of continued reliance on weapons of mass destruction for security. If this process can be sustained and furthered, if all nuclear powers become involved, and if the proliferation of nuclear weapons is arrested, then we may be beginning to redress the awful imbalance of scale between ordinary human life and the level of destructive capability that weapons of mass destruction represent. But there is still much work to be done. At present, despite the real successes embodied in the arms control and disarmament agreements negotiated to date, the level of destructive capability continues to increase, rather than to decrease. So far these agreements have served only to slow this process; they have not yet reversed it.

RATIONALES FOR WEAPONS OF MASS DESTRUCTION

Although several kinds of weapons of mass destruction have been developed and deployed, and arms-control and disarmament agreements have been negotiated respecting many of these kinds of weapons, only for nuclear weapons has a large body of doctrine evolved regarding their possession and declaratory policy on their use. This section briefly surveys this body by contrasting the divergent views and their historical relationship. I see no reason why such views could not also be related to other weapons of mass destruction than nuclear weapons.

In the fifteen years following World War II, as first the United States and then the Soviet Union began to acquire sizable numbers of nuclear weapons, the declaratory policy regarding their use, at least for the United States, could be described as the threat of "massive retaliation." (I have placed the words inside quotation marks because they represent a pole or extreme of doctrinal thinking perhaps more than an actual policy of a real government.[12]) It was not necessary to state explicitly that the policy of "massive retaliation" would result in nuclear weapons being used against the civilian population of an adversary, nor even that the retaliation would necessarily include the use of nuclear weapons. Rather it could be inferred that nuclear weapons would be used in retaliation to a provocation. Moreover, the underlying policy was directed as much against conventional attack on Western Europe by the Warsaw Pact countries, and against adventurism in Asia by the Soviet Union and the People's Republic of China, as against a direct nuclear attack on the United States or its allies.

The rationale assumed for the possession of nuclear weapons under such a doctrine of massive retaliation was that they provided a guaranteed capability to respond to provocations in an overwhelming fashion by destroying much of an adversary's assets and that thereby they would deter such provocations. The concept is also known as deterrence by assured destruction, mutual assured destruction (U.S. versus U.S.S.R.), or as countervalue deterrence.

The opposite pole of doctrinal thinking about deterrence of and by weapons capable of mass destruction is perhaps best characterized by the term counterforce. Such a deterrence threatens retaliation by nuclear weapons in a manner more nearly like conventional weapons; part of the declaratory policy is an explicit identification of military targets as the principal objective to be struck. In this sense, weapons of mass destruction appear to be on a more continuous spectrum of the level of force with conventional weapons such as machine guns, artillery, or high-explosive bombs, and the treatment of weapons of mass destruction as being different in kind is not a particularly relevant concept.

This quite different approach to deterrence is perhaps best

enunciated in the well-known 1962 Ann Arbor speech by then Secretary of Defense Robert McNamara.[13] In considering this development, it is important to realize that by the time of that statement the military situation with respect to nuclear weapons had changed considerably from what it had been at the end of World War II and even in the middle 1950s when the declaratory policy of "massive retaliation" was set out. Even at the later date, the United States still had a clear preponderance of nuclear weapons; there had been, moreover, no need to accept the possibility of a high level of destruction of targets within the United States by the Soviet Union. While the threat of widespread civilian deaths was real, it was not then so explicit: the delivery of nuclear weapons was carried out by long-range bombers with reaction times measured in hours; they had the capability of pinpoint bombing accuracy; and there was the possibility of an effective air defense. But by 1962 Soviet destruction could presumably be visited upon the United States by ICBMs armed with thermonuclear warheads and possessing a flight time of about one-half hour. Since they were not accurate enough to be targeted against missile silos, their presumed targets would be cities, a situation which made the involvement of urban civilians, completely unconnected with any military force-in-being and utterly defenseless, a much more stark possibility.

Thus a declaratory policy of a response concentrating on military targets (presumably a response flexible enough to employ the amount of force necessary to achieve the military objective) could be construed as an attempt to reduce the possibility of a massive attack on the population of the United States by giving the opponent the understanding that less-than-all-out attacks would be met with less-than-all-out responses. Nevertheless, if such a lower-level response failed, the threat of all-out (massive) retaliation remained the "ace in the hole" upon which deterrence rested.

During the decade after McNamara's speech, the proposals he had put forth were not implemented in any detail. As nearly as could be discerned, the declaratory policy of the United States reverted to one of massive retaliation; indeed, as ballistic missiles were introduced into the strategic forces, it became more and more a policy of instantaneous retaliation against unspecified, but presumably areal (i.e., civilian) targets.[14] (While the concept of massive retaliation was described in terms of the *capability* of carrying out a certain level of destruction, I am not aware of any specific target or specific set of targets ever discussed publicly by U.S. officials. On the other hand, it is clear that the declaratory policy envisioned the possibility of the destruction of cities.[15])

At the close of the 1960s the rationale for possession of and declaratory policy concerning use of nuclear weapons was again brought into focus by the "ABM debate"; the question was whether to attempt to defend certain U.S. cities against ballistic missile attack by deploying anti-ballistic missiles, armed with nuclear warheads, to destroy incoming warheads. The technical difficulties of doing this in an effective manner, plus the political controversy over the wisdom of attempting to do so, finally led to reorientation of the ABM program. Emphasis was changed to defense of ICBM silos, so that in the event of a first strike with nuclear weapons against the United States enough ICBMs would be preserved to guarantee the possibility of retaliation.

Behind the considerations of the ABM debate were the assumptions that an attack on the United States would be sudden and massive, and that the response by the United States would be instantaneous and massive. This represented a return to a declaratory policy of deterrence by threat of massive retaliation. The difference from the statements of the 1950s was that the nature of the threat being deterred had become preeminently the possibility of the Soviet Union inflicting upon the United States (presumably first) the same type of damage that the United States was capable of visiting upon the Soviet Union (presumably in retaliation). The possibility of a "massive" U.S. response (and subsequent counterattack by the U.S.S.R.) to a conventional attack on Western Europe remained, but by now the famous 7,000 nuclear weapons designated for "tactical" use there were very much an established part of U.S. policy for dealing with the threat of attack against the NATO alliance, creating at least the possibility of avoiding the involvement of U.S. cities in the aftermath of a Western (nuclear) counterattack against an invasion by the Warsaw Pact countries.

At present, the question of a rationale for deterrence which, as a declaratory policy, incorporates a flexible response to provocation has again arisen, this time in the context of the retargeting policies announced in 1974 by then Secretary of Defense James Schlesinger.[16] The basis for this new policy is essentially the same as that underlying the 1962 McNamara statement.[17] The primary point seems to be introducing into the declaratory policy several possible levels of response below (or alongside) immediate commitment of a large fraction of the U.S. nuclear arsenal to the destruction of areal targets of the adversary. The flexible response or counterforce policy suggests that such lower level response would be directed primarily against military targets. However, a massive attack on the United States must continue to be deterred, and the threat of massive retaliation (assured destruction, countervalue response) continues to be viewed as the deterrent against this sort of attack.

ETHICAL QUESTIONS RAISED BY WEAPONS OF MASS DESTRUCTION

In light of the present world situation and of how we have come to it, as sketched above, what can be said, in ethical terms, about: (1) the continued possession of weapons of mass destruction; (2) declaratory policy toward their use; and (3) actual use of them; as well as (4) efforts to control, reduce, and eventually eliminate them?

At a minimum, these questions should be evaluated in the light of those ethical elements which constitute the just-war tradition. But I believe that these weapons' capacity for *mass* destruction necessitates the consideration of other ethical elements as well in order to address these questions adequately. In other words, weapons of mass destruction have sufficiently changed the world that they require a new ethical framework for their evaluation.

The just-war tradition has, in the past, governed the decision to use violence in a conflict between two independent and sovereign states, and, once war was begun, the manner in which that violence was used. To summarize the criteria, the war is just: (1) if the decision to prosecute it is taken by duly constituted authority; (2) if the intention is a good one; (3) if the use of force is proportional to the aims of the war; (4) if the force is used in a discriminate fashion (i.e., if it is limited to the combatants and excludes the civilian population); (5) if the expected end result is a situation better than that expected if force were not used (i.e., if success is expected); and (6) if all other means to resolve the dispute or problem have been tried and have failed.[18] It is important to note that these considerations are limitations,[19] not permissive prescriptions. The general position which they embody is one of abhorrence of any use of force; if force must be used, it is to be bounded severely. *All* of the criteria must be satisfied.

Nevertheless, the just-war tradition is prescriptive for when and how to resort to the use of force. But a situation in which the very application of the force in question might not be possible in *any* just manner was never contemplated. Moreover, since weapons of mass destruction had not been developed when the criteria were developed, the tradition never addressed the questions of whether it is right to possess and to have a declaratory policy on the use of, much less actually to use, weapons capable of mass destruction. Neither is it intended to be normative for the effort to better a situation of ongoing "peace," such as the world experiences today.

If war should begin, the just-war criterion of proportionality, as I have noted above, might apply in dealing with the use of weapons of mass destruction, to the extent that one can *define* an acceptable outcome of a war as being his own survival, even at the expense of the existence of the other state. But, as I also stated, the test of discrimination is much more questionable—in fact I do not believe that it can, in general, be met by weapons of mass destruction, because their use invariably runs the predictable risk of involving noncombatant civilians of the adversary state, as well as innocent bystanders to the conflict. Even if only one or two nuclear weapons are used, a firebreak will have been breached, and in such circumstances the risk of an avalanche of destruction from the further use of nuclear weapons would appear to be much greater. While such use might still cause a greater or lesser degree of destruction, and therefore be "better" or "worse," the relative merits of such a use can be considered "ethical" only by some dim caricature of ethics. The imagination cannot adequately comprehend this scene, since it is almost impossible to think through beforehand a judgment on values involving these levels of destruction. Moreover, the survivors, to whom the judgment might make a difference, might hardly care, so awful would the circumstances be.

In light of this bleak prospect for ethical distinctions once nuclear weapons are used in any quantities, and in light of the importance of avoiding the necessity for making them, it seems to me that the primary question for ethical choice today is not so much the question of how to use nuclear weapons if the world again reaches such a sad state of affairs, but rather how to get from our present situation to a better future without resorting to the use of weapons of mass destruction in the process.

In examining this primary question for ethical choice, there are five elements which I believe must be factored into our considerations, in addition to those of the just-war tradition. These are

1. The magnitude of the destructive power of weapons of mass destruction in relation to the ordinary scale of human activity
2. Stability in international relations
3. Technological change and its control
4. The paradox of non-proliferation
5. Evolution in political organization

Let us proceed to some reflections on these proposed additional criteria.

The magnitude of destructive power. This element is related to the traditional criteria of discrimination and proportionality. Weapons in earlier times had the (small) virtue of at least being understandable in terms of everyday human events. The range and firepower of even a weapon as destructive as a tank can be understood, without much mental extrapolation, from considering the range and firepower of a man on horseback carrying a spear. But the concept of a missile, five thousand miles away, capable of delivering, within the space of thirty minutes, complete devastation of an area measured in tens of square miles is so alien to the imagination that to comprehend it as a human event is difficult. And, therefore, to comprehend the moral issue posed by the possibility of destruction on this scale is difficult as well. Worse, it is not a question simply of imagining one city held hostage by one missile, but of attempting to comprehend thousands of such targets and weapons. Thus, the ethical issues involved in the retention of such capability, in rationales for a declaratory policy regarding its use, and in its actual use cannot be readily treated in normal moral terms. It is, therefore, necessary to be exceptionally tentative with respect to decisions which would perpetuate a situation so removed from the normal human scale. Further, the magnitude of destructive power suggests a heightened sense of urgency to the task of reducing the probability of using such power and of removing it as an operative force in world affairs.

Stability and international relations. The moral element of stability in international relations lies in whether such stability is a good thing for the world. Stability is much in vogue at present as a goal of strategic policy, since its opposite is thought to heighten the chances that nuclear weapons might actually be used. For example, analysts speak of stabilizing or destabilizing the U.S.-Soviet military relationship by the acquisition of a weapon system. But morally one must weigh this concern for stability against other possible consequences of this action in reinforcing the present international organization of the world. What is the moral value of a balance of terror?

Evidently the world is better off if the current arsenal of nuclear weapons is not used. It can, therefore, be argued that a declaratory policy which diminishes the likelihood that nuclear weapons will be used is, other things being equal, a better policy because it will lead to a more stable world and one freer of the threat of its own self-destruction. To say "other things being equal," however, assumes a great deal. To a poor peasant in an oppressed land, the concept of a stable balance of terror may not be worth a fig leaf since from his perspective the question at hand is securing the elementary requisites of life—food, clothing, shelter, education, and human rights. Nevertheless, on balance, the destructiveness of nuclear weapons would appear to warrant strenuous efforts to prevent the shaky relationships that currently pass for stability in international relations from worsening; indeed, it is clear that an elementary stability in these relations is necessary to allow states to resolve, in time, the antagonisms which have caused them to acquire and threaten to use nuclear weapons in the first place.[20]

Technological change. One stumbling block to stability has been the degree to which technology has provided a basis for the destructive power of weapons of mass destruction to be increased—both qualitatively and quantitatively—over the space of three decades. If it is assumed that the acquisition of nuclear weapons by any state is in itself undesirable because it increases instability in the world as a whole, and diminishes all nations' security (an assumption with which I am in agreement), then it must be concluded that the more such weapons are developed (which implies perpetuation of possession), the worse off the world is.

The need to bring an end to the further technological development of weapons of mass destruction is widely recognized and has been partially embodied in the existing complex of modern arms control agreements. In order to help complete this task, it remains for future agreements to control chemical weapons' production and stockpiling, stop the testing of nuclear explosives, control the testing of strategic nuclear weapon delivery systems, and set a ceiling on the total number of these delivery systems.

There is, however, another side to the question of technological change. Some analysts argue that some technological developments move toward making nuclear weapons more "discriminating," or perhaps more capable of use in a proportional manner, or less vulnerable and, therefore, more conducive to stability. On this point in particular opinions differ depending on which end of the spectrum of strategic rationales—countervalue or counterforce—is preferred by the analyst. I shall return to this point in the next section.

Moreover, there is an inevitable tension between the assumption that the most modern technologies must be used for the weapons which constitute a state's arsenal, and the assumption implicit in the enterprise of arms control that security is better served by finding a means to end this modernization. If the second assumption is correct and successful policies based thereon are implemented, an inevitable change in the role that force plays in international affairs lies at the end of the process. Imagine for a moment how dominant a role in international affairs violence would currently play if, in 1920, a fully verified arms-control agreement had been negotiated prohibiting all submarines and all military aircraft save for unarmed reconnaissance airplanes. Further, imagine that all test explosions of nuclear devices had been successfully prohibited after August 1945. Now project this sort of imagining three decades into the future, when technology which could be applicable to weapons is not likely to have remained frozen at 1976 levels. Such an exercise suggests that if the current efforts at controlling weapons of mass destruction prove to stand the test of time, and if technology in the civilian sector progresses at anywhere near the rate it has over the past thirty years, by the end of the century the relative role of force may be greatly diminished simply because the technology applied to weapons will have been restrained to a level no longer considered modern. That, I believe, would change the moral value of weapons of mass destruction in a positive direction. The relevance of conventional weapons might also be lessened if the nuclear weapons states led the way in negotiating agreements restraining their own capabilities at the upper end of the spectrum of possible violence. Indeed, the control of technological change in weapons development could lead to the conclusion that most uses of violence in international relations should be prohibited pursuant to reliable agreement.

The paradox of non-proliferation. The fourth new element having importance for an ethical evaluation of weapons of mass destruction is a paradox originating in the fact that nuclear weapons and other weapons capable of mass destruction are not universally possessed by states. It is all to the good that such weapons have not spread any further than they have because this state of affairs enhances the possibility of eventually freeing the world of them altogether. Yet a non-nuclear weapon state can plausibly argue that, from the standpoint of deterrence, it is being discriminated against, insofar as it cannot deter the use of nuclear weapons against itself. Thus the dilemma: if deterrence is legitimate, it should be legitimate for each sovereign state in the world; the fact of possessing weapons should not make a fundamental difference to the application of ethical principles insofar as the use, or deterrence of use, of force is concerned. On the other hand, it seems clear that the larger the number of states that acquire nuclear weapons (or chemical weapons for that matter) the greater the danger that eventually they will be used again and, therefore, the less are the long-range prospects for the success of deterrence. It would, therefore, appear either that the possession of such weapons is wrong per se and should be ended, or, if it is somehow right, that the world must suffer both the eventual universal acquisition of weapons of mass destruction and the attendant danger that sooner or later such weapons will be used.

The real world, of course, does not fit easily into these abstract notions. Nations are not equal, and ethical considerations are not likely to redress imbalances by themselves. I believe, however, that this dilemma of equal treatment with respect to ensuring security for supposedly sovereign and independent states can be resolved only by continuing and strengthening the policy of nonproliferation of weapons of mass destruction, since this policy is inevitably the more correct one from a standpoint of ethics. The necessary corollary (imposed by the fact of discrimination) is the moral necessity resting on states already possessing such weapons to adopt policies that reduce the reliance of any nation on such weapons for security. The nuclear weapon states party to the Non-Proliferation Treaty of 1970 implicitly recognized this corollary when they pledged themselves, in Article VI, to seek an end to the nuclear arms race and eventually general and complete disarmament.[21]

Evolution in political organization. The last "new" ethical element, implicit in much of the preceding discussion, is the necessity of adopting an evolutionary approach to history, at least with respect to how mankind is organized at the international level. It is possible to argue, proceeding from an evolutionary point of view, that humanity, grouped for the moment into nations, may not have to rely forever on the threat of using weapons of mass destruction in order to prevent their use.

The technology of mass destruction has brought about an inconsistency between the capabilities of the world's political organization and the morality with which international affairs are conducted. In terms of both knowledge and physical possession, weapons of mass destruction have rendered the ideas of independence and sovereignty suspect, but the international structure has not yet proven capable of bringing these weapons under effective control. In face of the *knowledge* of weapons of mass destruction, can present political arrangements between nations be sustained without reliance on the *possession* of these weapons for the security of (some of) the member states? Is it even possible within these arrangements to work out reliable measures for proceeding from the present situation to a future more desirable one in which the threat of mass destruction plays a diminished or nonexistent role (even though the knowledge about such destructive power cannot itself be destroyed)?

The answers to these questions cannot be known definitively at present, but clearly if current efforts to control weapons capable of mass destruction can be sustained and furthered, and if the other nuclear powers can become involved, and if proliferation is arrested, then, within a relatively short time, the world may begin to experience the actual implementation of a conscious decision to reject at least the upper reaches of organized violence inherent in the possession of weapons capable of mass destruction. This phenomenon would be such a revolutionary phenomenon for mankind that we can hope that inherent in it would be the seeds of the vision necessary for choosing a proper course of action for the future development of humanity's political organization, in particular if this would involve the replacement of the present structure of 150 nations, all (in theory) equal and independent. For the moment, it would appear that working within the present framework of arms-control forums offers the best hope for progress in the effort that could produce this revolution.

The abolition of slavery may serve as an example for those who would lose patience. Less than twelve decades ago it was still practiced as an accepted institution in much of the United States. Weapons of mass destruction have been on the world scene for roughly half that time, and nuclear weapons for only a quarter. But I do not believe the eradication of nuclear weapons and other mass-destruction weapons will take humanity the long centuries required to abolish slavery. In fact, biological weapons have been effectively eradicated, and progress has been made toward the same end in dealing with nuclear weapons.

To summarize, these five new elements, together with the just-war criteria, must be taken into account in seeking an answer to the crucial ethical question of how best to bring about the goals of preventing the use of and abolishing weapons of mass destruction. If these weapons are, in fact, used, although there may still be a semblance of ethics in arguing that it is better to kill "only" several millions instead of several hundreds of millions of persons, deterrence will be worth about as much as the Maginot Line. Worse, it is difficult to imagine how, after such a failure, it would be possible to deter the next use and the next millions of deaths. Deterrence can be said, finally, to have succeeded only if it leads to a world free from the presence of weapons of mass destruction. And the elaboration of an ethical framework which hastens the outcome of a world thus freed appears to me to be the most important ethical enterprise of those involved in attempting to come to grips with the possession, declaratory policy, and actual use of weapons of mass destruction. These five new elements, I believe, are relevant to building such a framework, in a world whose knowledge and technology allow nations to possess these weapons.

THE MORAL DIMENSION OF DETERRENCE AND DECLARATORY POLICY

In this section, I further discuss declaratory policy on the use of weapons of mass destruction, particularly the policy of massive retaliation or assured destruction, in light of an ethical framework expanded to include my five new elements in addition to those of the just-war tradition. To do so, however, requires some additional discussion of the ethics of the actual use of weapons of mass destruction and the ethics of possessing these weapons in the first place.

Assuming that nuclear weapons or other weapons of mass destruction are possessed and a decision is taken to use them, then deterrence has failed. The term "deterrence" is taken to mean prevention of the massive use of force that is potentially available in the arsenals of weapons possessed by the United States, the U.S.S.R., and other powers. "Deterrence" can be formulated in much broader terms, of course, since there are other actions that states wish to prevent, such as conventionally armed attack on Western Europe, or renewed hostilities in the Middle East. But given the fact that weapons of mass destruction (and the knowledge and materials needed to produce them) are not a monopoly, the most important problem is how to prevent the emergence or the continuation of conditions in international relations that would precipitate any use of such weapons, or, at the very least, their use on a large scale.

It seems unquestionable that, if nuclear weapons are used upon the failure of deterrence, then, *at least up to some level,* we are better off the fewer that are used, the lower their yields, the less radioactivity they produce, and the fewer the casualties they cause. But even up to that level, as discussed in the preceding section, it is extremely difficult to make a case that the actual use of nuclear weapons would meet the criteria of discrimination and proportionality, in particular if such use were directed against cities; use would involve indiscriminate elements (radioactivity being the inescapable one) and also might be disproportionate to any good to be achieved. (One might argue that the use of a single nuclear weapon in an isolated instance to destroy the missile silo of an adversary—including a missile, one hopes—would be acceptable morally even taking these factors into account. I doubt, however, that such a possible use is a very realistic one.[22]) And *above some level* of release of nuclear explosive energy, with its associated products of blast, heat, and radioactivity, the resulting damage may be visited upon humanity as a whole. This level is probably not precisely quantifiable, but it is clear from present knowledge about the consequences of nuclear explosions that any use involving thousands of weapons would appear to be unjustifiable, regardless of the scale of provocation.[23] It might also not make much difference to the survivors whether more or fewer weapons were used. And even if such a use of nuclear weapons were to avoid altogether targeting urban populations and the "infrastructure" of human society—art treasures, universities, historical sites—the exposure of people who have no relation whatever to the hostilities to environmental, somatic, and genetic effects resulting from the exchange would itself appear to render this level of use morally unacceptable.

But a more basic ethical problem lies in the assumption upon which my consideration of the ethics of actual use is based: Science and technology now being available to permit their possession, weapons of mass destruction are physically in the possession of several nations. One can further assume that such weapons are a permanent fixture of human "civilization" and then seek to evaluate ethically both how to use them and how best to avoid their use. *Or*, one can assume that the physical possession of such weapons is an evil that must be tolerated *temporarily*, and, in addition to evaluating their use, one can, more importantly perhaps, evaluate alternative policies for deterrence *using the perspective of seeking an end to the need for deterrence*. Such an evaluation would balance the evil of threatening use against the relative potentiality of various deterrence strategies for maintaining international stability as a political context which permits careful negotiation for the gradual elimination of weapons of mass destruction. It is from this latter perspective that the following paragraphs discuss what then becomes an interim declaratory policy of deterrence.

My proposal here is that ethicians need to think of weapons of mass destruction in a different fashion, a fashion that includes the political utility of the possession of such weapons in bringing about their non-use. In previous ages, just-war theorists have discussed the political and moral criteria which govern the resort to arms and their subsequent utilization. The just-war tradition served as a politico-moral doctrine for the *military* use or non-use of arms. At present it appears necessary to elaborate an ethical structure for deterrence which would establish criteria governing the *political* use or non-use of weapons of mass destruction.

Important to an understanding and moral evaluation of a deterrence policy which relies on the capability for assured destruction of another country—in particular the destruction of its population and the industrial base—is the awareness that nuclear weapons and other weapons of mass destruction are in some sense different in kind from other weapons. (In the case of incendiaries, the difference lies in use *en masse*, as opposed to an isolated application of the basic weapon.) This awareness is exploited in measuring the capability in terms that have no proportion to immediate military goals—population or industrial assets. Furthermore, deterrence by threat of massive retaliation takes into account the fact that, at present, numbers of weapons of mass destruction exist in the arsenals of several states, not just one. The deterrence policy attempts to respond to the existence of such arsenals by threatening, in response to sufficient provocation, destruction at *some* level, ranging up to damage that is overwhelming in its magnitude and that corresponds to the power of these essentially different weapons.

In ethical consideration of declaratory policy, it seems to me that the most important feature of assured destruction deserving ethical consideration is the ambiguity inherent in this policy: The adversary cannot be certain of the intended targets or the level of actual response. In this fashion, the policy would appear to meet the ethical criteria of the just-war tradition by leaving unsaid what the actual targets might be in a response using weapons of mass destruction, despite the fact that the capability might be measured in terms of ability to destroy a certain level of population or industrial assets. (Alternative policies of deterrence by assured destruction are possible: for example, a threat of a certain and all-out response to any attack by an adversary, however limited. But if such a variant of the threat specifically aims to destroy cities, it seems morally unjustifiable on the grounds that the criterion of discrimination, at least, is violated.)

At the other end of the spectrum of declaratory policy is the concept of flexible response, which suggests that a limited provocation will be met with a limited response and a more massive provocation will warrant a more massive response. This approach of more precisely correlating the size of the response to the size of the provocation appears to be based on an assumption that the destructiveness of nuclear weapons and other weapons of mass destruction exhibits much more of a continuity with the destructiveness of conventional weapons than advocates of the concept of assured destruction will admit. Moreover, the discussion of this policy generally assumes, in the "eye-for-an-eye" sort of response it envisages, that the adversary will initially attack military targets. But if the adversary attacks "only" one or two civilian targets (for example, New York and Los Angeles), the announced limited response would have to be against a different kind of target if the declaratory policy is to avoid the same ethical difficulty confronting an explicit threat to attack cities in the assured destruction policy (that the contemplated response would be indiscriminate).

Proponents of assured destruction such as Herbert Scoville[24] argue, in addition, that a flexible response approach involves a greater risk that nuclear weapons may actually be used in conflict, because the explicit threat of their use at a lower level seems more plausible and, therefore, more likely. And, they argue, because nuclear weapons are weapons of mass destruction, any such limited use would exacerbate the risk that the control of their use would break down, with the parties to the conflict arriving (perhaps even more rapidly) at the same level of destruction than if they had initially relied on a declaratory policy of assured destruction.

It seems clear to me that the ethical considerations governing the possession of and declaratory policy for the use of nuclear weapons in peacetime are not those which would govern their actual use in time of war. Proceeding in this vein, the primary ethical attraction of the declaratory policy of assured destruction, considered apart from the ethics of actually using weapons of mass destruction (which would engender admitted and enormous evils), is that by this policy the use of such weapons can more likely be avoided. It preserves a respect for the "quantum jump" between use of conventional weapons and weapons of mass destruction, and it facilitates the process of controlling and eventually eliminating the military threats against which the threat of the use of nuclear weapons is the deterrent. Moreover, the ambiguity in terms of which the threatened response is set forth preserves the moral possibility that, if deterrence fails, use of nuclear weapons will be minimized.

A proponent of a declaratory policy based on flexible response need not disagree with a proponent of assured destruction over how to assign ethical priorities for specific steps toward controlling and eliminating weapons of mass destruction. What ethical differences are there, then, between the adherents of these opposite ends of the declaratory policy spectrum?

First, advocates of flexible response cite the immorality of threatening to attack civilians directly as a reason to declare a preference for targeting military assets. It seems to me that assured destruction must indeed avoid this noncombatant threat, as can be done by remaining ambiguous as to intended targets. Second, if the implementation of the flexible response approach requires improved weapons systems, this corollary, which implies further delay in abolishing these weapons, constitutes a moral liability of the policy. This disadvantage can only be justified by demonstrating some foreseen advantage in terms of security (such as an advantage in arms-control negotiations). In other words, proponents must show that if their policy requires new weapons[25] these would be a more valuable contribution to preventing the use of weapons of mass destruction than a policy which does not require any new such weapons. To the extent that flexible-response arguments for increased or refined weaponry constitute an obstacle to negotiating arms limitation agreements (which the weaponry is sometimes aimed at influencing in the first place!), I believe the moralist will be led to conclude that assured destruction would be the preferable approach to deterrence. A third ethical consideration is presented by the argument that a flexible-response policy will help to restore deterrence if it fails, or to prevent a partial failure of deterrence from becoming complete. Finally, the effect of such a policy on the proliferation of weapons of mass destruction must be evaluated. Not much has been developed in the literature on the moral factors involved in the last two points.[26]

In sum, the differences between the two approaches center on the questions of how to improve deterrence, and how to move *beyond* deterrence by working, in peacetime, to reduce the possibility of using weapons of mass destruction, and ultimately to eliminate it (currently, at least, by achieving substantive international arms-control agreements).

The assured-destruction position can be viewed as resting on the claim that a capability to inflict the defined level of damage, stated in ambiguous terms with respect to what the actual policy of implementation will or might be, gives the best means of allowing movement toward the goal of security without reliance on weapons of mass destruction, because it does not require further technical developments which could move in the opposite direction—higher yield weapons, more weapons, the threat of a first strike. From this standpoint, the flexible response position can be viewed as deficient to the extent: (1) that it mandates new technological developments which increase the adversary's perception of a first-strike threat to himself; (2) that it prolongs the time before an upper limit can be placed on total weapons capabilities or a reduction begun in these capabilities; and finally (3) that it suggests a lower threshold for initiating the use of nuclear weapons in a conflict. Given these factors, the concept of deterrence by assured destruction appears, on balance, to have a structure that makes it an ethically defensible position from which to work toward the goal of eliminating the need for deterrence.

CONCLUSION

In the final analysis, do ethical judgments really play a role in what to do about weapons of mass destruction? Without doubt, the answer is an affirmative one. Moral judgments—judgments of value—were made in electing to develop, test, and produce nuclear, chemical, and biological weapons and exploit them for political and security purposes. The same kind of judgment has been and will be made in electing to regulate, reduce, and eliminate these weapons as factors in international relations.

This paper has described an ethical structure which builds on, but goes beyond, the just-war tradition and which provides a solution to the problem of how to justify the *temporary* possession of weapons of mass destruction. Within this structure, it appears that a case can be made for a declaratory policy of deterrence which relies on a capability to carry out assured destruction, provided that the threat to do so is stated in ambiguous terms.

However, the five new elements in this ethical structure—the magnitude of destructive power, stability, technological change, non-proliferation, and evolution in political organization—lead directly to the conclusion that weapons of mass destruction must be eliminated in as short a time as possible. This conclusion, not an answer to the question of what declaratory policy is better, is the one that ought to be foremost in the mind of thinker and practitioner alike.

NOTES

1. These elements are discussed further below; see also Francis Winters, "Ethics, Diplomacy and Defense," in this volume. More complete descriptions of the just-war tradition are suggested in the bibliography.
2. See Philip Noel-Baker, *The Arms Race: A Programme for World Disarmament* (London: Atlantic Books, 1958), especially chapter 28, "What Are the Weapons of Mass Destruction?" pp. 315–19. In addition, the Outer Space Treaty, Article IV, prohibits the orbiting and the stationing in outer space of "nuclear weapons or any other kinds of weapons of mass destruction." The Seabed Treaty, Article I, contains a similar prohibition with respect to the ocean floor. The preamble of the Biological Weapons Convention refers to weapons of mass destruction "using chemical or bacteriological (biological) agents." For text of the treaties see note 4 below.
3. Frederic J. Brown, *Chemical Warfare: A Study in Restraints* (Princeton, N.J.: Princeton University Press, 1968), pp. 200–22.
4. A useful source book for treaty texts is *Arms Control and Disarmament Agreements: Texts and History of Negotiations*, U.S. Arms Control and Disarmament Agency Publication 77 (Washington, D.C.: U.S. Government Printing Office, February 1975).
5. Regarding efforts to control aircraft, see "Air Warfare," Chapter IVA in L. Oppenheim, *International Law*, H. Lauterpacht, ed., 7th ed. (London: Longmans, Green and Co., 1952), 2: 516–33; and Trevor N. Dupuy and Gary M. Hammerman, eds., *A Documentary History of Arms Control and Disarmament* (New York: R. R. Bowker Company, 1973), sections 33, 58.
6. See SIPRI [Stockholm International Peace Research Institute], *Incendiary Weapons* (Cambridge, Mass.: MIT Press, 1975), p. 81.

7. As stated in note 2, these are the terms in which the Outer Space Treaty and the Seabed Treaty define nuclear weapons.

8. But see J. B. Knox, T. V. Crawford, and W. K. Crandall, *Potential Exposures from Low-Yield Free Air Bursts*, Lawrence Livermore Laboratory Report UCRL-51164 (University of California, Livermore, Calif., 1971). This report discusses potentially high dose rates from even a one kiloton all-fission air burst at distances on the order of 100 kilometers.

9. For a revised estimate of casualties at Hiroshima and Nagasaki and a description of increased mortality in the population exposed to these bombs even today, see *New Scientist* (April 15, 1976): 115.

10. See *Arms Control and Disarmament Agreements*.

11. Ibid.

12. It was a statement by then Secretary of State John Foster Dulles which led to the adoption of the term as descriptive of U.S. policy. His actual words were "local defenses must be reinforced by the further deterrent of massive retaliatory power" (Address before the Council on Foreign Relations on "The Evolution of Foreign Policy," *Department of State Bulletin* 30 [January 12, 1954]: 108). See also Michael A. Guhin, *John Foster Dulles: A Statesman and His Times* (New York: Columbia University Press, 1972), pp. 221–39.

13. *Department of State Bulletin* 47 (July 9, 1962): 64–69.

14. See Peter C. Wagstaff, "An Analysis of the Cities-Avoidance Theory," *Stanford Journal of International Studies* 7 (Spring 1972): 162–72. See also A. C. Enthoven, "1963 Nuclear Strategy Revisited," in this volume.

15. Enthoven, "1963 Nuclear Strategy Revisited."

16. James Schlesinger in an address to the Overseas Writers Association, Washington, D.C., January 10, 1974. See also "Schlesinger Tells Newsmen U.S. ICBMs being Retargeted," Transcript EPF-42, U.S. Information Service, Washington, D.C., January 10, 1974, as quoted in Desmond Ball, "Déja Vu: The Return to Counterforce in the Nixon Administration," California Seminar on Arms Control and Foreign Policy, University of California, Los Angeles, 1975.

17. See Ball, "Déja Vu."

18. See Robert McAfee Brown, *Religion and Violence*, The Portable Stanford (Stanford: Stanford Alumni Association, 1973), pp. 19–20; Sydney D. Bailey, *Prohibitions and Restraints in War* (London: Oxford, 1972), pp. 15–16; and Winters, "Ethics, Diplomacy and Defense," as well as this volume's bibliography.

19. Brown, *Religion and Violence*, p. 20.

20. For some interesting comments on deterrence and stability see Jerome D. Frank, "Psychological Aspects of the Nuclear Arms Race," *Bulletin of the Atomic Scientists* 32 (April 1976): 22–24.

21. Article VI states that "each of the Parties to the Treaty undertakes to pursue negotiations in good faith on effective measures relating to cessation of the nuclear arms race at an early date, and on a treaty on general and complete disarmament under strict and effective international control."

22. This question is also raised by Lynn E. Davis, "Limited Nuclear Options: Deterrence and the New American Doctrine," *Adelphi Papers* 131 (London: International Institute for Strategic Studies, 1975), p. 22.

23. For a discussion of these consequences, see *Long-Term Worldwide Effects of Multiple Nuclear-Weapons Detonations*, a report contracted by the U.S. Arms Control and Disarmament Agency (Washington, D.C.: National Academy of Sciences, 1975).

24. See Herbert Scoville, "Flexible MADness?" *Foreign Policy*, no. 14 (Spring 1974): 164–77, and reprinted in this volume.

25. Although such new weapons may be relatively less vulnerable or less destructive (i.e., more discriminate), they remain weapons of mass destruction.

26. For a brief discussion of the political impact of flexible response on proliferation of nuclear weapons see G. W. Rathjens, "Flexible Response Options," *Orbis* 18 (Fall 1974): 677–88.

APPENDIX A

Selective Bibliography: Political-Military Issues

Compiled by John C. Baker

For a reader who is only just becoming familiar with this subject, much background concerning the issues in the current debate is given in the article by Ted Greenwood and Michael L. Nacht, and the transcript of *The Advocates* television program inserted into the *Congressional Record* by Senator Thomas J. McIntyre.

The case for more flexible strategic options and counterforce weapon improvements is made by the following authors: Fred C. Iklé, Bruce Russett, Michael M. May, William C. Moore, and Edward Luttwak. The best sources for the official arguments can be found in President Nixon's report of May 3, 1973, and especially Defense Secretary James R. Schlesinger's *Annual Defense Department Report FY 1975.*

Criticism of many aspects of the new strategic doctrine is well made by the following authors: Wolfgang K. H. Panofsky, Herbert Scoville, Jr., Barry Carter, and the Federation of American Scientists.

FUNDAMENTAL WORKS ON NUCLEAR STRATEGY AND ARMS CONTROL

Gray, Colin S. "The Arms Race Phenomenon." *World Politics* 24 (October 1971): 39–79.

Mr. Baker is editor of *Arms Control Today*, a monthly publication of the Arms Control Association, Washington, D.C.

Halperin, Morton H. *Defense Strategies for the Seventies*. Boston: Little, Brown and Co., 1971.

Harkabi, Y. *Nuclear War and Nuclear Peace*. Jerusalem: Israel Program for Scientific Translations, 1966.

Kahn, Herman. *Thinking About the Unthinkable*. New York: Avon Books, 1962.

Lambeth, Benjamin S. "Deterrence in the MIRV Era." *World Politics* 24 (January 1972): 221–42.

Martin, Laurence. *Arms and Strategy: The World Power Structure Today*. New York: David McKay Company, 1973. (See especially chap. 1, "The Central Nuclear Balance," pp. 11–33.)

Quanbeck, Alton H., and Blechman, Barry M. *Strategic Forces: Issues for the Mid-Seventies*. Washington, D.C.: The Brookings Institution, 1973.

Schelling, Thomas C., and Halperin, Morton H. *Strategy and Arms Control*. New York: The Twentieth Century Fund, 1961.

Snyder, Glenn H. *Deterrence and Defense*. Princeton: Princeton University Press, 1961.

STRATEGIC NUCLEAR DOCTRINE AND THEORY

Arbatov, G. A. "The American Strategic Debate: A Soviet View." *Survival* 16 (May/June 1974): 133–34.

Carter, Barry. "Nuclear Strategy and Nuclear Weapons." *Scientific American* 230 (May 1974): 20–31.

Federation of American Scientists. "Solution to Counterforce: Land-based Missile Disarmament." *Federation of American Scientists Public Interest Reports*, February 1974.

Gelb, Leslie H. "Debate on U.S. Nuclear Policy: Just What is Strategic Superiority?" *New York Times*, July 30, 1974.

Greenwood, Ted, and Nacht, Michael L. "The New Nuclear Debate: Sense or Nonsense?" *Foreign Affairs* 52 (July 1974): 761–80.

Iklé, Fred C. "Can Nuclear Deterrence Last Out the Century?" *Foreign Affairs* 51 (January 1973): 267–85.

Luttwak, Edward. "Nuclear Strategy: The New Debate." *Commentary* 57 (April 1974): 53–59.

May, Michael M. "Some Advantages of a Counterforce Deterrence." *Orbis* 14 (Summer 1970): 271–83.

McIntyre, Sen. Thomas J. "Nuclear Policy Debate." *Congressional Record*, March 28, 1974, S4663–4668. (A reprint of

The Advocates television debate, "Should We Develop Highly Accurate Missiles and Emphasize Military Targets rather than Cities?" which featured Robert Ellsworth advocating the *pro* case and Barry Carter advocating the *con* case.)

McNamara, Robert S. "The United States and Western Europe: Concrete Problems of Maintaining a Free Community." A speech delivered at the commencement exercises, University of Michigan, Ann Arbor, Mich., June 16, 1962. Reprinted in *Vital Speeches of the Day* 28 (August 1, 1962): 626–29.

Moore, Col. William C. "Counterforce: Facts and Fantasies." *Air Force Magazine* 57 (April 1974): 49–52.

Nixon, President Richard M. *U.S. Foreign Policy for the 1970's: Shaping a Durable Peace.* A report to the 93rd Cong., 1st sess. Washington, D.C.: Government Printing Office, May 3, 1973. (See especially pp. 182–86.) (For the previous presidential foreign policy reports, see especially February 18, 1970, pp. 121–22; February 25, 1971, pp. 173–74; and February 9, 1972, pp. 157–58.)

Panofsky, Wolfgang K. H. "The Mutual Hostage Relationship Between America and Russia." *Foreign Affairs* 51 (October 1973): 109–18.

Schlesinger, Secretary of Defense James R. *Annual Defense Department Report FY 1975.* Washington: Government Printing Office, 1974. (See especially Section IIA, "The Basis for the Strategic Forces," pp. 25–45.)

———."Remarks before the Overseas Writers Associates Luncheon." International Club, Washington, D.C., January 10, 1974. Excerpts reprinted in *Survival* 16 (March/April 1974): 86–90.

Scoville, Jr., Herbert. "Flexible MADness?" *Foreign Policy*, no. 14 (Spring 1974), pp. 164–77.

U.S. Congress, Senate, Budget Committee. *The 1976 First Concurrent Resolution on the Budget*, vol. 2. Hearings, 94th Cong., 1st sess. Washington, D.C.: Government Printing Office, 1975, pp. 847–992. (See especially the discussions of U.S. strategic policy by Paul Nitze, Jeremy Stone, and Paul Warnke, pp. 957–92.)

———.Foreign Relations Committee. *U.S.-U.S.S.R. Strategic Policies.* Hearings, 93rd Cong., 2nd sess. Washington, D.C.: Government Printing Office, 1974. (A detailed presentation of the new U.S. strategic doctrine by Defense Secretary James R. Schlesinger.)

HISTORIES OF U.S. STRATEGIC AND ARMS CONTROL POLICIES

Arms Control: Readings from Scientific American. With introductions by Herbert York. San Francisco: W. H. Freeman and Co., 1973.

Enthoven, Alain C., and Smith, K. Wayne. *"How Much Is Enough?" Shaping the Defense Program, 1961–1969.* New York: Harper and Row, 1971.

Huntington, Samuel P. *The Common Defense: Strategic Programs in National Politics.* New York: Columbia University Press, 1961.

Moulton, Harland B. *From Superiority to Parity: The United States and the Strategic Arms Race, 1961–1971.* Westport, Conn.: Greenwood Press, Inc., 1973.

Problems of Modern Strategy. Foreward by Alastair Buchan. New York: Praeger Publishers, 1970.

Roberts, Chalmers M. *The Nuclear Years: The Arms Race and Arms Control, 1945–70.* New York: Praeger Publishers, 1971.

York, Herbert F. *Race to Oblivion: A Participant's View of the Arms Race.* New York: Simon and Schuster, 1970.

STRATEGIC ARMS LIMITATION NEGOTIATIONS

Carter, Luther. "Strategic Arms Limitation (1): The Decades of Frustration." *Science* 187 (January 31, 1975): 327–30.

Kruzel, Joseph. "SALT II: The Search for a Follow-On Agreement." *Orbis* 17 (Summer 1973): 334–63.

Newhouse, John. *Cold Dawn: The Story of SALT.* New York: Holt, Rinehart and Winston, 1973.

Nitze, Paul H. "SALT: The Strategic Balance Between Hope and Skepticism." *Foreign Policy*, no. 17 (Winter 1974–75), pp. 136–56.

———. "Vladivostok and SALT II." *The Review of Politics* 37 (April 1975): 147–60.

Scoville, Jr., Herbert. "Beyond SALT One." *Foreign Affairs* 50 (April 1972): 488–500.

U.S., Congress, Senate, Foreign Relations Committee. *Strategic Arms Limitation Agreements.* Hearings, 92nd Cong., 2nd sess. Washington, D.C.: Government Printing Office, 1972.

U.S., Arms Control and Disarmament Agency. *Arms Control and Disarmament Agreements: Text and History of Negotiations.* Washington, D.C.: Government Printing Office, February 1975.

STRATEGIC WEAPONS SYSTEMS

General Works

Legault, Albert, and Lindsey, George. *The Dynamics of the Nuclear Balance.* Ithaca, N.Y.: Cornell University Press, 1974.

Martin, Laurence. *Arms and Strategy: The World Power Structure Today.* New York: David McKay Company, 1973.

Ruina, J. P. "U.S. and Soviet Strategic Arsenals." In *SALT: The Moscow Agreements and Beyond.* Edited by Mason Willrich and John B. Rhinelander. New York: The Free Press, 1974.

Tsipis, Kosta. "The Accuracy of Strategic Missiles." *Scientific American* 233 (July 1975): 14–23.

York, Herbert. "Multiple-Warhead Missiles." *Scientific American* 229 (November 1973): 18–27.

Cruise Missiles

Shapley, Deborah. "Cruise Missiles: Air Force, Navy Weapon Poses New Arms Issue." *Science* 187 (February 7, 1975): 416–18.

Tsipis, Kosta. "The Long-Range Cruise Missile." *Bulletin of the Atomic Scientists* 31 (April 1975): 14–26.

Land-Based Ballistic Missiles

Hepfer, Brig. Gen. John W. "M-X and the Land-Based ICBM." *Astronautics & Aeronautics* 13 (February 1975): 57–61.

Nuclear Missile Submarines and Antisubmarine Warfare

"Antisubmarine Warfare." *The Strategic Survey, 1970.* London, 1970, pp. 14–15.

Garwin, Richard L. "Antisubmarine Warfare and National Security." *Scientific American* 227 (July 1972): 14–25.

Scoville, Jr., Herbert. "Missile Submarines and National Security." *Scientific American* 226 (June 1972): 15–27.

Scoville, Jr., Herbert, and Hoag, David C. "Ballistic Missile Submarines as Counterforce Weapons." In *The Future of the Sea-Based Deterrent.* Edited by Kosta Tsipis, Anne H. Cahn, and Bernard T. Feld. Cambridge, Mass.: The MIT Press, 1973.

Tsipis, Kosta. *Tactical and Strategic Antisubmarine Warfare.* Cambridge, Mass.: The MIT Press, 1974.

Strategic Systems for Verification and Surveillance:

Carter, Luther J. "Strategic Weapons: Verification Keeps Ahead of Arms Control." *Science* 187 (March 14, 1975): 936–39.

Greenwood, Ted. "Reconnaissance and Arms Control." *Scientific American* 228 (February 1973): 14–25.

Klass, Philip J. *Secret Sentries in Space.* New York: Random House, 1971.

Scoville, Jr., Herbert. "A Leap Forward in Verification." In *SALT: The Moscow Agreement and Beyond.* Edited by Mason Willrich and John B. Rhinelander. New York: The Free Press, 1974, pp. 160–82.

EFFECTS OF NUCLEAR WEAPONS

Heer, David M. *After Nuclear Attack: A Demographic Inquiry.* New York: Frederick A. Praeger, Publishers, 1965.

U.S., Congress, House, Committee on Foreign Relations, Subcommittee on Arms Control, International Organizations and Security Agreements. *Analyses of Effects of Limited Nuclear Warfare.* 94th Cong., 1st sess., September 1975.

U.S., Arms Control and Disarmament Agency. *Worldwide Effects of Nuclear War . . . Some Perspectives.* Washington, D.C.: Government Printing Office, 1976.

SOVIET STRATEGIC POLICY

Erickson, John. *Soviet Military Power.* London: Royal United Services Institute, 1971.

Holloway, David. "Strategic Concepts and Soviet Policy." *Survival* 13 (November 1971): 364–69.

Kolkowicz, Roman; Gallagher, Matthew P.; and Lambeth, Benjamin S.; with Clemens, Jr., Walter C.; and Colm, Peter W. *The Soviet Union and Arms Control: A Superpower Dilemma.* Baltimore: The Johns Hopkins Press, 1970.

Lambeth, Benjamin S. "The Sources of Soviet Military Doctrine." In *Comparative Defense Policy.* Edited by Horton, Rogersen, and Warner. Baltimore and London: Johns Hopkins University Press, 1974, pp. 200–16.

Wolfe, Thomas W. "Soviet Interests in SALT." In *SALT: Implications for Arms Control in the 1970s.* Edited by William R. Kintner and Robert L. Pfaltzgraff, Jr. Pittsburgh: University of Pittsburgh Press, 1973.

TACTICAL NUCLEAR WEAPONS POLICY

Bennett, W. S.; Sandoval, R. R.; and Shreffler, R. G. "A Credible Nuclear-Emphasis Defense for NATO." *Orbis* 17 (Summer 1973): 463–79.

Brenner, Michael. "Tactical Nuclear Strategy and European Defense: A Critical Reappraisal." *International Affairs* 51 (January 1975): 23–42.

Canby, Steven. *The Alliance and Europe: Part IV, Military Doctrine and Technology*. Adelphi Papers, no. 109. London: International Institute for Strategic Studies, 1975.

———."Damping Nuclear Counterforce Incentives: Correcting NATO's Inferiority in Conventional Military Strength." *Orbis* 19 (Spring 1975): 47–71.

Cliffe, Trevor. *Military Technology and the European Balance*. Adelphi Papers, no. 89. London: International Institute for Strategic Studies, 1972. (See especially pp. 3–7, 29–35.)

Kemp, Geoffrey. *Nuclear Forces for Medium Powers: Part I: Targets and Weapon Systems*. Adelphi Papers, no. 106. London: International Institute for Strategic Studies, Autumn 1974.

Martin, Laurence. *Arms and Strategy: The World Power Structure Today*. New York: David McKay Co., 1973. (See chap. 6, "Tactical Nuclear Weapons," pp. 131–41.)

———. "Theatre Nuclear Weapons and Europe." *Survival* 16 (November/December 1974): 268–76.

Nelson, Gaylord. "Report on Tactical Nuclear Weapons." *Congressional Record*, July 20, 1971, S11625–11628.

Polk, James H. "The Realities of Tactical Nuclear Warfare." *Orbis* 17 (Summer 1973): 439–447.

Record, Jeffrey. "To Nuke or Not to Nuke: A Critique of Rationales for a Tactical Nuclear Defense of Europe." *Military Review* 54 (October 1974): 3–13.

Schlesinger, Secretary of Defense James R. *The Theater Nuclear Force Posture in Europe: A Report to the United States Congress in Compliance with Public Law 93–365*. Washington, D.C.: Department of Defense, May 1975.

Scott, John F. "What We Know, and What We Don't Know, About Tactical Nuclear War." *Air University Review* 25 (July/August 1974): 51–54.

U.S., Congress, Senate, Foreign Relations Committee. *Nuclear Weapons and Foreign Policy*. 93rd Cong., 2nd sess. Washington, D.C.: Government Printing Office, 1974.

U.S., Congress, Senate, Foreign Relations Committee. *U.S. Security Issues in Europe: Burden Sharing and Offset, MBFR and Nuclear Weapons*. 93rd Cong., 1st sess. Washington, D.C.: Government Printing Office, 1973.

Wohlstetter, Albert. "Threats and Promises of Peace: Europe and America in the New Era." *Orbis* 17 (Winter 1974): 1107–44.

NUCLEAR PROLIFERATION

The Arms Control Association and the Carnegie Endowment for International Peace. *NPT: Paradoxes and Problems*. Washington, D.C.: The Arms Control Association, 1975.

Bloomfield, Lincoln P. "Nuclear Spread and World Order." *Foreign Affairs* 53 (July 1975): 743–55.

Epstein, William. "The Proliferation of Nuclear Weapons." *Scientific American* 232 (April 1975): 18–33.

Maddox, John. *Prospects for Nuclear Proliferation*. Adelphi Papers, no. 113. London: International Institute for Strategic Studies, 1975.

Myrdal, Alva. "The High Price of Nuclear Arms Monopoly." *Foreign Policy*, no. 18 (Spring 1975): 30–43.

Quester, George H. "Can Proliferation Now be Stopped?" *Foreign Affairs* 53 (October 1974): 77–97.

———. *The Politics of Nuclear Proliferation*. Baltimore and London: The Johns Hopkins University Press, 1973.

SIPRI (The Stockholm International Peace Research Institute). *The Nuclear Age*. Stockholm and Cambridge, Mass.: Almqvist and Wiksell in collaboration with the MIT Press, 1974.

REFERENCE WORKS

Each year the U.S. Department of Defense produces three documents which contain a substantial amount of information concerning defense policy, current weapon programs, and estimates of Soviet and Chinese capabilities. These documents are the Secretary of Defense's *Annual Defense Department Report;* the *Military Posture* statement of the Chairman of the Joint Chiefs of Staff; and the statement entitled *Department of Defense Program of Research, Development, Test and Evaluation.*

Widely used nonofficial sources of facts and figures on military force levels include *The Military Balance*, published by the International Institute for Strategic Studies (IISS), London, and the

World Armaments and Disarmaments: SIPRI Yearbook published by the Stockholm International Peace Research Institute (SIPRI), Stockholm. Both these organizations also provide a number of annual studies on various defense and arms-control subjects.

Information of the capabilities of specific weapon systems can be found in *Jane's Aircraft*, *Jane's Weapon Systems*, and *Jane's Fighting Ships*, published in London. Also see the *World Missile Yearbook*, published by *Flight International*, London. A useful introduction to the subject of strategic missiles is available in the following articles: Ian Smart, *Advanced Strategic Missiles: A Short Guide*, Adelphi Papers no. 63 (London: Institute for Strategic Studies, 1969); "The Accuracy of Missile Systems," in *Strategic Survey 1969* (London: Institute for Strategic Studies, 1970), pp. 30–33; and Kosta Tsipis, "The Accuracy of Strategic Missiles," *Scientific American* 233 (July 1975): 14–23.

Information and facts concerning the details of the effects of nuclear explosions can be found in a volume prepared for the U.S. Department of Defense: Samuel Glasstone, ed., *The Effects of Nuclear Weapons* (Washington, D.C.: U.S. Government Printing Office, April 1962). For a less technical treatment of the same subject, see Thomas L. Martin, Jr., and Donald C. Latham, *Strategy for Survival* (Tucson: The University of Arizona Press, 1963), pp. 56–133 and 296–352; and Vice-Admiral B. B. Schofield, "The Employment of Nuclear Weapons at Sea," *RUSI: Journal of the Royal Institute for Defense Studies*, May 1963, pp. 168–71.

Excellent reference material on U.S. involvement in arms-control and disarmament activities may be found in the U.S. Arms Control and Disarmament Agency's *Arms Control and Disarmament Agreements: Texts and History of Negotiations* (Washington, D.C.: U.S. Government Printing Office, 1975); and *SALT Lexicon* (Washington: U.S. Government Printing Office, 1974). For background material on arms negotiations, see the annual volume entitled *Documents on Disarmament*, prepared by the Arms Control and Disarmament Agency.

APPENDIX B

Selective Bibliography: Ethical Issues

Compiled by Scott G. Michael

OVERVIEWS

While development of just-war theory from antiquity through the nuclear age is characterized by diversity of inspiration, context, and effect, there exist several major surveys of the subject, comprehensive in varying degrees, which provide general background and a broad frame of reference for further study. Most include substantial material on divergent Christian doctrines and secular law traditions.

Bainton, Roland. *Christian Attitudes Towards War and Peace.* New York: Abingdon Press, 1960.

Eppstein, John. *The Catholic Tradition of the Law of Nations.* Washington, D.C.: Catholic Association for International Peace, 1935. (Emphasizes mechanics of doctrinal development within the Church.)

Long, Edward LeRoy, Jr. *War and Conscience in America.* Philadelphia: Westminster Press, 1968. (Distinguishes just-war, crusade, and agonized-participation traditions. See especially pp. 22–47.)

McKenna, Joseph C. "Ethics and War: A Catholic View." *American Political Science Review* 54 (September 1960).

Mr. Michael is a student at the School of Foreign Service, Georgetown University.

Ramsey, Paul. *War and the Christian Conscience*. Durham, N. C.: Duke University Press, 1961. (Includes material on World Council of Churches policy, current Protestant thought, and contemporary applications of theory.)

Regout, Robert. *La doctrine de la guerre juste de Saint Augustin à nos jours d'après les Théologiens et les Canonistes Catholiques*. Paris: A. Pedone, 1935.

Rommen, Heinrich A. *The Natural Law*. Translated by T. Hanley. St. Louis: Herder, 1947. (Gives doctrine in broader context of natural law tradition. See especially part 1, "History of the Idea of Natural Law.")

Vanderpol, Alfred. *La guerre devant le christianisme*. 3rd ed. Paris: A. Tratin, 1911.

———. *Droit de guerre d'après les Théologiens et les Canonistes du Moyen Age*. Paris: A. Tratin, 1911.

———. *La doctrine scholastique du droit de guerre . . . avec une biographie de l'auteur*. Edited posthumously by Emile Schemon. Paris: A. Pedone, 1919.

Windass, Stanley. *Christianity versus Violence: A Social and Historical Study of War and Christianity*. London: Sheed and Ward, 1964.

ORIGINS AND DEVELOPMENTS IN THEORY AND LAW

Although boundaries may blur, several distinct periods emerge in the development of just-war theory. Each period reflects the influence of various contemporary religious, ideological, and socio-political forces; furthermore, the thought of different eras finds modes of expression diverse in tone and substance. Just-war theory cannot be studied in a vacuum—Protestant thought, secular thought, and the positive-law tradition in international law are factors crucial to a full understanding of the theory's growth.

Development Through the Augustinian Era

Bainton, Roland. *Christian Attitudes Towards War and Peace*. New York: Abingdon Press, 1960. (Includes numerous references to the influence of biblical and classical traditions. See especially chaps. 1-5.)

Miller, Patrick D. *The Divine Warrior in Early Israel*. Cambridge, Mass.: Harvard University Press, 1973. (Includes many references to the influence of biblical tradition.)

Augustinus, Aurelius. *The City of God.* Translated by Marcus Dods. New York: The Modern Library, 1950. (See especially book 1, pp. 3–39, 85–87, 104–6, 175–76; also pp. 683–85. The works of Augustine mark the emergence of the Christian just-war tradition. For further references on Augustinian thought, see the subsection on noncombatant immunity below.)

Deane, Herbert A. *The Political and Social Ideas of St. Augustine.* New York: Columbia University Press, 1963. (See especially chap. 5. For a constrasting view of Augustine, see the R. S. Hartigan titles listed under noncombatant immunity below.)

The Middle Ages, Aquinas, and the Natural Law

The social changes from the time of Augustine to that of Aquinas were of course profound; the period, characterized by the growth of church power in feudal society and the development of complex rules embodied in the chivalrous code, defined concepts and built foundations for classic just-war theory.

Aquinas, Thomas. *Summa Theologica.* 3 vols. London: R. & T. Washbourne; New York: Benziger Brothers, 1912–22. (For references and interpretation see Russell below.)

———. *Treatise on Law.* Chicago: Regnery Company, 1963. (See especially "Of the Natural Law."

Blake, E. O. "The Formation of the Crusade Idea." *Journal of Ecclesiastical History* 21 (January 1970): 11–31. (Covers the period of Popes Gregory VII and Urban II.)

Finch, George Augustus. *Sources of International Law.* Washington, D.C.: Carnegie Endowment for International Peace, 1937. (See especially pp. 15–29.)

Keen, M. H. *The Laws of War in the Late Middle Ages.* London: Routledge & Kegan Paul, 1965.

Kennelly, Dolorosa, C. S. J. "The Peace and Truce of God." Ph.D. diss. University of California, Berkeley, Calif., 1963. (Discusses the Council of Constance, 1095.)

O'Connor, Daniel John. *Aquinas and Natural Law.* London: Macmillan, 1967.

Russell, Frederick H. *The Just War in the Middle Ages.* Cambridge: At the University Press, 1975. (Describes Decretalists and other Church and scholastic development; also references for Aquinas's *Summa.*)

Southern, R. W. *Western Society and the Church of the Middle Ages.* Baltimore: The Johns Hopkins Press, 1970.

Walters, LeRoy B., Jr. "The Just War and the Crusade: Antitheses or Analogies." *Monist* 57 (October 1973): 584–94.

Classic Just-War Theory and the Development of International Law

The Renaissance saw the increasing codification of just-war theory as a combination of secular tradition and Church (scholastic) thought. Yet with the Reformation and the growth of nation-states, the seventeenth and subsequent centuries saw the growth of a body of secular international law which, while drawing upon just-war theory, supplanted that tradition long abused by hypocritical rulers.

Overviews

Dempsey, Paul Donan. "The Genesis of the Principle of Humanity in the Literature of the Law of War During the Seventeenth Century." M.A. diss., Georgetown University, Washington, D.C. (Covers especially Grotius and Hobbes.)

Johnson, James T. *Ideology, Reason, and the Limitation of War: Religious and Secular Concepts, 1200–1740.* Princeton, N. J.: Princeton University Press, 1975.

Scott, James Brown. *The Catholic Conception of International Law: Vitoria and Suarez.* Washington, D.C.: Georgetown University Press, 1934. (See chaps. 1, 2, 12.)

Walters, LeRoy Brandt, Jr. "Five Classic Just-War Theories: A Study in the Thought of Thomas Aquinas, Vitoria, Suarez, Gentili, and Grotius." Ph.D. diss., Yale University, New Haven, Conn., 1971.

Source Materials

Gentili, Alberico. *De Jure Belli Libri Tres.* The Classics of International Law, vol. 2, no. 16. Oxford: The Clarendon Press, 1925. (Covers the causes, prosecution, and cessation of war.)

Grotius, Hugo. *De Jure Belli ac Pacis Libri Tres.* The Classics of International Law, vol. 2, no. 3. Oxford: The Clarendon Press, 1925.

Suarez, Francisco. *Selections from Three Works of Francisco Suarez, S. J.* The Classics of International Law, vol. 2, no. 20. Oxford: The Clarendon Press, 1944. (See especially "On Charity," pp. 800–868.)

Vattel, Emmerich. *The Law of Nations or the Principles of Natural*

Law, vol. 4, pt. 3. Washington, D.C.: Carnegie Institution of Washington, 1916.

Vitoria, Francisco de. *De Indis et de Jure Belli Relectiones.* Translated by John Pawley Bate in *The Spanish Origins of International Law.* Oxford: The Clarendon Press, 1934. (See especially pp. 173–243.)

International Law: Nineteenth Century to World War I

In the era of "social Darwinism" and imperialism, the "value-free," "scientific" trend came to international law on war. Contrasting this trend, which fell in the chaos of attrition warfare from 1914 to 1919, were multilateral attempts to limit war along just-war lines.

Baker, Joseph Richardson. *The Laws of Land Warfare Concerning the Rights and Duties of Belligerents as Existing on August 14, 1914.* Washington, D.C.: U.S. Government Printing Office, 1919.

Carnegie Endowment for International Peace. *The Hague Conventions of 1899 and 1907 Respecting the Laws and Customs of War on Land.* Washington, D.C.: Carnegie Endowment for International Peace, 1915.

Fuller, Col. J. F. C. *The Reformation of War.* New York: E. P. Dutton and Company, 1923. (Epitomizes the degeneration of the secular and is replete with race theory. See especially pp. 56–74.)

THE JUST-WAR THEORY IN WORLD WAR II AND THE NUCLEAR AGE: RECONSTRUCTION AND CHALLENGE

World War II brought the advent of "total war," "unconditional surrender," and "the Bomb." War was fought on a scale and in terms unprecedented. The just-war theory, especially the element of noncombatant immunity, was once again confronting those concerned about war and morality. In the years since World War II, the question has become whether to reconstruct or abandon the just-war theory.

World War II: The Question of Limits

Three writers show concern that limits were lost during the war:

Ford, John C., S.J. "The Morality of Obliteration Bombing." *Theological Studies* 5 (1944): 261–309: Reprinted in *War and Morality*. Edited by Richard A. Wasserstrom. Belmont, Calif.: Wadsworth Publishing Co., 1970.

Kennan, George. *American Diplomacy, 1900–1950*. Chicago: University of Chicago Press, 1951. (See pp. 101–3 on "total victory.")

———. *Memoirs*, vol. 1. Boston: Little, Brown and Company, 1967. (See pp. 309–10.)

———. *Russia and the West Under Lenin and Stalin*. Boston: Little, Brown and Company, 1961. (See pp. 366–68.)

Ryan, John K. *Modern War and Basic Ethics*. Milwaukee: The Bruce Publishing Company, 1940. (Maintains just-war principles; sees build-up of armaments as a dangerous, uncomprehended move away from the just-war position.)

Three writers defend violations of just-war standards in World War II:

Brandt, R. B. "Utilitarianism and the Rules of War." In *War and Moral Responsibility*. Edited by Marshall Cohen. Princeton, N.J.: Princeton University Press, 1974.

Hare, R. M. "Rules of War and Moral Reasoning." In *War and Moral Responsibility*. Edited by Marshall Cohen. Princeton, N.J.: Princeton University Press, 1974.

Walzer, Michael. "World War II: Why Was This War Different?" In *War and Moral Responsibility*. Edited by Marshall Cohen. Princeton, N.J.: Princeton University Press, 1974.

Noncombatant Immunity in the Nuclear Age

Literature on this topic cannot easily be divided along clear lines. Some works support just-war criteria outright; others purport to do so. Some writers challenge the non-combatant concept. Most works fit into the maintenance/challenge schema indicated below. Notes indicate special variations or stresses.

Maintenance of Just-War Standards

Anscombe, Elizabeth. "War and Murder." In *War and Morality*. Edited by Richard A. Wasserstrom. Belmont, Calif.: Wadsworth Publishing Company, 1970.

Cohen, Marshall. "War and Its Crimes." In *Philosophy, Morality, and International Affairs*. Edited by V. Held, S. Morgenbesser, and T. Nagel. New York: Oxford University Press, 1974.

Johnson, James T. "The Meaning of Non-Combatant Immunity in the Just War/Limited War Tradition." *Journal of the American Academy of Religion,* June 1971, pp. 151–70.

Murphy, Jeffrie G. "The Killing of the Innocent." *Monist* 57 (October 1973): 527–50.

Murray, John C., S. J. *Morality and Modern Warfare.* New York: Council on Religion and International Affairs, 1959. (Opposes R. Niebuhr, pp. 27–28; Thompson, p. 21.) Same theme appears in *We Hold These Truths.* Garden City, N.Y.: Doubleday, 1964, p. 263.

Nagel, Thomas, "War and Massacre." In *War and Moral Responsibility.* Edited by Marshall Cohen. Princeton, N.J.: Princeton University Press, 1974.

Ramsey, Paul. *The Limits of Nuclear War: Thinking About the Do-Able and The Un-Do-Able.* New York: Council on Religion and International Affairs, 1963.

Russett, Bruce. "Short of Nuclear Madness." *Worldview* 15 (April 1972): 31–37.

Thiesen, Sylvester P. "Man and Nuclear Weapons." *The American Benedictine Review,* September 1963, pp. 365–84, 389–90.

Weber, Theodore. *Modern War and the Pursuit of Peace.* New York: Council on Religion and International Affairs, 1968. (Specifically refutes O'Brien and also Hartigan).

Challenge to Just-War Standards

Bennett, Jonathan. "Whatever the Consequences." *Analysis* 26 (January 1966). (Opposes Murphy.)

Falk, Richard A. *Law, Morality and War in the Contemporary World.* New York: Praeger Publishers, 1963. (Seeks "stability"; finds deterrence "necessary but insufficient.")

Gessert, Robert A. and Hehir, J. Bryan. *The New Nuclear Debate.* New York: Council on Religion and International Affairs, 1976.

Hartigan, Richard Shelly. "Non-Combatant Immunity: An Analysis of Its Philosophical and Historical Origins." Ph.D. diss. Georgetown University, Washington, D.C., 1964.

———. "Non-Combatant Immunity: Its Scope and Development." *Continuum* 3 (Autumn 1965). (Refers to Frs. Ryan and Ford.)

———. "Non-Combatant Immunity: Reflections on Its Origins and Present Status." *Review of Politics* 29 (April 1967): 204–20.

———. "St. Augustine on War and Killing: The Problem of the Innocent." *Journal of the History of Ideas* 27 (April–June 1966).

(See Ramsey's *War and the Christian Conscience*, chap. 2, for opposing viewpoint.)

Iklé, Fred C. "Prevention of Nuclear War in a World of Uncertainty." *Department of State Bulletin*, 70, March 25, 1974, pp. 314–18.

Kissinger, Henry A. *Nuclear Weapons and Foreign Policy*. New York: Harper for the Council on Foreign Relations, 1957. (See esp. chaps. 5–7, on limited war. He favors limiting nuclear war to minimize noncombatant injury, but technical arguments that limited nuclear strategies inflict serious noncombatant injury place his theory in opposition to just-war criteria.)

Noble, Cheryl. "Political Realism, International Morality, and Just War." *Monist* 57 (October 1973). (Analyzes Kissinger's *A World Restored*, as it relates to these themes.)

O'Brien, William V. "Nuclear War and the Law of Nations." In *Morality and Modern Warfare*. Edited by William Nagle. Baltimore, Md.: Helicon Press, 1960.

———. *Nuclear War, Deterrence, and Morality*. New York: Newman Press, 1967. (Finds adherence to noncombatant immunity not a precondition for a just nuclear defense.)

———. *War and/or Survival*. Garden City, N.Y.: Doubleday Company, 1969. (Says extremism of idealists and realists blocks progress.)

Thompson, Kenneth W. *Christian Ethics and the Dilemmas of Foreign Policy*. Durham, N.C.: Duke University Press, 1959. (Opposes Murray, pp. 136–44; also see pp. 19–20, 41–50, 64–65, 70–71, 96–98, 101–2.)

Wasserstrom, Richard A. "On the Morality of War." In *War and Morality*. Edited by R. A. Wasserstrom. Belmont, Calif.: Wadsworth Publishing Co., 1970.

International Law in the Nuclear Age

Bailey, Sidney. *Prohibitions and Restraints in War*. London: Oxford University Press, 1972.

Carnegie Endowment for International Peace. *Law of Armed Conflicts*. New York: Carnegie Endowment for International Peace, 1971.

Greenspan, Morris. *The Modern Law of Land Warfare*. Berkeley, Calif.: University of California Press, 1959. (Reviews post-Geneva law.)

Schwarzenberger, Georg. *International Law*. Vol. 2, Armed Conflict. London: Stevens and Sons, Ltd., 1968.

United Nations, General Assembly, Secretariat. "Respect for Human Rights in Armed Conflicts: Part I," (A/9215, vol. 1) November 7, 1973, pp. 17–20. (Catalogs legal restrictions on killing civilians.)

Church Doctrine and Critique

Since World War II, the Roman Catholic Church has strengthened its position against war, reinforcing limits within the just-war theory while narrowing the just causes once embodied in the theory.

Abbott, Walter M., S. J., ed. *The Documents of Vatican II*. New York: America Press, 1966. (See pp. 291–97.)

Feeney, Margaret M. *Sword of the Spirit; Just War? Papal Teaching on Nuclear Warfare with a Scientific Commentary*. Hinckley, Leics, Walker, 1958.

Horman, Karl. *Peace and Modern War in the Judgment of the Church*. Translated by Caroline Hemsath. Westminster, Md.: Newman Press, 1966. (Treats developments from World War II through Pope John XXIII.)

John XXIII. *Pacem in Terris*. New York: America Press, 1963.

Murray, John C., S. J. *Morality and Modern War*. New York: Council on Religion and International Affairs, 1959. (Details policies of Pius XII.)

Paul VI. *Populorum Progressio. The Pope Speaks*, 12:144–172, 1967.

Tucker, Robert W. *Just War and Vatican Council II: A Critique*. With commentary by Ralph Potter, Paul Ramsey, et al. New York: Council on Religion and International Affairs, 1966.

American Policy and the Just War

Johnson, James T. "Just War, the Nixon Doctrine and the Future Shape of American Military Policy." In *The Yearbook of World Affairs 1975*, vol. 29. London: Stevens and Sons, Ltd., 1975.

Rapaport, Anatol. *Strategy and Conscience*. New York: Harper & Row, 1964. (Exposes subjectivity and uncertainty concealed by games theory and modern strategy.)

Schelling, Thomas C. *The Strategy of Conflict*. Cambridge, Mass.: Harvard University Press, 1960, pp. 50–57, 87.

Tucker, Robert W. *The Just War: A Study of Contemporary American Doctrine*. Baltimore: The Johns Hopkins Press, 1960.

Von Weizaecker, Carl-Friedrich Freiherr. "The Ethical Problem of Modern Strategy." In *Problems in Modern Strategy*. New York: Praeger Publishers, 1970.

Winters, Francis X., S. J. "Ethical Considerations and National Security Policy." In *Report of the Commission on the Organization of the Government for the Conduct of Foreign Policy*, vol. 7, appendix W, no. 2. Washington, D.C.: U.S. Government Printing Office, June 1975, pp. 293–99.

———. "Morality in the War Room." *America*, February 15, 1975, pp. 106–10.

Revolution, Counterinsurgency, and the Just War

Arendt, Hannah. *Crises of the Republic*. New York: Harcourt Brace Jovanovich, 1972, pp. 1–47. (Discusses wars of intervention and counterinsurgency.)

Berryman, Phillip. "Latin American Liberation Theology." *Theological Studies* 34 (September 1973): 357–95.

"Can Counterinsurgency War Be Conducted Justly?" Paper prepared for meeting of the American Society of Christian Ethics in Evanston, Ill. January 21, 1966.

Furniss, Edgar S. *Counterinsurgency: Some Problems and Implications*. New York: Council on Religion and International Affairs, 1966.

Gutiérrez, Gustavo. *A Theology of Liberation*. Translated by Sister Caridad Inda and John Eagleson. Maryknoll, N.Y.: Orbis Books, 1973.

———. "Notes for a Theology of Liberation." *Theological Studies* 31 (1971).

Hartigan, Richard Shelly. "Urban Riots, Guerilla Wars and Just War Ethics." In *The Religious Situation*. Edited by Donald R. Cutler. Boston: Beacon Press, 1968.

Kenny, Denis. "Wars of National Liberation: A Catholic Response." *Worldview* 16 (February 1973): 35–39. (States the church should establish communication and listen.)

Ramsey, Paul. "The Just Revolution." *Worldview* 16 (October 1973): 37–40.

Overall Reconstruction and Alternatives

Reconstruction

Arendt, Hannah. *Crises of the Republic.* New York: Harcourt Brace Jovanovich, 1972, pp. 105–198.

Butterfield, Herbert. *Christianity, Diplomacy and War.* London: The Eppworth Press, 1953.

Cochran, Charles L. "The International Law of War and Moral Law." *Catholic World* 214 (November 1971): 71–73.

Eliot, Gil. "How Wars Have Ended." *Worldview* 17 (March 1974): 20–22 (Finds the Westphalian system not useful for modern nuclear realities.)

Hehir, J. Bryan. "Non-Violence, Peace, and the Just War." *Worldview* 12 (June 1969). (Reviews Douglass's *The Non-Violent Cross.)*

Jenkins, Iredell. "The Conditions of Peace." *Monist* 57 (October 1973): 507–26. (Encourages thinking in terms of peace and planning for it, but not fleeing from war.)

Johnson, James T. "Ideology and the *Jus ad Bellum.*" *Journal of the American Academy of Religion* 41 (June 1973): 212–28. (Wants to restore justice to *jus ad bellum;* critical of first-use/second-use dichotomy.)

———. "Rationalizing the Hell of War." *Worldview* 17 (January 1974): 43–47. (Responses to pacifist Gordon Zahn.)

———. "Toward Reconstructing the *Jus ad Bellum.*" *Monist* 57 (October 1973): 461–88.

Little, David. "Moral Discourse Under Fire." *Worldview* 15 (January 1972): 31–38.

Meyerowitz, Henri. *Le principe de l'égalité des belligérents devant le droit de la guerre.* Paris: A. Pedone, 1970. (Says the concept of justice has been lost from twentieth-century international law.)

Morganthau, Hans. *Politics Among Nations.* New York: A. Knopf, 1967, pp. 219–49.

Osgood, Robert E., and Tucker, Robert W. *Force, Order and Justice.* Baltimore: The Johns Hopkins Press, 1967, pp. 215, 290–301, 302–22.

Potter, Ralph. *War and Moral Discourse.* Richmond: John Knox Press, 1970. (See especially pp. 51–54.)

Ramsey, Paul. *The Just War: Force and Political Responsibility.* New York: Charles Scribner's Sons, 1968.

———. *War and Christian Conscience*. Durham, N.C.: Duke University Press, 1961.
Winters, Francis X., S. J. *Politics and Ethics*. New York: Paulist Press, 1975, pp. 101–121.
———. "The Violence of Truth." *Worldview* 17 (January 1974): 21–26.

Alternatives

De George, Richard T. *Soviet Ethics and Morality*. Ann Arbor, Mich.: University of Michigan Press, 1969 (Gives interesting comparison and contrast.)
Douglass, James. *The Non-Violent Cross: A Theology of Revolution and Peace*. New York: Macmillan, 1969.
Earle, William. "In Defense of War." *Monist* 57 (October 1973): 551–69.
Holmes, Robert L. "On Pacifism." *Monist* 57 (October 1973): 487–506.
McSorley, Richard, S. J. *Kill for Peace?* New York: Corpus Books, 1970. (See especially pp. 29–41.)
Stone, Julius. *Aggression and World Order*. London: Stevens and Sons, 1958. (Rejects just-war elements in international law as meaningless.)
Yoder, John. *The Politics of Jesus*. Grand Rapids, Mich.: Eerdmans, 1972, pp. 241–46. (Consistently disavows use of violence for political goals.)
Zahn, Gordon C. *An Alternative to War*. New York: Council on Religion and International Affairs, 1963. (Takes a pacifist position.)

APPENDIX C

Glossary of Nuclear Weapons and Arms Control Terminology

by John C. Baker

Accidental attack An unintended attack which occurs without deliberate national design as a direct result of a random event, such as a mechanical failure, a simple human error, or an unauthorized action by a subordinate.

Accidents Measures Agreement An agreement between the United States and the Soviet Union which went into force September 30, 1971. In the agreement both countries pledged to improve their organizational and technical safeguards against accidental or unauthorized use of nuclear weapons; to give immediate notification to the other should the risk of nuclear war arise from such incidents; and to give advance notification of missile launches.

ACDA The U.S. Arms Control and Disarmament Agency.

Active defense The type of defense that seeks, by use of defensive missiles or airplanes, to intercept an offensive missile or bomber before it reaches its targets.

Air-to-surface missile (ASM) A missile launched from an airborne carrier against a target on the ground.

Antiballistic missile (ABM) Either: (a) a defensive missile designed to intercept and destroy or neutralize an incoming warhead/reentry vehicle; or (b) in a broader sense, the whole system of launchers, radars, computers, and missiles designed to defend some specified target or geographic area against ballistic missile attack.

Anti-Ballistic Missile (ABM) Protocol An extension of the initial ABM Treaty which further restrained both the United States and the Soviet Union to the deployment of 100 ABM launchers and interceptors at only one site apiece. The United States chose to maintain its site in North Dakota, in defense of its land-based ICBM bases, while the U.S.S.R. chose an ABM defense of Moscow. The agreement was signed in July 1974.

Anti-Ballistic Missile (ABM Treaty) A treaty between the United States and the Soviet Union which limited each nation to two ABM launching sites, at least 1,300 kilometers apart, with no more than 100 ABM launchers and interceptors at each. The agreement, which was signed May 1972, was the result of the Strategic Arms Limitations Talks (SALT) negotiation; it was modified and extended by the *Anti-Ballistic Missile Protocol.* See also *Standing Consultive Commission.*

Antisubmarine warfare (ASW) The type of defensive warfare whereby an attempt is made to combat the unique advantages of the submarine. There are five basic steps: detection; classification or identification; localization; attack; and the final destruction of the submarine. Tactical ASW generally refers to combat against submarines which are threatening sea lanes or a surface fleet with conventional torpedoes or cruise missiles. *Strategic ASW* aims at destroying the adversary's submarines which carry strategic nuclear missiles.

Arms control International action, formal or informal, which places limitations on armed forces, armaments, or military expenditures. This may include restrictions on the use, levels, or deployment of weapons or forces, as well as other actions to prevent the spread of weapons. Also actions or measures for preventing, controlling, or terminating hostilities.

Assured destruction capability The ability (or a very high degree of confidence that one has the ability) to inflict some specific level of damage on an adversary. This level is generally equated with the ability to destroy an adversary's population and industry, but not his military forces. During the later years of Robert S. McNamara's tenure as secretary of defense, *assured destruction* was formalized as a measurement of the adequacy of U.S. strategic force levels, and an *assured destruction capability* was generally considered to be the forces required to destroy 20 to 25 percent of the population and 50 percent of the industrial capacity of the Soviet Union. See also *mutual assured destruction.*

Attack submarine A submarine that does not carry strategic nuclear missiles and is used to attack conventional warships or to hunt down and destroy ballistic-missile submarines.

B-1 A long-range strategic bomber, under development by the United States, which will be able to penetrate Soviet air defenses at low levels to reach its targets. The B-1 will carry nuclear bombs, as well as short-range nuclear missiles, and will eventually replace the older B-52 bombers.

B-52 A large, intercontinental subsonic bomber which the United States procured in the early 1960s.

Backfire A longe-range bomber presently being procured by the U.S.S.R. Suitable for regional nuclear missions, the Backfire is also reported to be capable of intercontinental missions if provided with sufficient air-to-air refueling capability.

Badger (TU-16) A Soviet intercontinental subsonic twin-turbojet aircraft.

Ballistic missile Any missile which does not rely on aerodynamic surfaces to produce lift; consequently it follows a ballistic trajectory (i.e., one resulting only from the effects of gravity and aerodynamic drag) when thrust is terminated.

Ballistic Missile Early Warning System (BMEWS) A U.S. electronic defense network, based in Greenland, Scotland, and Alaska. It was established in the early 1960s in order to give early warning of incoming transpolar ballistic missiles.

Bargaining chip Willingness to pursue a weapons program primarily for its utility in ongoing arms-control negotiations. A bargaining chip implies a program which will be eventually given up or halted in exchange for a favorable concession from the other side.

Bear (Tu-20) A Soviet four-engine turboprop intercontinental strategic bomber.

Biological Weapons Convention An international agreement which prohibits the development, production, and stockpiling of bacteriological (biological) and toxin weapons.

Bison (Mya-4) A Soviet four-engine turbojet intercontinental strategic bomber.

Blackout A phenomenon caused by a nuclear explosion in space. Radar rays are reflected, refracted, or absorbed in blackout areas.

Blast The airborne pressure pulse (shock-wave) initiated by the rapid expansion of hot gases produced by an explosion.

Catalytic war A war resulting from an act of a vengeful, ambitious, or desperate smaller power that provokes two great powers to go to war with the intention of destroying each other.

Circular error probability (CEP) A measure of the accuracy of offensive missile attacks on point targets. It is the radius of a circle around the target within which half the attacking warheads can be expected to fall. Consequently, the smaller a missile's CEP, the more likely it will destroy its target.

Cold launch The technique of ejecting a missile from a silo before full ignition of the main engine, sometimes called pop-up. Ballistic missiles are launched from submarines in this manner, and some of the new ICBMs of the U.S.S.R. may also be capable of being cold launched. This type of launch technique allows more room in the silo, which can be used either for larger missiles or for more hardening of the silo; it also leaves the silo relatively undamaged after the launching and thus available for reloading.

Collateral damage The damage to surrounding resources, military or not, as the result of actions or strikes directed specifically against enemy forces or military facilities.

Command Data Buffer System A computer system, being introduced in the United States, which allows rapid retargeting of ICBMs. The system is presently being emplaced on all 550 Minuteman III ICBMs which carry multiple warheads.

Comprehensive Test Ban (CTB) A possible addition to the present Partial Test Ban Treaty. It would extend the PTBT by banning underground nuclear testing, thus prohibiting any nuclear testing at all.

Conference of the Committee on Disarmament (CCD) Located in Geneva, it is the principal forum for multilateral arms-control negotiations on such subjects as chemical-biological weapons, a comprehensive nuclear test ban, and the seabed treaty.

Countercombatant strategy A strategy which emphasizes nuclear strikes against the conventional and strategic military forces of the adversary and the avoidance of nuclear damage to nonmilitary targets, such as cities.

Counterforce strike An attack aimed at an adversary's military capability, especially his strategic military forces (such as air bases and ICBM silos).

Countervalue strike An attack aimed at an opponent's cities or industrial capability. Also known as a *countercity strike.*

Coupling The linking of a lower level conflict, such as military aggression in Europe by Warsaw Pact countries, to the use of U.S. strategic deterrent forces.

Crisis stability A strategic-force relationship such that

neither side has any incentive to initiate the use of strategic nuclear forces in a crisis situation.

Cruise missile A missile powered by rocket or jet engines which flies within the atmosphere like an airplane along most of its trajectory. *Conventional cruise missiles* carry nonnuclear warheads and have short ranges. *Strategic cruise missiles* carry nuclear warheads and can travel over 1,000 kilometers.

Damage Denial The ability to preclude any significant damage from an opponent's nuclear attack.

Damage-limiting capability The ability to minimize the damage that a nuclear attack could cause if deterrence were to fail.

D-class submarine A new Soviet strategic missile submarine which is being deployed to carry the SS-N-8 SLBM; it has a 4,200 nautical mile range.

Decoy An aid designed to complicate the problem presented to a system defending against penetration. A decoy simulates a vehicle carrying a warhead, thus increasing the number of targets with which a defender must contend. Numerous decoys may be used.

Depressed-trajectory missile A ballistic missile fired at a much lower angle than usual. Such a missile rises above the line-of-sight radar horizon at a later stage of flight than a normal parabolic trajectory, making detection and interception more difficult. This capability is gained at the expense of reduced payload and lessened accuracy.

Deterrence The strategy which seeks to persuade an opponent that, in his own interest, he should avoid certain courses of action; in the nuclear sense, the opponent is to be convinced that the costs and risks attendant to aggression clearly outweigh any calculable gains to be drawn from such aggression.

Disarmament The reduction or elimination of military forces and armaments, especially by formal or informal international action.

"Disarming" first-strike A nuclear attack which would destroy or disable nearly all of an adversary's nuclear forces and would reduce the amount of damage his surviving nuclear force could produce to an "acceptable" level.

Dual-capable systems Weapon systems capable of delivering either conventional or nuclear warheads.

Electromagnetic Pulse (EMP) Waves produced by a nuclear explosion. They can severely disrupt radar and radio transmissions.

Electronic countermeasures (ECM) Actions taken to prevent or reduce an enemy's effective use of equipment and tactics employing or affected by electromagnetic radiations; they also exploit the enemy's use of such radiations.

"Empty hole problem" The possibility that should a nation decide to launch a counterforce attack against another's ICBM force, the adversary might chose to launch the endangered ICBMs (probably upon receiving radar warning of nuclear attack), thereby leaving only empty silos to be destroyed. See also *Launch-on-warning.*

Equivalent Megatonnage (EMT) A measure used to compare the destructive potential of various combinations of nuclear warhead yields against relatively soft targets. It includes compensation for the fact that blast damage from a nuclear explosion does not increase proportionally with the size or yield of the nuclear explosion.

"Essential Equivalence" As defined by former Secretary of Defense James R. Schlesinger, the requirement that the United States must not allow the U.S.S.R. to develop major asymmetries in the basic factors that determine strategic force effectiveness. These factors include throw-weight, accuracy, yield-to-weight ratios, reliability, and other factors which contribute to the effectiveness of strategic weapons and to the perceptions of other nations of the relative power balance between the United States and Soviet Russia. The term does not mean that the two nations must maintain exact equivalence in any particular category of strategic force, only a rough balance in the *sum* of all factors.

Fallout The process of particles contaminated with radioactive material from a nuclear explosion falling back to the earth's surface. Also applied in a collective sense to the contaminated particular matter itself.

FB-111 A U.S. supersonic bomber.

Fireball The luminous sphere of hot gases produced by a nuclear explosion.

Fire storm A phenomenon occuring in very large fires. The updraft produced by the fire causes winds to blow in toward the fire from all directions. In such a situation, virtually all combustible material within the area covered by the fire is burned.

First-strike The launching of an initial strategic nuclear attack before the adversary has used any nuclear weapons himself. See also *"Disarming" first-strike.*

First use The launching of an initial nuclear attack against the conventional forces of the enemy after a conventional war is in progress.

Forward-based systems (FBS) U.S. aircraft and other systems which could deliver nuclear strikes against the U.S.S.R. from bases outside the United States. These systems are designed primarily for missions in Western and Central Europe in support of NATO ground forces.

Fractional orbiting bombardment system (FOBS) A missile that achieves an orbital velocity but then fires a set of retrorockets before the completion of one revolution in order to slow down its reentry system and to drop the warhead that it carries into a normal ballistic trajectory toward a target on the earth's surface. This capability generally requires that a smaller payload than usual be carried with less accuracy.

G-class submarine A Soviet diesel-powered submarine which can carry two or three ballistic missiles.

Galosh The designation for the Soviet ABM system which is emplaced around Moscow.

General war Armed conflict between the major nuclear powers in which the total resources of the belligerents are employed and the national survival of a major belligerent is in jeopardy. See also *Limited war.*

Geneva Protocol of 1925 An international agreement which prohibits the use of chemical and biological weapons in warfare.

H-class submarine A Soviet nuclear-powered submarine which carries an average of three missiles.

Hardening The process of protecting land-based missiles or bombers from the blast effects of nuclear weapons by the building of missile silos or structures with concrete and earth so as to withstand the blast, heat, or radiation from a nuclear explosion.

Hard-point defense ABM defenses designed to protect ICBM sites or other hardened facilities that possess a relatively high degree of ability to withstand the effects of a nuclear explosion.

Hard target Any facility which is able to withstand a substantial degree of overpressure (generally hundreds of psi). Such targets usually include hardened command and control centers, missile silos, and warhead storage bunkers. See also *Overpressure.*

Hedge A system or weapons program which is developed or deployed as an insurance against the possible failure of a more central program or weapon system.

"Hot line" A direct communication link between the heads of the U.S. and U.S.S.R. governments for use in times of emergency. Its purpose is to minimize the possibility that nuclear accidents, ambiguous incidents, or unauthorized actions might lead to the outbreak of nuclear war. Originally a wire telegraph circuit, the system was updated in 1971 to a satellite communication circuit.

Inertial guidance system The basic guidance system for ballistic missiles. It is capable of detecting and correcting deviations from a planned trajectory and/or velocity.

Intercontinental ballistic missile (ICBM) A multistage rocket capable of delivering nuclear warheads at a long range (4,000 miles or more).

Intermediate-range ballistic missile (IRBM) A ballistic missile with a range of roughly 1,500 to 4,000 nautical miles.

Invulnerability The condition in which a military force is protected from destruction by an enemy counterforce attack. Invulnerability for nuclear forces is sought in several ways including: dispersal, warning systems, mobility and concealment, and hardening.

Kiloton (KT) A unit of explosive force equivalent to that produced by 1,000 tons of TNT. See also *Megaton* and *Yield*.

Launch-on-warning A doctrine calling for the launch of ballistic missiles as soon as a missile attack against them is detected and before the attacking warheads reach their targets. See also *"Empty hole problem."*

Limited or controlled response The deliberate and limited employment of nuclear weapons against a specific set of targets.

Limited war (a) Armed conflict short of general war, exclusive of incidents, involving the overt engagement of the military forces of two or more nations; (b) a war fought for limited objectives; or (c) a war limited as to geography, weapons employed, participants, or objectives. See also *General war*.

Maneuverable reentry vehicle (MaRV) A system where a missile carries single or multiple warheads which are able to change course during the final phase of their flight to their targets. There are two types of MaRVs. One is designed specially to penetrate ABM defenses and is known as an *ABM evader*. The other is the *"terminal guidance"* MaRV, which is a warhead of very high accuracy, suitable for counterforce attacks.

Medium-range ballistic missile (MRBM) A ballistic missile with a range of 600 to 1,500 nautical miles.

Megaton (MT) A measure of the yield of a nuclear weapon equivalent to one million tons of TNT. One megaton equals 1,000 kilotons. See also *Kiloton* and *Yield.*

Minuteman ICBM A U.S. solid-fueled ICBM. About 1,000 are currently in the arsenal: 450 Minuteman IIs, which carry a single warhead; 550 Minuteman IIIs, which each carry three MIRVs.

Missile attack assessment system (MAAS) This system is currently being installed to give the United States a high-confidence strategic warning system which can determine where a strategic missile attack originated and for what targets it is intended.

Missile site radar (MSR) Part of the U.S. ABM system which performs the functions of surveillance and detection, target track, missile track, and command for the Sprint and Spartan ABM missiles.

Mobile ICBM An ICBM which can be moved in order to reduce its vulnerability to attack. The term usually connotates a *land-mobile ICBM* (i.e., one which may be transported by truck or train). Yet a mobile ICBM may be placed in other media, such as an *air-mobile ICBM*, which is dropped from a large aircraft and then ignited.

Multilateral Force (MLF) A proposal made by the United States during the early 1960s to provide NATO with a sea-based nuclear missile force. The ships were to be manned by a mixed crew from several NATO nations. The plan was strongly criticized by the U.S.S.R., which feared that the scheme would give the NATO countries (especially West Germany) access to nuclear weapons. The proposal was eventually shelved.

Multiple independently-targetable reentry vehicle (MIRV) A system in which a missile carries several warheads which are capable of being directed against the same number of widely separated targets.

Multiple reentry vehicle (MRV) A system in which a single missile carries multiple warheads that are not independently targeted but are dispersed in a "shotgun" manner over a general target area.

Multiple warhead Any system in a missile which carries more than one nuclear warhead. See also *Maneuverable reentry vehi-*

cle, Multiple reentry vehicle, and *Multiple independently-targetable reentry vehicle.*

Mutual Assured Destruction (MAD) A general strategic doctrine based on the ideas that strategic stability is enhanced between two nuclear powers once they both develop second-strike capabilities and that this stability is undermined if either side is able to significantly threaten the strategic deterrent forces of the other side. Critics have used the acronym MAD on the basis that this doctrine's declaratory policy threatens enemy cities as a means of maintaining the maximum deterrent effect.

Mutual deterrence The situation that develops between two nuclear powers when each is deterred from attacking the other because the damage expected to result from the victim's retaliation would be unacceptable.

Mutual force reductions (MFR) Arms-control concepts for Europe that would provide for reduction in the military forces of NATO and the Warsaw Pact countries.

M-X A U.S. strategic weapons development program which is examining possible alternatives to the present land-based ICBM force. The three under consideration include an air-mobile ICBM system, a land-mobile ICBM, and a larger and more accurate fixed-silo ICBM.

Nautical Mile A unit of length used by naval and air forces. It is the length of one minute of latitude, and one nautical mile equals 1.15157 statute miles or 1.853248 kilometers.

National means of verification Techniques for monitoring compliance with the provisions of an agreement which are under national control (as opposed to bilateral or multilateral control). These techniques generally include surveillance satellites and radar systems.

NAVSTAR A system of satellites under development which will eventually provide highly accurate navigational information for aircraft, submarines, missiles, and other systems.

Nike-X A U.S. ABM system, designed in the early 1960s to use the long-range Zeus missile and the short-range Sprint missile in combination with the various radars. The Nike-X system was not deployed and was followed by the Sentinel ABM system.

No-First-Use A general pledge taken by nuclear-weapons countries not to be the first to use nuclear weapons.

Non-Proliferation Treaty (NPT) An international treaty

aimed at preventing the spread of nuclear weapons while expanding the benefits of nuclear energy to all nations. Nonnuclear signatories have undertaken a pledge not to acquire nuclear weapons and nuclear-weapons states have agreed not to assist nonnuclear countries in acquiring nuclear weapons.

Nth country problem The possibility of the diffusion of nuclear weapons to an indeterminate ("N") number of countries through the development of independent capabilities or the acquisition of nuclear weapons from existing nuclear powers.

Nuclear Free Zone Areas in which the production and stationing of nuclear weapons are prohibited.

Nuclear parity A condition in which opposing nations possess approximately equal nuclear capabilities.

Nuclear sharing A policy whereby a major nuclear power makes nuclear weapons available to an ally while retaining a right of veto over the use of the weapons.

Nuclear superiority (a) The advantage given by possession of a nuclear striking force so large that it would be credible that its possessor might use it in retaliation to conventional aggression and still have sufficient nuclear capability to carry out a second-strike response; (b) a situation in which one side in a strategic confrontation possesses a significantly greater number of strategic delivery systems.

On-Site inspection (a) Examination of an area or installation to determine whether a violation is occurring at that location; (b) examination of the area where a seismic event has occurred, in order to determine whether it was an earthquake or an explosion.

Overpressure The pressure produced by a nuclear explosion in excess of normal air pressure. Usually measured in pounds per square inch.

Over-the-Horizon radar (OTH) A long-range ballistic missile warning system that uses radar waves which are reflected back and forth between the earth's surface and the ionosphere, and can therefore propagate over the horizon.

Partial Test Ban Treaty (PTBT) An international agreement signed in 1963 by the United States, the Soviet Union, Great Britain, and many nonnuclear-weapons countries. It prohibits the testing of nuclear weapons in any part of the atmosphere, outer space, or underwater; continued testing was allowed underground.

Passive defense A defense against a nuclear strike by either removing the targets in question from offensive reach or protecting them against the effects of nuclear explosions; thus the effects of an attack can be absorbed without great damage. Efforts in this category include civil defense programs (such as fallout shelters), as well as the hardening of missile silos.

Payload The weight that the rockets of a missile are required to lift; this includes both the weight of the booster stage of the missile and the reentry vehicle with its warhead package. See also *Throw weight.*

Peaceful nuclear explosives (PNEs) Nuclear devices which are used for peaceful purposes such as nuclear excavation and stimulation of underground natural gas formations.

Penetration aids (PEN AIDS) Devices to aid the entry of aircraft or missiles through the enemy's active defenses. Penetration aids for missiles include decoys, chaff, and electronic jammers.

Perimeter acquisition radar (PAR) A long-range radar of the Sentinel and Safeguard ABM systems. It is used for the initial detection and tracking of incoming offensive warheads.

Permissive Action Link (PAL) The hardware and methods by which a designated official retains control of a nuclear weapon and by which the freedom of action of the custodian may be limited and controlled.

Point Defense Defense of a limited geographical area. The term now usually refers to the defense of ICBM silos.

Polaris (a) The first generation of U.S. ballistic missile submarines which are nuclear powered; or (b) the first generation of submarine-launched ballistic missiles (SLBMs) which the Polaris submarines carry.

Poseidon An advanced U.S. submarine-launched missile that replaced the earlier Polaris SLBMs. The Poseidon SLBMs have a longer range, better accuracy, and carry MIRVs.

Preemptive strike A first strike against an adversary's offensive forces, population, or industry, in anticipation of a nuclear attack by him.

Preventive war A war initiated in the belief that a military conflict, while not imminent, is very probable, and that to delay active hostilities would involve greater risk than beginning them oneself.

Psi (pounds per square inch) The measure commonly used to determine the capability of an object to withstand overpressure. Unprotected objects, such as human beings and buildings, are destroyed by 10 psi or less, while hardened military targets, such as hardened missile silos, may withstand between 100 to 1,000 psi.

SA-5 A Soviet ground-to-air missile which has been extensively deployed.

Safeguard ABM The modification of the Sentinel ABM system announced by President Richard Nixon on March 14, 1969. It differs from the earlier *Sentinel ABM system* in that it was designed primarily to protect ICBM sites and ultimately to provide only light defense of population centers.

Sanguine A proposed U.S. communications systems which would use extremely low-frequency radio waves to communicate with nuclear missile-and-attack submarines at deep depths in the oceans.

Seabed Treaty An international treaty which prohibits the emplacing of nuclear weapons upon the seabed of the oceans.

Second-strike capability The capability to carry out a major nuclear attack on an adversary after absorbing a first strike.

Semiautomatic Ground Environment (SAGE) A U.S. defense system designed to provide instantaneous information by computer for air defenses.

Sentinel The U.S. ABM system approved by President Lyndon Johnson. It was capable of protecting cities against small-scale attacks and potentially expandable into a "thick" system offering protection against larger attacks. See also *Safeguard ABM*.

Shoot-look-shoot missile control system A system whereby the impact areas of nuclear warheads are determined (presumably by satellite monitoring), and subsequent missiles are launched only against those targets not hit the first time. The aim is to increase the efficiency of counterforce operations, albeit at the cost of some delay in sorting out enemy missile sites.

Short-range armed missile (SRAM) An air-to-surface missile first deployed on U.S. strategic bombers in the early 1970s. This missile is used by the bombers to penetrate enemy air defenses and attack targets.

Silo A fixed-site emplacement which is usually hardened for the protection of land-based ICBMs.

Single Integrated Operational Plan (SIOP) The name given to U.S. strategic war plans which would direct the country's nuclear forces in a time of nuclear conflict.

Soft target Any object which can be destroyed by a low level of overpressure produced by a nuclear explosion. Most objects are "soft targets," including people, cities, aircraft, and ships. See also *Psi.*

Sound Surveillance Systems (SOSUS) A fixed underwater surveillance system used by the United States to monitor the movements of Soviet missile and attack submarines.

Soviet ICBMs The present Soviet ICBM arsenal includes the *SS-11*, a liquid-fueled missile comparable in size to the U.S. Minuteman; the *SS-13*, the first Soviet ICBM to employ solid fuel (also similar to the U.S. Minuteman in size and payloads); and the *SS-9*, a very large liquid-fueled ICBM capable of carrying a warhead between 12 to 25 megatons. The new generation of Soviet ICBMs beginning to be deployed include the *SS-17* and *SS-19*, liquid-fueled missiles which are larger than the *SS-11* which they may replace; the *SS-16*, a solid fuel ICBM which may be a mobile ICBM; and the *SS-18*, a possible larger replacement for the *SS-9*s. All the new Soviet ICBMs have been flight-tested with MIRVs.

Spartan A long-range exoatmospheric antimissile missile, which is a part of the U.S. ABM system.

Sprint A short-range endoatmospheric antimissile missile, which is a part of the U.S. ABM system.

Stable deterrence A situation in which potentially opposing nuclear powers have available weapons systems so numerous and diversified that no single power or combination of powers can hope to upset the balance either through war or through technological innovation. See also *Deterrence* and *Mutual Assured Destruction.*

Standing Consultive Commission (SCC) A U.S.-U.S.S.R. commission established in accordance with the provisions of the ABM Treaty which will provide a forum for the discussion of questions relating to the compliance of the two parties to the obligations of the treaty.

Stellar inertial guidance (SIG) A guidance system which uses stars as reference points.

Strategic alert A status of heightened readiness in preparation for a strategic attack.

Strategic Arms Limitation Talks (SALT) A series of negotiations between the United States and the U.S.S.R. which began in Helsinki in November 1969. These negotiations seek to limit and eventually reduce both offensive and defensive strategic arms. In 1972 these negotiations resulted in the *ABM Treaty* and the *Interim Offensive Weapons Accord.*

Strategic forces Forces which have the capability of delivering nuclear weapons against targets on the territory of a potential adversary; also, defensive forces designed to defend against such attacks.

Strategic stability This term generally refers to a relationship in which neither nuclear power has an incentive to initiate the use of strategic nuclear weapons. As used by former Defense Secretary Schlesinger strategic stability is composed of two aspects: (a) *crisis stability*, which means that neither country has an incentive to launch a nuclear strike even during a crisis situation; and (b) *force stability*, which means that neither side perceives the necessity to undertake major new arms programs in order to avoid being placed at a "perceived" strategic disadvantage in some measure of strategic force effectiveness.

Strategic superiority See *Nuclear superiority.*

Tactical nuclear weapons Nuclear weapons designed to be employed against enemy targets in a limited conflict or a battlefield context. Often these weapons are of shorter range than those which are designed for strategic operations.

Tallinn line A defensive surface-to-air missile system deployed by the U.S.S.R.

Terminal defense A defense designed to intercept a missile during the final phase of its trajectory.

Theater nuclear forces A somewhat broader term generally than *tactical nuclear weapons*, including nuclear forces which might be used in a nuclear battlefield context, such as SLBMs, which are otherwise categorized as strategic nuclear forces.

Threshold Test Ban (TTB) An agreement concluded between the United States and the U.S.S.R. in 1974, which seeks to limit underground nuclear testing for weapons development purposes to 150 kilotons or less.

Throw weight The maximum useful weight which has been flight tested on the boost stages of a missile. In contrast with *payload*, the weight of the booster stage of the missile is not included in the calculation of throw weight. Throw weight is also an indication of the potential application of the missile's capability for carrying multiple warheads, as well as the size of the yield of these warheads.

Titan II A large, liquid-fueled U.S. ICBM, which carries a warhead of several megatons.

Treaty of Tlatelolco (Also known as the *Latin America Nuclear Free Zone Treaty*). This treaty seeks to limit the spread of nuclear weapons by preventing their introduction into this region.

Triad The basic structure of the U.S. strategic deterrent force: the land-based ICBM force; the strategic bomber force; and the submarine missile fleet.

Trident (Formerly known as *underwater long-range missile system (ULMS)*. A new nuclear missile submarine and two new SLBMs, which will eventually replace the present Polaris/Poseidon missile submarine force. The Trident submarine is larger than the Polaris and will carry 24 SLBMs. The Trident I missile will be MIRVed and will have a longer range (about 4,000 nautical miles) than the present Poseidon SLBMs. The Trident II missile will be even larger and have a range of about 6,000 nautical miles.

Variable-range ballistic missile (VRBM) Missiles which are capable of an intercontinental range but can be targeted for much shorter ranges as well.

Verification The process of determining the degree to which parties to an agreement are complying with the provisions of the agreement.

Warhead That part of a reentry vehicle containing the nuclear explosives, fuses, and other components necessary for a nuclear explosion.

Weapons of mass destruction Weapons capable of a high order of destruction or of being used in such a manner as to destroy large numbers of people. Nuclear, chemical, and biological weapons are usually included under this term.

X-ray kill The mechanism by which X-rays from an ABM nuclear explosion destroy or neutralize reentry vehicles at great distances.

Y-class submarines A modern Soviet nuclear-powered submarine which has sixteen SLBM launchers.

Yield The total effective energy produced in a nuclear explosion, usually expressed in terms of the number of tons of TNT that would have to be exploded to produce the same amount of energy. Nuclear explosion effects include nuclear radiation, thermal radiation, and blast. See also *Kiloton* and *Megaton.*

Yield-to-weight ratio The explosive force of a nuclear weapon relative to its weight, or destructive power per pound of the warhead.

APPENDIX D

Reason, Morality, and Defense Policy

Alain C. Enthoven

Since the detonation of the first nuclear weapons, a consensus has developed to the effect that the traditional Christian doctrine of the just war has been rendered obsolete. There is a great diversity of view within this consensus, both in the motives for rejecting the traditional doctrine and in the conclusions to be drawn from its rejection. For example, there are the pacifists, for whom nuclear weapons provide a new argument against a competing moral theory. Nuclear weapons also prove to them what they believed all along, that the only rational and moral course is to disarm completely, even if unilaterally.

There is another school that resembles the pacifists, at least in the belief that universal and lasting peace is a realistic short-term goal for national security policy. But for this group, peace will be maintained by the awful mechanism of the balance of terror, instead of being maintained by good will and disarmament. This school argues that a stable balance of terror, based on invulnerable nuclear striking forces aimed at the cities of the enemy, will make war impossible. This line of thought is the source of much of the most violent objection to civil defenses, counterforce strategy (i.e., a strategy based on the attempt to defeat the enemy's forces rather than to destroy his cities), and active air and antimissile defense, on the grounds that such preparations may "make nuclear war possible." Thus we have the curious phenomenon of pacifists and nuclear deterrers uniting in opposition to civil de-

---

Reprinted with permission from *America* 108 (April 6 and 13, 1963).

fense. It is clear that to justify a policy based exclusively and deliberately on attacks on enemy cities, one must do away with the traditional Christian doctrine of the just war.

A third group, which might be called the "realists," wants to eliminate moral restraints from the conduct of warfare, and joins in the rejection of the traditional doctrine. If all means of warfare are immoral, as this group would have it, there is no basis for moral restraint, and all decisions can be made on the basis of "military necessity."

Although I do not doubt that the holders of these views have found substantial and compelling reasons for their beliefs, I still believe in the validity and relevance of the traditional Christian doctrine. Military force as an instrument of the policies of nations is not about to be abolished, and attempts to base our morality on the dream that it will be are doomed to irrelevance. By setting its sights too high, such a moral doctrine will fail to accomplish anything of value. Nor has the "balance of terror" stopped all armed aggression. Nuclear weapons have not deterred unjust Communist aggression in Korea, Hungary, or South Vietnam, though fortunately they have so far imposed an uneasy truce at the nuclear level. As a response to the unjust aggression that is occurring and will in all probability continue to occur, we must have usable military force.

Love of our neighbors obliges us to take an active part in the preservation of their lives and freedom and in the creation of conditions in which they can work out their own salvation. One of the great challenges of the nuclear age is how to make military force usable—both morally and practically—in the defense of our lives and freedom.

Although there are distinguished examples to the contrary, many of the theologians, moralists and others writing on the problem of morality and modern war do not have an adequate factual understanding of the key issues of defense policy. They consequently tend to develop their analyses on the basis of oversimplified assumptions that do not describe accurately the actual choices faced by defense policy makers. And too often they conclude with such sweeping statements as: "Thermonuclear war is mass murder"—which are not particularly helpful to the defense policy maker who is trying to do the right thing by both his country and his conscience.

It is with these thoughts in mind that I offer the following description of current U.S. defense policy, presented not in moral terms, but in the practical terms in which these policies have been developed and defended by defense policy makers. In Part One, I describe the general themes underlying current defense policy and the way they have worked themselves out in the build-up of our nonnuclear forces. However, the problems of nonnuclear and nuclear strategy are closely interrelated and cannot be understood in isolation. Therefore, Part Two . . . will contain a description of our policies and objectives in preparation for the possibility of a nuclear war.

I

There are three related themes underlying and uniting our defense policies today. They are, first, deterrence of aggression; second, freedom for the President to select and apply the amount and kind of force appropriate to the threat at hand; and third, the controlled use of force. In the nuclear age, military force will be too dangerous to use if our objectives are not carefully chosen and limited at each step of a conflict, and if the force cannot be used in a controlled and deliberate way to achieve precisely the objectives being sought. To fight for unlimited objectives, or to fight in an uncontrolled way, would almost surely bring on almost unlimited destruction.

In order to give the President the freedom of action required to be able to limit appropriately the use of force, current defense policy emphasizes flexibility, options, and choice. One of its main objectives is to make available to the President a range of military responses appropriate for each threat to our security, so that he can apply force adequate to accomplish the objectives at hand without any unnecessary damage or loss of life, and while holding to a minimum the risk of escalation to a more destructive level of conflict.

Some years ago, there was much public debate as to whether limited war was possible. The theory and practice of strategic bombing in World War II, the use of the atomic bombs, and the unconditional-surrender policy left in their aftermath a widespread belief that war could only be total. This belief persisted long after the armed resistance to Communist aggression in Greece and Korea. Of course, total war remains possible. But as time goes by, and the size and destructive power of nuclear arsenals increase, total war between nuclear powers will more and more mean total destruction. It is my own opinion that with the widespread realization of this fact will come the general belief that all wars should be limited. At no time should we deliberately choose to fight an unlimited, uncontrolled war. The "limited-war/general-war" dichotomy that has crept into our language may be harmful if it suggests that there is a kind of war that it makes sense to fight without limits, though, of course, the limits that we adopt will have to depend on the threat and on our objectives.

What this means, in practice, is that we are working to acquire a flexible, balanced defense posture giving us capabilities for the selective use of force for all kinds of conflict, from counterinsurgency and antiguerrilla warfare through large-scale conventional (nonnuclear) warfare, through major thermonuclear war. Although the choice of the amount and kind of force to be applied in any circumstances is bound to be a difficult one, we would like to make it possible in all cases, if I may borrow a phrase from *The Mikado*, "to make the punishment fit the crime."

Keeping the use of force appropriately limited requires control. The range, speed, and destructiveness of modern weapons make this problem both more urgent and more difficult than it has ever been before. More than ever before, this means that the President must have communication and control facilities to provide him with timely and accurate information on the course of events and to permit him to communicate his decisions in a similar manner. It also means that the military forces must be responsive to his direction, even in considerable detail. To use President Kennedy's words: "Our weapon systems must be usable in a manner permitting deliberation and discrimination as to timing, scope, and targets in response to civilian authority."

Moreover, when force is being applied, the military action must not be allowed to control events and compel the President's decisions; rather, it should be the other way around. To borrow a term from missilery, our use of military force in the Cold War must be command-guided, not inertially guided.

This belief may be contrasted to the view that "peace is peace and war is war" and that, in war, military necessity is the only valid criterion for decision. Certainly, the requirements of the military commander must be considered very seriously, both because our security requires success in whatever armed conflicts are thrust upon us and because the lives of our soldiers are involved. Still, the President must be free to weigh them against other requirements and decide what is best for the security of the

United States. This principle was important before nuclear weapons; it has taken on added importance in the nuclear age.

This was one of the hard lessons of the Korean War. The United States had to relearn to fight for limited objectives. There were reasons which the original military commander found very compelling for expanding the scope of the conflict. But in the President's judgment, to expand the conflict would have risked touching off another world war, which would have left both the South Koreans and ourselves far worse off than the final outcome that actually was achieved. The President must be in a positon to make and enforce such judgments.

The same principle of control was applied in a thoroughgoing way in the recent Cuban crisis. Each military move was, in effect, a carefully formulated message from the President to Khrushchev, intended to convince him that the United States would use military force to the extent necessary to achieve removal of the offensive weapons. But each move was also intended to convince him that he could withdraw without armed conflict, if he would withdraw. Because each move was a carefully formulated message, all moves had to be carefully controlled from the White House. All this was summarized by the President in the words:

> Our arms must be subject to ultimate civilian control and command at all times, in war as well as peace. The basic decisions on our participation in any conflict and our response to any threat—including all decisions relating to the use of nuclear weapons, or the escalation of a small war into a large one—will be made by the regularly constituted civilian authorities.

Because of the importance of such control, a great deal has been done in the Defense Department in the past two years to strengthen and make more secure the means of high-level command and control of forces.

How have these themes worked themselves out in the development of our defense program? One of the most important ways has been in the recent and large build-up in our conventional or nonnuclear forces.

To understand properly the importance of the build-up of nonnuclear forces, it is necessary first to understand that there is a very great difference between nuclear weapons and nonnuclear weapons. Nuclear weapons are not simply high explosives writ large. Their destructive power makes them a completely new kind of military force which must be understood and related to our national security objectives in new ways. Hiroshima was destroyed by a 20-kiloton bomb. We now have weapons a thousand times that size. Roughly 2.5 million tons of TNT were dropped on Germany in World War II. One B-52 can now deliver many times that amount of destructive power, and we have the ability to deliver the equivalent of thousands of millions of tons intercontinentally. Besides the familiar effects of blast and heat, these weapons can cover many thousands of square miles with deadly radioactive fallout. All this is familiar.

There has been in recent years the development of small nuclear weapons having yields equivalent to a few thousand tons of TNT or less. The day will come, if it has not come already, when there will be nuclear weapons of smaller yield than the largest high explosive weapons. When that day comes, will there no longer be a distinction between nuclear and conventional weapons? Some have argued to that effect. But they are mistaken. There is and will remain an important distinction, a "fire break" if you like, between nuclear and nonnuclear war, a recognizable qualitative distinction that both combatants can recognize and agree upon, if they want to agree upon one. And in the nuclear age they will have a very popular incentive to agree upon this distinction and limitation: because if they do not, there does not appear to be another easily recognizable limitation on weapons—no other obvious "fire break"—all the way up the destructive spectrum to large-scale thermonuclear war.

Adequate nonnuclear forces are important. It is for this reason that, in the past two years, we have increased the number of active, combat-ready Army divisions from 11 to 16, and our active, tactical air wings from 16 to 21. It is for this reason that we have more than doubled the annual rate of procurement of Army equipment, that we have speeded up the tempo of modernization of our tactical air forces, and that we have increased our outlays on naval shipbuilding. Moreover, it is for this reason that we are now urging our NATO allies to increase the size and effectiveness of their conventional forces.

Strong nonnuclear forces are required because there are many situations in which the use of nuclear weapons would be inappropriate. For the same reasons that a sledge hammer does not make a good substitute for a fly swatter, nuclear weapons are not a good substitute for nonnuclear forces against a wide range of military threats. Even if they could be used to apply the minimum force required to achieve our objectives, their use would risk triggering escalation to a more and unnecessarily destructive level of conflict.

A nation or an alliance which maintains a strong nuclear posture combined with weak nonnuclear forces thereby puts itself at a great disadvantage in the confrontation with another power that has both strong nuclear and strong nonnuclear forces. This will be true no matter how strong and effective are its nuclear forces, provided that the other power maintains a secure "second strike" nuclear retaliatory capability, that is, a force capable of surviving a nuclear attack and of destroying the enemy's society in a retaliatory blow. Because nuclear war is so destructive, the use of nuclear weapons must be reserved only for the most desperate circumstances. But if the nuclears have to be reserved for vital issues, the side with the strong conventional forces is likely to be able to have its way on all issues less than vital. The side without adequate conventional forces will have no means for effective resistance in such confrontation. The side with conventional forces can use "salami slice" tactics, or make its aggression piecemeal, in the confidence that it will be able to have its way on all but life-and-death matters. This is the kind of threat we have been facing in Berlin. The danger in piecemeal aggression is that erosion in the position of the free world over the years can end in world domination by the Communists.

Put alternatively, the President will be in a weak bargaining position indeed if he is confronted by the Communist bloc with a choice between suicide or surrender, holocaust or humiliation. In order to resist aggression and defend our freedom, the President must have more attractive alternatives. Without conventional forces, our choice when faced with aggression may be "Red or dead"; conventional forces help to deter aggression, and, if deterrence fails, they can give us the opportunity to fight to stay alive and free.

Nevertheless, the build-up in our conventional forces has been costly and controversial. Two main lines of argument have been advanced against it. The first is that it weakens our nuclear resolve. In effect, it is a message to Khrushchev telling him that we are afraid or unwilling to use nuclear weapons, and that he can commit aggression against us with the expectation that we will not use them. Of course, pushed to an extreme, such an argument would say that we ought to abolish the U.S. Marine Corps. But the argument is defective.

It is not so important to convince an aggressor that we will use nuclear arms. The important thing is to convince him that we will use whatever force is necessary to preserve our freedom. In many cases, that will be nonnuclear force. Sole or excessive reliance on nuclear weapons may tempt him to believe that we will not fight for less than vital issues. The danger is that each issue can be made less than vital. Aggression can be made piecemeal and in small enough pieces so that succumbing always looks attractive by comparison with thermonuclear war. Isn't Berlin Khrushchev's "last territorial demand in Europe"?

In fact, reflection on the problem should convince most reasonable men that the threat of the ultimate use of nuclear weapons, if required, is much more credible to an aggressor who sees that to accomplish his objective he must first defeat a large and effective conventional force. If he succeeds in doing that, the issue is likely by then to be vital for the defender.

Still, some argue that we should try to convince our adversaries that we would use nuclear weapons even in situations in which it is irrational to do so. Interestingly enough, Khrushchev himself has recently attacked this principle as a policy for the Communist bloc, and, in attacking him, the Chinese Communists have none the less acknowledged the enormous destructiveness of nuclear war. When it is clear that the Communists know the facts of nuclear destructiveness, it would seem foolish for us to base our strategy on the pretense that we do not. The trouble with trying to exploit "the rationality of irrationality," as theorists of bargaining and conflict call this, is that it simply is not a viable policy in the long run for a democracy, especially a democracy with allies. We must have defense policies that make sense to well-informed citizens, both in the United States and among our allies. Moreover, threats to blow ourselves up along with the aggressor are not likely to be credible. Rather, the most credible kind of threat is the threat that we will do what in the event will be most in our interest to do. In the case of piecemeal nonnuclear aggression, that will be to apply conventional forces.

The other main line of argument against the buildup of our conventional forces is that it will be fruitless, extremely costly and unable to achieve the objective of adequacy because we are so badly outnumbered by the Communist hordes. These arguments, though widely believed, are not supported by the facts. Conventional military strength requires fighting men; it also requires that the men be fed, clothed, and equipped with effective weapons and other materiel. Equipping and supporting armies requires wealth and industrial production. The NATO allies outnumber the members of the Warsaw Pact in population, men under arms, and even foot soldiers in active army forces. In the dire straits into which mismanagement has plunged their economy, the Chinese Communists appear to be far from being able to provide modern and effective equipment for an army the size of our own. Moreover, the gross national products of the United States and our allies are more than twice the same total for the Soviet Union and its allies; in terms of industrial production, the ratio is more than two and one-half to one. What all of these facts suggest is that, although substantial sacrifice may be involved for us and our NATO allies in equipping ourselves with adequate conventional forces, proportionally the sacrifice is much smaller for us than it is for our adversaries. Although we do need to strengthen our conventional forces some, the extra costs are not large. We have already paid the entry fee into the "nonnuclear club." It is now largely a matter of making fully effective the force levels we have already agreed to provide.

A related argument has it that limiting conflicts to nonnuclear weapons puts us at a disadvantage because of our numerical inferiority, and that we need to use nuclear weapons as an equalizer in all but the smallest of armed conflicts. Leaving aside the undesirable character of the equalization they accomplish, and the unresolved question of whether the use of nuclear weapons is to our military advantage if the other side replies in kind, let me point out that our wealth and technology confer on us some important advantages in nonnuclear combat. Indeed, the effectiveness of modern nonnuclear arms is so great that they can offset substantial numerical inferiority in isolated situations in which we might be numerically inferior. The ability to produce such arms in quantity is a key determinant of the effectiveness of a nation's nonnuclear forces.

In summary, conventional military force is usable force. In Korea and in the Cuban crisis, we found that the nonnuclear forces were the cutting edge of our military power. We can use conventional force with a minimal risk of self-destruction. Therefore, it provides a more credible deterrent to nonnuclear aggression. As the destructiveness of nuclear war increases, and as nuclear weapon systems become less vulnerable to sudden attack, the effectiveness of the threatened first use of nuclear weapons as a substitute for conventional forces will diminish, and we will have no sensible alternative to building up our conventional forces to the point at which they can safely resist all forms of nonnuclear aggression. Our forces will be adequate if we can never be forced because of weakness to be the first to have to resort to nuclear weapons.

II

Nuclear forces are not an effective substitute for adequate nonnuclear forces; neither are nonnuclear forces an effective substitute for adequate nuclear forces. Rather, the relationship between the two is one of complementarity. Now that the Communist bloc is armed with nuclear weapons, we cannot successfully fight conventional wars except under the umbrella of nuclear strength. This nuclear strength is required to deter the Communists from escalating a nonnuclear conflict which is not going well for them into nuclear war, and to convince them that an act of nuclear aggression would lead to their defeat, and possibly to the destruction of their society.

This, then, is the most important objective of our nuclear posture: to make thermonuclear war unlikely by deterring deliberate, calculated nuclear aggression. We also seek other objectives. We want to make accidental, unpremeditated, irrational nuclear war unlikely also. And if war does occur, we want to be able to bring it to a speedy termination on military terms favorable to ourselves, and we want to do what we can to limit the damage caused to ourselves and our allies. How do we go about pursuing those objectives?

First, we attempt to deter deliberate, premeditated attack by maintaining nuclear forces that can survive a surprise nuclear attack and strike back effectively afterward. This means relatively invulnerable weapon systems like Minuteman, Titan, and Polaris, and secure, protected, survivable command and control facilities that will enable our national leadership to survive an attack and direct the use of retaliatory forces against any aggressor.

There is a great deal of literature about, and many approaches to, the subject of nuclear deterrence. Some argue that, in the event of a nuclear attack on the Alliance, we should plan to retaliate strictly against Soviet cities. Others argue that we should plan to strike back only against Soviet military forces. Still others argue for both. Some believe that we should design our posture for an irrevocable commitment to a spasm of "massive retaliation." Our approach is based on options, deliberation, flexibility, and control. Rather than decide ahead of time which targets must be hit by which weapons, and then commit ourselves to it, our approach is to give the President a range of choices so that he can select the plan whose targets and timing of attacks are most appropriate to the circumstances at hand. I won't speculate here as to which nuclear response might be used in which circumstances. Nothing useful would be accomplished by doing so. But, let me make three observations about this policy.

First, it is a policy of strength, not weakness. It takes superior nuclear forces to be able to ride out any kind of attack and then retain the option to destroy most of the enemy's remaining military forces, should that be appropriate. It would be a policy of weakness to commit ourselves irrevocably to a spasm of nuclear retaliation against Soviet cities.

Second, this policy requires protected forces and secure command and control. It requires weapon systems like Minuteman, which is based underground in dispersed, blast-resistant silos, and Polaris, both of which can ride out a thermonuclear attack and be held in reserve in the environment of nuclear war. This is one of the reasons why the Defense Department's procurement of strategic weapon systems in the last two years has emphasized Minuteman and Polaris.

Third, this approach to nuclear deterrence illustrates the principle that, across the spectrum of conflict, military force is to be used for a purpose, and with deliberation and control. There is, to be sure, a danger of breakdown of control in the environment of thermonuclear war. But there is no point at which it makes sense to choose to abandon control. Even when it comes to thermonuclear weapons, if our weapons are to be used to keep us alive and free, their use must be controlled.

This emphasis on control has led the Defense Department, in the past two years, to emphasize the procurement of survivable, secure, redundant and internetted command, control, and communications facilities. For example, we now have a SAC command post with a general officer on board constantly airborne, 24 hours a day. For the top civilian authorities, we have the National Emergency Airborne Command Post, command posts on ships at sea, and various underground command posts, all tied together by protected communications. As well as making a major contribution to our ability to deter deliberate attack, this strengthened command structure has made an important contribution to reducing the hazard of such unlikely eventualities as unauthorized, accidental, or other unpremeditated attacks blowing up into large-scale thermonuclear war. And, along with many other safety precautions that we have taken, it is making much less likely the possibility of accidental or unauthorized use of nuclear weapons on our side.

I would like to emphasize this point, because some recent literature has suggested that there is a lack of concern among the military and civilian leaders of the Department of Defense for the safety and stability of our nuclear-weapons posture. This suggestion could not be farther from the truth. In fact, both our military and civilian leaders take this problem very seriously, and they have been willing to accept considerable costs to assure the compatibility of military readiness with the highest possible degree of safety.

But despite our best efforts, a war may still occur. In these dangerous and unpredictable times, it would be foolish to base our planning on the assumption that a thermonuclear war could never happen. Despite our best efforts, almost any kind of nuclear war would be an unprecedented disaster. But if such a war were thrust upon us, there are worthwhile things that could be done to mitigate its consequences. We are making preparations whose purpose is, in the event of war, to enable us to maintain a favorable military position, to bring the war to an end quickly, and to hold to a minimum the damage to our own population, to the population of our allies, and even, if possible, to those of our enemies. To limit the damage to our own and allied populations, we are making a combination of plans and preparations, including Civil Defense, active air and antimissile defense, and an ability to destroy what we can of the enemy's offensive weapons. Let me explain each one.

The largest part of our Civil Defense program is fallout shelters for our population. One of the most destructive effects of nuclear weapons is radioactive fallout. In a thermonuclear attack on the United States, many millions of people would die, even though they were far from the blast and thermal effects, simply from radioactive fallout. Although there are substantial uncertainties here, and the estimates vary widely depending upon the assumptions made, most studies suggest that while several tens of millions might die from the blast and thermal effects of a nuclear attack on the United States, because of fallout the total deaths could well be over a hundred million in the United States alone. In order to prevent this, the President has directed the Department of Defense to undertake an expanded Civil Defense program, which has as its first objective the provision of fallout shelters for all of our population.

Civil Defense is very important for many reasons. Without it, our active defenses and other preparations for survival in a thermonuclear war would be rendered meaningless. For example, if we defended our cities with impenetrable antimissile defenses, but had no fallout protection for the inhabitants, an attacker could still destroy all the people in those cities simply by surface-bursting thermonuclear weapons upwind and killing the people with fallout. If we do have a Civil Defense program, then active air and antimissile defenses can also make a very important contribution to our survival. Civil Defense is also necessary if we are to have any hope of limiting the effects of a major thermonuclear war and making possible a meaningful strategy of controlled use of nuclear weapons.

In addition to these measures, we are buying strategic retaliatory forces capable of knocking out those vulnerable elements of enemy nuclear striking power remaining after an attack has been launched against us. Of course, we are up against the limitation here that, after such an attack, our counterattacking forces are likely to be spent destroying many empty bases and launching sites. However, our studies to date suggest that, in such circumstances, it would still be likely that there would remain vulnerable forces that could be used against us in follow-up attacks, and that their timely destruction could help to limit the damage to the United States and our allies.

Beyond these measures, we are also opening up the option of maintaining effective deterrence after a nuclear war begins. This was described last spring by Secretary of Defense McNamara in an address at the University of Michigan. In his words:

> The United States has come to the conclusion that, to the extent feasible, basic military strategy in a possible general nuclear war should be approached in much the same way that more conventional military operations have been regarded in the past. That is to say, principal military objectives, in the event of a nuclear war stemming from a major attack on the Alliance, should be the destruction of the enemy's military forces, not of his civilian population.
>
> The very strength and nature of the Alliance forces make it possible for us to retain, even in the face of a massive surprise attack, sufficient

reserve striking power to destroy an enemy society, if driven to it. In other words, we are giving a possible opponent the strongest imaginable incentive to refrain from striking our own cities.

Questions arise as to whether nuclear war can be limited and controlled. First, can it? The answer depends on our will to make it so. With the protected weapon systems, command posts, and communications we are now acquiring, there is no technical reason why the use of nuclear weapons cannot be controlled in a nuclear war. The destructive power of their uncontrolled use should give all participants a strong incentive to find ways of avoiding it. Moreover, as both sides acquire protected forces like Minuteman and Polaris, the prospects are that neither side will be able to improve its military position by a sudden attack on the forces of the other. Then, if massive thermonuclear attack ever did make sense, it will do so no longer.

The other question is: "Should we try?" The argument against trying, one that has been used against Civil Defense, is that it weakens the "fire break" between nuclear and nonnuclear war. But any thermonuclear war would be such an unprecedented disaster that it is difficult to see how anything we could do to mitigate its consequences would effectively weaken the "fire break." And the disaster of an unlimited nuclear war would be too great to permit us not to take whatever measures we can to minimize its likelihood. Moreover, the principle of controlled and limited use of military force is indivisible. If we believe in control in some circumstances and not in others, it will become more difficult to maintain it in those circumstances in which we should. An emphasis on limitations in the use of force is desirable across the spectrum of conflict.

How are these policies related to the traditional Christian doctrine of the just war? According to that doctrine, the use of force to repress injustice can be justified—indeed, required—under certain conditions, including the following. First, the use of force must have a reasonable chance of success. Second, if successful, it must offer a better situation than the one that would prevail in the absence of the use of force. Third, the force that is used must be proportional to the objectives being sought (or the evil being repressed). For this to be satisfied, peaceful means of redress must have failed. Fourth, the force must be used with the intention of sparing noncombatants and with a reasonable prospect of actually doing so.

It is interesting to observe that the potentially catastrophic character of thermonuclear war has forced practical decision-makers, reasoning in a secular context, to adopt a set of criteria very much like those of the traditional Christian doctrine and to apply them to the design of the military posture of the United States. Now, much more than in the recent past, our use of force is being carefully proportioned to the objectives being sought, and the objectives are being carefully limited to those which at the same time are necessary for our security and which do not pose the kind of unlimited threat to our opponents in the Cold War that would drive them to unleash nuclear war. In the past, before nuclear weapons, deliberate limitations in the use of force did not present much of a practical problem because of the limited destructive power of nonnuclear weapons. Nuclear weapons have now given such constraints great practical importance.

Within the broad policy of armed resistance to aggression, which is one of the alternatives open to us, and in terms of the moral criteria of the traditional Christian doctrine, I think it is fair to say that we have made considerable progress. Of course, this is not to say that we have gone as far as we can go.

On the other hand, is the traditional doctrine still relevant in the nuclear age? A question to consider in one's critical thought on this problem is whether the view that the traditional doctrine is obsolete is based on an overemphasis on unlimited nuclear war, perhaps on an identification of all armed conflict with it. An unlimited nuclear war is an extreme on a broad spectrum of possible armed conflicts. Of course, it is a very important extreme because of its disastrous consequences, but it is not the whole spectrum. In fact, it is only one among many possible kinds of thermonuclear war. It would be a mistake to apply reasoning based on this extreme to all kinds of armed resistance to aggression and injustice. It is important to recognize this, for if our thinking is unclear on this point, and if we identify any use of armed force with unlimited destruction, we are likely unnecessarily to disarm ourselves and leave ourselves victims of Communist aggression.

It is clear that we have elected to retain the threat of use of nuclear weapons in our own defense and that of our allies. We thereby consciously accept the risk that we will have to use them. Some people believe that we should reject the use of nuclear weapons altogether. Before accepting such a judgment, one should consider carefully the full implications of such a decision. We do have worldwide responsibilities. Many millions of people depend for their lives and freedom on our military strength. In this respect, the United States is in a very different position from any other country in the free world.

Moreover, as Christians, bidden by Christ to love our neighbors, are we not still bound by the precepts that bound the first Christian warriors? Indeed, the moral imperative upon us may be much stronger, for the evil against which we are defending our neighbors, ourselves and even, hopefully, the people of the Communist bloc—that is, totalitarianism and compulsory, atheistic materialism enforced by the machinery of the modern police state—is much greater. Critics of the traditional doctrine applied to the nuclear age like to point out that we are no longer fighting with bows and arrows. They should bear in mind that we are not defending ourselves against a Christian king of Russia.

The moral problems raised by preparation for modern warfare, which are inseparable from the whole question of national-security policy, are extremely complex and difficult. We can neither escape them nor hope to understand them fully. Clearly, all proposed answers should be offered with a certain amount of caution. But, in that spirit, it does seem to me reasonable to suggest that current U.S. defense policy, which emphasizes deterrence, control, and the use of the appropriately limited amount of force, represents a good reconciliation of the traditional doctrine with the facts of life in the nuclear age. We have achieved some success with the controlled use of force. We are still alive and free today, and the missiles are out of Cuba. We are running great risks, to be sure, but would the risks be ameliorated by laying down our arms? It is tragic that nations must at times resort to armed force to resolve their differences. War is destructive, and it has evil consequences. But our defense posture is being designed to make war less likely and less destructive. I am not suggesting that we can make war and violence desirable. The question is whether we have a better alternative.

In sum, I have defended our policies on the grounds that they make sense. Can they also be defended on the grounds that they are moral? Viewed with perspective, the two should be the same.

Index

The index was prepared by Maureen L. Canick and Renee P. Johnson.